SOUL IN SEOUL

SOUL IN SEOUL

African American Popular Music and K-pop

CRYSTAL S. ANDERSON

University Press of Mississippi / Jackson

The University Press of Mississippi is the scholarly publishing agency of
the Mississippi Institutions of Higher Learning: Alcorn State University,
Delta State University, Jackson State University, Mississippi State University,
Mississippi University for Women, Mississippi Valley State University,
University of Mississippi, and University of Southern Mississippi.

www.upress.state.ms.us

The University Press of Mississippi is a member
of the Association of University Presses.

Copyright © 2020 by University Press of Mississippi
All rights reserved

First printing 2020

∞

Library of Congress Cataloging-in-Publication Data

Names: Anderson, Crystal S., author.
Title: Soul in Seoul: African American popular music and K-pop / Crystal S. Anderson.
Description: Jackson: University Press of Mississippi, 2020. | Includes bibliographical references and index.
Identifiers: LCCN 2020010046 (print) | LCCN 2020010047 (ebook) | ISBN 9781496830098 (hardback) | ISBN 9781496830104 (trade paperback) | ISBN 9781496830111 (epub) | ISBN 9781496830128 (epub) | ISBN 9781496830135 (pdf) | ISBN 9781496830142 (pdf)
Subjects: LCSH: Popular music—Korea (South)—African American influences. | Popular music—Korea (South)—History and criticism.
Classification: LCC ML3502.K6 A64 2020 (print) | LCC ML3502.K6 (ebook) | DDC 781.63/164095195—dc23
LC record available at https://lccn.loc.gov/2020010046
LC ebook record available at https://lccn.loc.gov/2020010047

British Library Cataloging-in-Publication Data available

CONTENTS

Acknowledgments vii

Introduction ix

1
"Listen to the Music": African American Popular Music and K-pop 3

2
"A Song Calling for You": Korean Pop Groups 43

3
"Soul Breeze": Korean R&B Groups and Soloists 89

4
"Rewriting the Résumé": Mainstream Korean Hip-hop Artists 119

Conclusion 147

Discography 161

References 163

Index 183

ACKNOWLEDGMENTS

This book is the result of years of love for K-pop and support from a number of individuals and institutions. I would like to thank Gary Okihiro, who encouraged me to pursue the project and assured me that I had something of value to contribute. I wish to thank my KPK: K-pop Kollective crew, especially Kaetrena Davis Kendrick and cofounder Kuylain Howard, who participated in endless conversations about K-pop. I would also like to thank the organizers of KPOPCON and KCON, who provided opportunities for me to think through my work with the fans who make K-pop possible, as well as the numerous universities that invited me to talk about K-pop. I would also like to thank my colleagues at *hellokpop*, particularly Jung Bae, who encouraged me to "listen to everything." This book would not be possible without the regular interaction of other fans who help keep me current with the wide world of K-pop music, so I thank the "Facebook Ladies," D. BryAnn Chen, Carla Walker, and O. L. Wilson. I'd like to thank my fellow academics who challenged, inspired, and provided opportunities for me to share my work, including Michelle Cho, Shilpa Dave, Robert Ku, Yasue Kuwahara, Jade Kim, Doobo Shim, Heijin Lee, Valentina Marinescu, Sherrie Ter Molen, Lori Morimoto, LeiLani Nishime, David Oh, Myoung-Sun Song, and Tasha Oren. Many thanks goes to my permanent cheering squad: Anne Choi, Eric Ashley Hairston, Jackie Modeste, Renee Nick, and Jonathan Page. Last but not least, I truly thank my family for my love of music and for providing multiple households where music was always playing.

INTRODUCTION

BTS, a seven-member male pop group, broke into the mainstream American cultural consciousness in 2017 through a series of high-profile accomplishments for the contemporary Korean popular music known as K-pop. BTS stands for Bangtan Sonyeondan, which initially meant Bulletproof Boy Scouts, or Bangtan Boys, and later, Beyond the Scene. The group's song "DNA" (2017), a song with all-Korean lyrics, entered *Billboard*'s Hot 100 chart. The group performed on the American Music Awards, then appeared on several American television shows, including *The Late Late Show*, *Jimmy Kimmel Live!*, and *The Ellen Show*. The group even garnered an award for its social media savviness. At the same time, these accomplishments revealed the group's clear connections to American hip-hop, which started early in its career. Prior to its newfound popularity in the United States, BTS starred in its own reality television show in 2014, *BTS American Hustle Life*. The group traveled to the United States and received mentoring from several American rappers. Such experiences bolstered the group's relationship with hip-hop culture and formed the foundation for its later success: "Besides writing and producing most of their work, the group also touches on a myriad of social and political issues in their tracks, including mental health and the class divide.... The attempt to cultivate a sense of authenticity was also evident in the group's earlier years. In 2014, BTS spent time in Los Angeles so that they could boost their hip-hop credibility with the help of rappers Coolio and Warren G." (Ming 2017). The remix of "Mic Drop" (2017), a collaboration with music producer Steve Aoki and rapper Desiigner, was released to acclaim in the United States, with one version featuring "the rapper's fast-talking, trap-laden delivery" (Herman 2017b).

However, BTS's gestures to American hip-hop only scratch the surface of the extent to which African American popular music informs K-pop. *Soul in Seoul: African American Popular Music and K-pop* examines ways that contemporary

Korean popular music cites musical and performative elements of African American popular music culture as well as the ways that fans outside of Korea construe these citations. K-pop represents a mode of Korean popular music that emerged in the 1990s with global aspirations and combines musical elements from Korean and foreign cultures, particularly black American popular music culture. This definition of K-pop goes beyond "idols," or the highly visible pop groups that sing and dance, to include other kinds of artists that fall under the K-pop umbrella, including Korean R&B artists and hip-hop acts. They all exhibit intertextualities that simultaneously emulate instrumentation and vocals of R&B genres of African American popular music and enhance the R&B tradition by employing Korean musical strategies that mix multiple genres. Global fans, functioning as part of K-pop's music press, deem such citational practices as authentic. K-pop artists also cite elements of African American performance in music videos that disrupt limiting representations. Such intertextuality makes K-pop a branch of a global R&B tradition. Korean pop groups participate in that tradition through cultural work that enacts a global form of crossover informed by black American music strategies. Korean R&B artists engage a global tradition through authenticity that takes R&B beyond the traditional black/white racial binary. Korean hip-hop practitioners share in the R&B tradition by promoting its innovative music aesthetics.

Considering K-pop as a part of a global R&B tradition results in increased attention to its music aesthetics, reveals the authenticating function of fans, and shows the diversity of global influences on K-pop and its culture and the global impact of African American cultural production. While K-pop has gained attention for the stunning visuals and complex choreography of its "idol" groups, music remains the primary appeal for global fans and is the primary site that reveals the impact of African American music traditions on K-pop. At the same time, fans are largely responsible for K-pop's global spread, not just as consumers but also as critical content producers. Recognizing this global reach and the bi-directional flows of culture disrupts homogenizing and generalizing approaches to K-pop.

K-pop, Intertextuality, and Music Aesthetics

K-pop exhibits an intertextuality that results from a hybridity that blends African American popular music with Korean music strategies. *Soul in Seoul* puts the music front and center through a consideration of music reviews and song descriptions that reveal how K-pop simultaneously embraces and enhances the R&B tradition. In doing so, the book represents a novel approach to K-pop beyond lyric and musicological analyses.

K-pop is certainly due a comprehensive examination, given the diversity of genres represented by the over seven hundred groups and solo artists that have debuted since its emergence in the 1990s. Under the K-pop umbrella, my book focuses on contemporary Korean pop, R&B, and mainstream hip-hop artists (as opposed to underground artists) with substantial careers that span several years (in some cases decades) and who have produced substantial discographies. A comprehensive review of their discographies covers deep cuts in addition to promotional tracks, providing a picture of a group's distinct style, including the use of different kinds of vocals (by singers and rappers) and musical instrumentation from a variety of genres of African American popular music. This review also captures how such performers cite African American popular music culture over time. Such citational practices represent deliberate and intentional references to music elements, as well as participation in existing musical traditions. They also represent an alternative to cultural appropriation as a way of describing K-pop's interaction with other cultures. Going beyond the idea of cultural dilution or imitation, citational practices capture the variety of ways that K-pop engages its musical source material.

The book's examination of K-pop music incorporates song descriptions that reflect the ways both fan audiences and music journalists talk about popular music. In *Listening to Popular Music: Or, How I Learned to Stop Worrying and Love Led Zeppelin*, Theodor Gracyk (2007) refers to "everyday aesthetics" that value the way we ordinarily interact with art: "If the traditional analyses of an aesthetic attitude emphasizes a disinterested contemplation of a distinct object, the new aesthetic directs us to look for aesthetic rewards in any directed awareness of a situation. We should expect to find aesthetic value in any appreciative perceptual experience" (38). Global fans of K-pop express a "directed awareness of a situation" by writing reviews that describe songs in relation to music they already know or marvel at some new take. This approach to cultural production is contextualized by the field of popular music studies, which in *Understanding Popular Music* Roy Shuker (2001) situates within the larger field of cultural studies. This is a mode of cultural studies "where 'culture' is simultaneously the ground on which analysis proceeds" as well as "the object of study" (Grossberg, Nelson, and Treichler 1992, 5). My analysis of K-pop music uses the interpretative and evaluative elements of cultural studies methodology, which links it to other popular music studies books, including Imani Perry's *Prophets in the Hood: Politics and Poets in Hip Hop* (2004) and Mark Anthony Neal's *Songs in the Key of Black Life: A Rhythm and Blues Nation* (2003).

K-pop's citational practices reveal a mode of intertextuality with African American popular music where K-pop artists draw on specific artists and emulate their distinctive styles. Such practices mirror a brand of intertextuality grounded in African American expressive culture that thrives on exchange and influence, according to John P. Murphy (1990): "Creativity in such a language environment is not based on a concept of complete originality (if such a thing is possible), but on repetition and variation, where meaning depends as much on the transformation of existing material as it does on originality" (9). I find a similar dynamic at play in K-pop's citation of black American popular music, where K-pop songs emulate musical elements of R&B genres, but with a difference. By examining how specific K-pop artists engage with the style of specific R&B artists, *Soul in Seoul* interrogates how K-pop broadens particular styles of R&B. Examining the citation by particular K-pop artists of particular American R&B artists also makes lines of influence clear.

Soul in Seoul's focus on song descriptions, with attention to intertextuality and music genealogy, represents a novel approach to the study of K-pop music, one that goes beyond lyrical and musicological analysis. Lyrical analysis represents a particular conundrum for a large constituency of fans who live outside of Korea and do not speak Korean. Most K-pop songs are in Korean with smatterings of English phrases or choruses. Some fans do not even look up translations and others rely on translations that vary in quality and accuracy. Yet, lyrics are not the only way an audience experiences music. Gracyk (2007) adds that "the *music* is designed to reward listening in advance of a decision about the song's subject matter. . . . When listeners respond but do not care or cannot tell what the message is, the response is what we broadly characterize as aesthetic" (62). My study heeds Mark Katz's (2014) call to value the sound of music, for "people engage with music primarily as sound rather than text" (25). It is the same reason why audiences can enjoy instrumental versions of songs with lyrics.

By focusing on song descriptions, my book also diverges from musicological approaches to K-pop, such as Michael Fuhr's *Globalization and Popular Music in South Korea: Sounding Out K-pop* (2016). Katz (2014) notes how musicological approaches focus on formal notation and graphical representation of the music: "To many musicologists, to study music is to focus on notes. . . . And for many, these notes come from works in the Western classical tradition, written often, but not always by white men who are currently dead, and which manifest themselves in the form of scores" (24–25). Not only are most audiences unfamiliar with such formal approaches to popular music, some may question the application of methods developed for classical music to popular music. Moreover, because the audience is a significant part of K-pop culture, it makes sense to examine the music as its audience hears it. This means that song descriptions may also include emotional responses as part of the critical appraisal by fans: "Much popular music is largely a music of the body and emotions, and its influence cannot easily be reduced to simple consideration of its formal musical qualities" (Katz 2014, 22). Musicological approaches often overlook this dimension of the musical experience.

Because it focuses on the impact of the aesthetics of the music, *Soul in Seoul*'s approach also differs from more sociohistorical approaches to black American popular music. These examinations of black popular music reflect what Gracyk (2007) describes as the sociohistorical valuation of music, which suggest "that *every* evaluation of every piece of music (including 'aesthetic' evaluation) can and should attend to social and political values" (49). In *What the Music Said: Black Popular Music and Black Public Culture*, Mark Anthony Neal (1999) defines black popular music largely by its sociohistorical meanings: "Soul music represented the construction of 'hypercommunity' in that both physical and metaphysical notions of space and community, and all the political and social meanings that underlie such formations, converge within its aesthetic sensibilities. Thus, soul music became the ideal artistic medium to foreground the largest mass social movement to emerge from within the African American experience" (40). Neal defines black popular music genres like soul by their role in the civil rights movement. In doing so, he promotes the idea that popular music's primary meaning is social or political in nature. Similarly, Nelson George (1988) links the "death" of R&B largely to the economic impact of corporate expansion in *The Death of Rhythm and Blues*: "Crossover came to dominate all discussions of black music and, eventually, the music itself. In the process, much of what had made the R&B world work was lost, perhaps some of it forever" (147). Central to that crossover was the decline in the black independent record label: "There were many forms of crossover, each of which fed on the others to alter the way the business of black music is conducted. A wave of major label signings from the early to mid-seventies decimated the independents, costing them not just top performers and writers but administrative personnel as well" (George 1988, 147, 148). George links the way music sounds (i.e., its appeal to a mass audience beyond African Americans) to economic shifts that affected the music's production. But this overlooks the aesthetics of the music itself. Sociohistorical approaches to the study of black popular music are important. However, *Soul in Seoul* focuses on the impact of musical innovations as well as how those innovations are perceived by audiences around the world.

Authentic Engagement

Music is only one part of viewing K-pop as part of a global R&B tradition. Through their critical production, fans function as part of K-pop's music press and confer authenticity on K-pop's citations of R&B. *Soul in Seoul* focuses on global fans writing music reviews in English, a subset of a larger global fandom. By focusing on fan critical production, the book contributes new perspectives to fandom studies and East Asian popular culture, which tend to focus on fan attitudes and behavior.

Intertextuality makes the audience key to how performers make their influences obvious. In other forms of black American popular music like jazz, it can be seen this way: "By invoking and reworking music that is familiar to the audience, the jazz performer involves the audience in the process and makes it meaningful for those who recognize the sources" (Murphy 1990, 9). Mainstream music publications, online Korean entertainment platforms, and individual blogs that feature fan reviews have generated a large body of critical reception of K-pop, long before many scholarly sources took up the subject. My study focuses on global fans, or fans located outside of Korea, who write in English. Many are also non-Korean speakers. For some fans, English becomes a default common language. Some online fan clubs with members from multiple countries insist that participants use English. Several K-pop media outlets utilize English as their common language, even though the comments below stories may be in multiple languages.

Such fans may be consumers of K-pop, but they are also very familiar with the musical trajectories of individual groups. While they may lack technical musical knowledge, their reviews consistently relate K-pop to other influences and recognize its connections to the styles and artists of black American popular music. This critical activity occurs on the Internet, making reviews easily accessible and influential to overall perceptions of K-pop. In *Popular Music: The Key Concepts*, Roy Shuker (2017) notes the importance of the audience to intertextuality: "While many consumers may, at least implicitly or subconsciously, accept such preferred readings, it must be kept in mind that it is not necessarily true that the audience as a whole do so. In particular, subordinate groups may reinterpret such textual messages, making 'sense' of them in a different way" (348). Such fans join those who write about music for popular, commercial outlets. They are part of the "music scene," which Richard Peterson and Andy Bennett (2004) describe as a site "in which clusters of producers, musicians and fans collectively share their common musical tastes and collectively distinguish themselves from others" (1). The website of

The Journal of Popular Music (n.d.) recognizes "the insights and expertise of critics, journalists, and those in the industry" as well as "critical assessments of recordings or performances that place them in a wider historical, musical, or cultural context" that may be produced by nonprofessionals. The critical function of fan reviewers distinguishes them from other fans and places them closer to those who provide musical commentary in mainstream media. Such individuals also make up a "music press," a critical music community that includes general writers who produce "reviews of contemporary recordings, artist profiles/interviews, and, most commonly, lifestyles and associated gossip" (Shuker 2001, 84). With the impact of the Internet in the dissemination of K-pop, the music press or music scene includes those who write about music on individual blogs as well as writers who write for mainstream and K-pop media outlets. This connection between the music and the mass listener is particularly significant for popular music; Allan F. Moore (2012) notes that popular songs are created "always with an ear to a particular listening public" and "will only attract that public if they can resonate with potential listeners" (3). Fan reviews describe what the fans hear, and often their reaction to what they hear. As a result, *Soul in Seoul* examines how fans recognize K-pop's citational practice in their own interpretative discourse.

Such fan reviewers also represent a transcultural community. Using animation fans as an example, Sandra Annett (2011) suggests that a transcultural community "allows participants with diverse perspective, who may not be equals in terms of language ability or social status in a given collaboration, to exchange views on media works they enjoy in a many-to-many forum of communities" (174). Like these animation fans, the global K-pop community that writes reviews in English makes up a community that traverses national boundaries. The focus on critical production of fans extends work in transcultural fandom and K-pop beyond a specific nation or region. Some scholarship deemphasizes the transculturality in fandom by focusing on particular regions or countries. In their introduction to *East Asian Pop Culture: Analyzing the Korean Wave* (2008), Chua Beng Huat and Koichi Iwabuchi (2008) utilize "a more systematic comparative analysis, both in terms of its reception and consumption in different locations, and in terms of a comparison with similar genre entertainment from other parts of East Asia" (7). Similarly, in their introduction to *K-pop—The International Rise of the Korean Music Industry* (2015), JungBong Choi and Roald Maliangkay (2015) conclude that "fans of various age, gender, ethnicity, or nationality would have different interest in and expectations from K-pop. . . . The primary site of concern for international fans is their own locality and its cultural milieus" (7). The focus on fans in the East Asian region overlooks the common production of global audiences beyond East Asia, which is as important as studies of local communities.

Rather than drawing on fan behavior, my study follows other scholarship in fan studies by focusing on cultural production in the form of reviews created by this imagined global community of K-pop fans. In *Textual Poachers: Television Fans and Participatory Culture*, Henry Jenkins (2013) identifies fan cultural production as one of five levels of fan activity, one where "fans create works that speak to the special interests of the fan community" (279). JungBong Choi (2015) identifies fans of K-pop as content producers who "curate, manage, and catalyze the formation of the Hallyu phenomenon" (42). The K-pop fan reviewer is an active listener and producer of interpretative commentary in the form of music reviews posted on individual blogs as well as those published by online Korean entertainment media outlets. The critical precursor to such fan production is the fanzine and other critical media produced by fans, which Peterson and Bennett (2004) note "have long served as an important resource for fans of particular genres of music, offering a channel of communication, for example, for the exchange of information about their favorite performers, performances, production techniques, and so on" (11). Such reviews reveal the ability of fans to recognize the musical influences in songs and describe the styles of individual artists because they have a deep knowledge of a large portion of their body of work.

By focusing on the way the content produced by fans confers authenticity, my study embarks on new directions in East Asian fandom studies, which tend to focus on fan attitudes toward the fandom object. Several studies of K-pop rely on ethnography or qualitative methods to uncover the motives behind the actions of K-pop fans. *Korean Masculinities and Transcultural Consumption: Yonsama, Rain, Oldboy, K-pop Idols* by Jung Sun (2011) argues that Singaporean fans of pop singer Rain "embrace the cultural hybridity of Rain's global masculinity, employ advanced media technology to produce and consume *mugukjeok* images of Rain, and frequently cross national and cultural borders in pursuit of the leisure and the entertainment that are provided by their consumption of Rain's overseas concerts" (76). This examination focuses on the behavior of Rain's fans as an exemplar of a particular mindset, for Jung Sun (2011) argues that such behavior "can be understood as driven by the new consumer lifestyles of the new rich that become the basis for an emerging 'cultural Asia'" (75). While these approaches interpret the behaviors of fans as one response to K-pop music, *Soul in Seoul* interprets critical fan production, artifacts of their engagement with the music.

Disruption of Globalization

Viewing K-pop as part of a global R&B tradition reveals the diversity of influences on K-pop and its culture and the global impact of African American cultural production, thereby disrupting homogenizing forms of globalization. Examining the influence of African American popular music, an American ethnic mode of cultural production, adds an additional dimension to the influences on K-pop beyond generalized Western or American cultural forces. The transnational American studies lens detects a different array of influences compared to the focus on economic and political forces often utilized in Korean studies. It also provides a vision of African American cultural production beyond the United States.

Because of the way that R&B music, an American cultural production, informs K-pop, *Soul in Seoul* uses a transnational American studies lens. My definition of K-pop highlights the influence of foreign music cultures, particularly African American popular music cultures, which represent a distinct American musical tradition and reflect the ways that American cultures travel. In her 2004 presidential address to the American Studies Association, Shelly Fisher Fishkin (2005) described the transnational turn in American studies and envisioned ramifications for the field: "We are likely to focus less on the United States as a static and stable territory and population whose most characteristic traits it was our job to divine, and more on the nation as a participant in a global flow of people, ideas, texts and products" (24). Such a turn impacts the way we see cultural production of the United States interact with other cultures: "We need to understand the cultural work that forms originating in the United States do in cultures outside this country" (Fishkin 2005, 33). Such impact relies on the migration not only of people but also of cultural production like African American music. A hybridized form itself, black American popular music is simultaneously shaped by and pushes back against mainstream American cultural forces and as a result, represents a complex mode of interaction with American culture and an interesting model for other global cultures. In particular, African American popular music has a long tradition of travel and impact. In the introduction to *Black Cultural Traffic: Crossroads in Global Performance and Popular Culture*, Kennell Jackson (2005) notes how the movement of black culture can significantly impact the culture of other places. He points to the spread of African aesthetics in art as a result of colonialism: "It was cataclysmic because African art altered the paradigm for the representation of the human body in many arts in the West" (21). Similarly, R&B genres alter the way that post-1990 Korean popular music looks and sounds. This is the result of the influx of an American music tradition.

Much like Western art was impacted by African art aesthetics, K-pop music videos reflect the influence of distinct African American performance aesthetics in choreography, styling, and other visuals. While music videos promote music, Diane Railton and Paul Watson (2011) argue in *Music Video and the Politics of Representation* that the music video is both "a distinct media form with its own patterns of production, codes and conventions of representation, and complex modes of circulation" and "a key site through which cultural identities are produced, inscribed and negotiated" (10). Music videos are particularly salient for the study of K-pop, not only because they focus on the appearance of the artists but also because they transcend the language barrier by working in images that global audiences can consume.

In placing my analysis of K-pop within a transnational American studies context, *Soul in Seoul* pursues a different perspective compared with scholarship in Korean studies focused on Hallyu, or the Korean wave. Studies of the Korean wave initially focused on Korean television drama and film, with little or no coverage of K-pop. Chua and Iwabuchi's (2008) seminal collection *East Asian Pop Culture: Analysing the Korean Wave* focuses solely on Korean television dramas and their impact on largely East Asian locations. Do Kyun Kim and Min-Sun Kim's *Hallyu: Influence of Korean Popular Culture in Asia and Beyond* (2011) extends its analysis to Korean television and film in locations outside of East Asia to include the Middle East but does not feature a single chapter on Korean popular music. Other scholarship in Korean studies focus more on economic forces that impact K-pop and less on the music itself. Sangjoon Lee and Abé Mark Nornes (2015) note that later studies contextualize K-pop within "an economic experience encircling such trends as economic liberalization, deregulation, and the heightened mobility of capital, commodities, services, and labor around the world" (11). K-pop music like Psy's "Gangnam Style" represents "a ready-made export": "Under conditions of globalizing market forces in a digital age, 'Gangnam Style' has become a 'cool' cultural brand promoting Korean exports ranging from mobile phones to cosmetics to consumer electronics" (Nye and Kim 2013, 34). Within such scholarship, K-pop represents a commodity no different from a car or cellphone that can be marketed globally or utilized politically. By contrast, my study centralizes K-pop as cultural production and how global fans make meaning from it.

Other approaches view K-pop largely within a Korea-centric political context. Ingyu Oh (2013) argues that K-pop embodies a unique globalization process: "The localization process therefore includes a special (or Korean) staging formation for boy and girl bands previously unheard of in other countries" (401). Here, K-pop functions as a vehicle for political goals within the Korean wave, characterized by the production and distribution of Korean cultural production globally, initially to East Asia and later to the rest of the world. Such distribution began with Korean films, television, and music, and spread to fashion, cuisine, and other aspects of culture. In the wake of a major economic crisis in the 1990s, Korea developed a culture industry designed to promote Korean culture. The Korean government utilizes the Korean wave to encourage the recognition of Korean culture. As a result, scholars view cultural production such as K-pop as part of a larger political project. Some scholars utilize a neoliberalist framework to examine the cultural products that operate according to the whims of the free market (Yoon 2009). Others point to what they perceive as exploitative industry practices reflected in lawsuits over long contracts, long work days, and lack of profit-sharing for artists, characterizing K-pop merely as a commodity to be consumed. Some scholars focus on the political implications of the Korean wave for K-pop as a tool of soft power. Nye and Kim (2013) describe soft power as "attraction that makes others want what you want," and "co-opts people rather than coerces them" (31). While the global spread of K-pop has economic and political implications, we also need to understand how forces not captured by approaches commonly utilized in Korean studies scholarship influence K-pop. Only by looking at the cultural production itself can we parse the different ways that different cultures shape K-pop. African American music culture may emerge from a Western country that engages in particular globalizing strategies, but it also belongs to a global tradition that offers alternatives to those very globalizing strategies.

Moreover, examining the global impact of African American popular music expands our consideration of black popular culture beyond the United States. From blues and jazz to soul and hip-hop, African American popular culture exerts a great influence on American culture. It is contextualized by the particular historical and cultural experiences of African Americans who exist in a racialized society. At the same time, the cultural production of African Americans has had tremendous global impact beyond the United States, and in the process develops multiple meanings for multiple audiences. By exploring the global impact of these cultures, *Soul in Seoul* complements scholarship that examines the global movement of black American popular culture and its influence on East Asian music cultures. In *Babylon East: Performing Dancehall, Roots Reggae, and Rastafari in Japan*, Marvin D. Sterling (2010) considers "a range of ways in which Japanese perform Jamaican culture, including in gendered, class-based, ethnic, local, national, and transnational terms" and focuses his analysis, "especially in the international context, on race and particularly blackness" (23). In *Hip-Hop Japan: Rap and the Paths of Cultural Globalization*, Ian Condry

(2006) notes that the spread of hip-hop represents a different kind of globalization: "In contrast to symbols of cultural globalization, such as Coca-Cola, Disney, Nike, and McDonald's, which take their cues from huge multinational corporations, hip-hop in Japan draws attention to an improvisatory working out of a cultural movement in language and among peer-groups of a particular generation of youth" (12). *Soul in Seoul* also joins other scholarship on the treatment of R&B outside the United States, including *Black Popular Music in Britain Since 1945*, edited by Jon Stratton and Nabeel Zuberi (2014), and *How Britain Got the Blues: The Transmission and Reception of American Blues Style in the United Kingdom* by Roberta Freund Schwartz (2007).

Soul in Seoul positions itself within popular music studies, fan studies, and transnational American studies to examine K-pop as part of a global R&B tradition. In doing so, it draws attention to K-pop's musical aesthetics, the authenticating function of fans, and the disruption of homogenizing forms of globalization. Subsequent chapters of the book redefine K-pop with a focus on hybridity, which reveals citational practices that draw on African American popular music and are confirmed as authentic by fans who function as part of K-pop's music press. They also examine how Korean pop, R&B, and hip-hop artists exhibit intertextuality with various musical elements of R&B.

• • •

Soul in Seoul begins with chapter 1, "'Listen to the Music': African American Popular Music and K-pop," which redefines K-pop with a focus on hybridity that reveals citational practices that draw on African American popular music and are confirmed as authentic by fans functioning as part of K-pop's music press. I argue that K-pop is a mode of Korean popular music that emerged during the 1990s with global aspirations and a hybridity that combines Korean and foreign musical cultures, particularly African American popular music. This definition goes beyond "idols"—the highly visible pop groups that sing, dance, and engage in extramusical activities—to capture the diversity of K-pop artists that share these characteristics. Historically, there has been limited interpersonal interaction between Koreans and African Americans. Yet, hybridity, K-pop's most salient characteristic, is largely informed by African American popular music. K-pop cites the musical and performative elements of the African American popular music tradition, including its distinctive vocals, innovative instrumentation, and eye-catching choreography and styling. These citational practices reflect intertextuality through the emulation of R&B genres as well as enhancement of that tradition through the use of Korean musical strategies that blend multiple genres and styles. K-pop's citational practices are deemed authentic by global fans who produce critical cultural production in the form of reviews. In doing so, they function as part of the music press for K-pop.

Chapter 2, "'A Song Calling for You': Korean Pop Groups," examines how Korean pop groups, or "idols," exhibit intertextuality by emulating R&B elements in catchy pop songs and enhancing the R&B tradition by infusing multiple genres within R&B songs and utilizing R&B musical elements throughout their careers. Korean pop groups emulate the R&B tradition by citing elements of funk, club, and urban R&B. While "idol" groups like g.o.d (Groove Overdose), 2PM, and Wonder Girls are on the same Korean entertainment label, they cite elements of R&B with very different results. Moreover, Korean and African American producers infuse K-pop with different varieties of R&B. At the same time, Korean pop acts like SHINee, Shinhwa, and TVXQ enhance the R&B tradition by mixing pop genres with R&B within individual songs as well as over the course of their careers. "Idols" also cite the choreography and styling elements of African American performance. Male pop artist Rain (Bi) emulates the dynamic performances of 1990 R&B singers, while K-pop girl group Wonder Girls draw on the retro styling of 1960s African American girl groups. Unlike other types of artists under the K-pop umbrella, Korean pop acts undergo a casting and training system that mirrors the one developed by African American music producer Berry Gordy, who employed image and music quality in the service of cultural work to achieve crossover success for African Americans. Like Gordy, Korean CEOs use this crossover success to shape the global image of their Korean artists. Combining R&B-inflected music and black promotional strategies makes Korean pop part of the global tradition of R&B.

While Korean pop groups incorporate R&B aesthetic elements within a pop context, chapter 3, "'Soul Breeze': Korean R&B Groups and Soloists," reveals that Korean R&B artists exhibit intertextuality by emulating the distinctive instrumentation and gospel-inflected vocals of R&B and enhance the tradition by invoking multiple R&B genres and styles. Korean pop and Korean R&B share similar origins. Groups like Fly to the Sky and 4MEN transitioned from "idol" groups to full-fledged R&B artists. Korean R&B vocal groups like Brown Eyed Soul emulate the R&B tradition by citing soul instrumentation, while Big Mama draws on female gospel-inflected vocals. Other Korean R&B artists enhance the tradition by drawing on and blending various styles. Park Hyoshin enhances the tradition by invoking multiple R&B male vocal styles, while Lyn invokes multiple genres and Zion.T blends R&B and hip-hop. In addition to musical citation, Korean R&B artists like Wheesung cite the dynamic performance style of African American music videos, while Big Mama's styling questions the representation of women in music video, much like African

American female singers. Through this intertextuality, Korean R&B artists reflect vocal authenticity in a global R&B tradition, expanding it beyond the black/white racial binary.

Like Korean R&B artists, Korean hip-hop groups who occupy the mainstream also come under the K-pop umbrella. Chapter 4, "'Rewriting the Résumé': Mainstream Korean Hip-Hop Artists," explores how these hip-hop groups exhibit intertextuality by emulating the R&B tradition through sampling and the use of R&B vocals and enhancing it by mixing multiple genres with hip-hop elements and using live instrumentation. Dynamic Duo emulates the R&B tradition through sampling and the use of R&B vocals, while Epik High and music producer Primary enhance it through eclectic citations of styles not commonly associated with hip-hop as well as the use of live instrumentation. Mainstream Korean hip-hop acts also cite limiting and liberating hip-hop tropes in music videos. Male hip-hop artist Jay Park invokes both a playful male swagger as well as reductive images of women, while female hip-hop artist Yoon Mi-rae draws on images of agency derived from African American female rappers. These Korean hip-hop artists participate in a globalized R&B tradition by promoting its innovative musical aesthetics.

BTS's rising popularity in the United States represents the continuation of the ways that K-pop functions as part of a global R&B tradition. As the book will reveal in detail, K-pop engages in citational practices that reveal intertextuality that involves both African American popular culture and Korean music strategies. Such citational practices are deemed authentic by fan critics who operate as part of K-pop's music press. By considering both the musical elements of K-pop and the response by fan critics, we can see how K-pop, as part of a global R&B music tradition, disrupts homogenizing modes of globalization.

SOUL IN SEOUL

1

"LISTEN TO THE MUSIC"
African American Popular Music and K-pop

Before BTS exploded into the American pop culture imagination in 2017, South Korean rapper Psy propelled K-pop to unprecedented worldwide recognition in the summer of 2012, when his video for the song "Gangnam Style" was the first to achieve over one billion views on YouTube. Since its release, it has garnered over two billion views. Psy was the first South Korean artist to chart at #1 on the iTunes Music Video Chart. He also won the Best Video Award at the MTV Europe Music Awards. Spurred by the popularity of his video, Psy embarked on a promotional jaunt in the United States that included a performance for President Barack Obama as well as appearances on several talk shows. However, his closing performance at the American Music Awards on November 18, 2012, raised a few eyebrows. It began with an introduction by will.i.am, member of the American group Black Eyed Peas, who referenced the millions of YouTube views received by "Gangnam Style." Psy's performance began with the now familiar intro to the song. Centered on the stage and surrounded by dancers, Psy performed the "horse dance" choreography for the majority of the song. Near the end of the song, the stage suddenly went dark and Psy whispered the phrase, "Hammer Time." The lights came up to reveal MC Hammer, a popular African American rapper and performer from the 1990s, standing next to Psy. Both entertainers then danced to a mix of Psy's "Gangnam Style" and MC Hammer's 1991 hit song, "2 Legit 2 Quit" (1991). During the performance, MC Hammer and Psy performed each other's signature choreography. While the performance may have amazed some, it was a given for Psy: "Psy admits that he's been a lifelong fan of Hammer so it wasn't hard for him to go Hammer-time at the AMAs. He tells CNN, 'Honestly, I practiced his move[s] 20 years ago, so I've done that for 20 years" (Schwartz 2012). Some may have dismissed the performance as a quirky, onetime gimmick for the AMAs, but the optics of the performance of MC Hammer's "2 Legit 2 Quit" and Psy's "Gangnam Style" gesture toward the more substantial links between black American popular music and K-pop music. Psy's comment suggests that he was well aware of MC Hammer's work, even as a Korean entertainer. While MC Hammer garnered fame during his heyday, his popularity did not rise to the level of his contemporaries, like Michael Jackson. So Psy's knowledge of MC Hammer's work was more than casual.

While Psy's success reveals hip-hop as a major influence on K-pop, R&B in general exerts an even greater influence. It not only influences Korean acts with obvious hip-hop connections, but even dedicated R&B and more pop-oriented performers. Rain (Jung Ji-hoon), also known as Bi, may be familiar as the lead in the 2009 film *Ninja Assassin*, but he also enjoys a thriving career in East Asia. He showed promise in the American market with two concerts in Madison Square Garden in 2006, when American media dubbed him the Korean Justin Timberlake and the Korean Usher, referencing two major R&B singers in the United States (Sontag 2006). Beginning in 2004, Park Jin-young, the CEO of JYP Entertainment, Rain's Korean agency at the time, consciously incorporated more R&B elements into Rain's music. Performing under the stage name "The Asiansoul" in Korea as an established artist himself, Park also had been writing and producing music for American R&B artists like Mase, Omarion, and Tyrese (H.-J. Shin 2009, 515). Several other Korean artists followed Rain in an attempt to gain a measure of success in the United States. Many of them drew from R&B genres. While Rain achieved a measure of success in the United States, several other Korean artists have not been able to do so. What is interesting is that they all draw from R&B genres. The Korean singer Se7en (Choi Dong-wook) is known for his soulful voice, as an online reviewer of his 2016 album *I Am Se7en* (2016) notes: "On 'Good Night,' we switch to a smooth R&B groove, punctuated with techno highlights. Everyone here is on point here, with Se7en's trademark vibrato and a mellow rap from Reddy. The vocal work here is fantastic, and Se7en does plastic soul as well as anyone" (eric_r_wirsing 2016). Wonder Girls, a Korean pop girl group, may have failed to garner the interest of teenagers, but their music drew attention to their use of R&B in their most popular song, "Nobody" (2007): "It revived the industry with a modern update to old school sounds that drew on Motown and the disco era for inspiration, which resulted in the single becoming one of the most popular Korean songs ever" (Herman 2017a). From R&B to pop singers, R&B has had a clear influence on K-pop.

In order to understand the meaning of the impact of black American popular music R&B on K-pop, we need to change our perceptions of it as trendy, teenage music. Defining K-pop with a focus on hybridity reveals citational practices that draw on African American popular music and are confirmed as authentic by global fans. This definition goes beyond "idols," or Korean performers who sing and dance, to capture the diversity of K-pop artists that transcend genre. Hybridity, K-pop's most salient characteristic, is largely informed by African American popular music and incorporates Korean musical strategies. As a result, K-pop reflects intertextuality through the emulation of R&B genres and enhancement of those genres through the application of Korean popular music aesthetics. Global fans, or fans located outside of South Korea, deem K-pop's citational practices authentic through music reviews. In doing so, they function as part of K-pop's music press.

Defining K-pop

Popular perceptions of K-pop based largely on "idol" groups and singers fail to capture the full extent of the diverse artists under its umbrella. My definition of K-pop goes beyond "idols" to include the range of K-pop artists that share other commonalities.

Popular Definitions of K-pop

Popular descriptions of K-pop narrowly focus on one aspect of K-pop and, as a result, fail to capture a more comprehensive view of the music. Some focus solely on "idols," overlooking the variety of non-idol performers that find themselves under the K-pop umbrella. Others define K-pop by the teenagers that make up the most visible part of its fan base, ignoring its appeal to a broader audience. Still others characterize K-pop solely by its commercial nature, overlooking recognition it acquires for its musical innovation and creativity.

For some, K-pop encompasses all Korean popular music. Writing for *Time*, Ben Cosgrove (2014) pens a story with the headline "K-pop Pioneers: The Kim Sisters Take America," and describes the group as "a kind of proto-K-pop group." This characterization retroactively applies the term K-pop to older forms of twentieth-century Korean popular music rather than the specific mode of post-1990 popular music that "K-pop" represents. Kim Chang Nam (2012) reminds us that "it would be inadvisable to jump to the hasty conclusion that K-pop is merely synonymous with Korean popular music in its most general sense.... The K-pop at the center of growing international interest in Asia and Europe is being applied to a specific form of popular music emerging in a particular period" (9).

When people think about K-pop, they tend to envision "idols," pop groups made up of attractive Korean performers who sing, dance, and cultivate enthusiastic fan bases while engaging in extramusical activities, such as acting in films and television, hosting music and variety programs, endorsing products, and participating in fashion magazine photo shoots. Recruited by large Korean entertainment agencies at young ages, these performers undergo extensive training for years. Some debut and continue to develop their vocal and dance abilities as well as other skills such as foreign-language proficiency and acting. David Bevan (2013) of the *Washington Post* defines K-pop as "an artform—closer to a science" where "prospective performers are recruited and sent through a specially designed, deeply competitive training program meant to prepare them for careers as global pop exports." This training program has been subject to critiques that point to excessively long exclusive contracts and demanding work conditions that require practice after school for the younger trainees and arduous promotion schedules for established groups that often take them away from their families. Critics also frequently describe K-pop "idols" by their appearance and performance. JungBong Choi and Roald Maliangkay (2015) describe K-pop as "a new standard of popular music that is characterized by, among other things, the visual appeal of its idols and performances, as well as by a significant degree of musical conservatism" (1). Writing for the *New Yorker*, John Seabrook (2012) focuses on the eye-catching choreography: "The performers are mostly Korean, and their mesmerizing synchronized dance moves, accompanied by a complex telegraphy of winks and hand gestures, have an Asian flavor, but the music sounds Western: hip-hop verses, Euro-pop choruses, rapping, and dubstep breaks." Using the "idols" as a foundation, others see K-pop as a genre. Michael Fuhr (2016) outlines K-pop's boundaries based on a global imaginary that "is shaped and reflected by multiple practices and textures, as have become evident, for example, in the flexibility of language use, in the multi-dimensional attractivity created by a 360-degree idol star system, in performance-centered songwriting, hook songs, *ppong* melodies, and in choreography and music videos" (118). Many of these characteristics described by Fuhr apply largely to "idols," who are known for their foreign language acquisition, choreography practice, and an emphasis on appearance. It is mostly idols who are employed by "a few talent agencies in place that can afford the investments and provide all facilities necessary to send talents through all of the manufacturing processes and maintain a whole career life cycle once they've made their debut" (Fuhr 2016, 76).

However, defining K-pop solely by "idols" overlooks the other kinds of solo artists and groups that fall under the K-pop umbrella. For example, "The Best K-pop Songs of 2017," a list compiled by Tamar Herman, Jeff Benjamin, and Caitlin Kelley (2017) at *Billboard* magazine, includes not only "idol" groups like EXO, BTS, and Red Velvet but also a number of non-idol acts like Akdong Musician, Loco, and IU. Akdong Musician is a brother-sister singer-songwriter duo represented by YG Entertainment, one of the "Big Three" Korean entertainment agencies that represents "idols," but they do not engage in choreography and their music is not "performance-centered." Loco is a Korean rapper represented by AOMG, an independent hip-hop label founded by Korean American rapper Jay Park, and Korean rapper Simon Dominic. IU, a female singer, was also featured on the *New York Times Magazine* "25 Songs That Tell Us Where Music Is Going" list in 2018. Lindsey Weber (2018) describes her as "one of K-pop's rare chart-topping singer-songwriters." Online East Asian music databases show that K-pop audiences recognize non-idol acts as part of K-pop. *jpopasia*, an online community for enthusiasts of Japanese popular music (J-pop), also features in-depth profiles of Korean R&B artists like Big Mama, Brown Eyed Soul, and Lyn, Korean electronic music groups like House Rulez, Korean rock groups like Jaurim and Nell, and Korean indie groups like Urban Zakapa and Standing Egg. A search for K-pop on *generasia*, a website that describes itself as "the largest Asian media wiki on the planet," brings back results that includes a similar range of artists. A definition of K-pop that only focuses on "idols" excludes artists like these, who are considered K-pop artists by critics and audiences alike.

Moreover, the boundaries between pop and other types of music in K-pop are more fluid than many expect. Pop groups often feature respected Korean rappers on tracks. Kim Hyun-joong, a member of the Korean pop group SS501, features rappers on his 2013 solo album *Round 3*. The promoted track, "Unbreakable," features respected Korean American hip-hop artist Jay Park. In 2017 Park signed with Roc Nation, the management company run by American rap mogul Jay-Z. Korean R&B artists also create tracks that feature Korean rappers. Big Mama, a female Korean R&B group, features veteran Korean hip-hop artist MC Mong (Shin Dong-hyun) on its track "Heaven" (2007). Veteran Korean hip-hop group Dynamic Duo features Naul from the Korean R&B group Brown Eyed Soul on its track "Chulchek" (2007). These artists work in different genres but they also work together. The artists themselves acknowledge K-pop's fluidity, as Tablo of the hip-hop trio Epik High suggests an interview: "Even K-pop influences us. Even K-pop of this time. A lot of people would be surprised by that. . . . Even the Wonder Girls [an "idol" group]. Or a lot of the songs that JYP [Entertainment] makes. I hear their stuff and it's not like that's my preferred choice of genre or whatever, but there's a lot in that music that I hear and I'm like, 'Wow, that's pretty cool,' you know?" (S.-Y. Kim 2011). Moreover, Korean television shows referred to as K-dramas expose global audiences to a wide variety of music that audiences describe as K-pop. Most K-dramas have an official soundtrack (OST), which brings together artists from different genres. The lead ballad for *Descendants of the Sun*, one of the most-watched K-dramas of 2016, is performed by Yoon Mi-rae, also known as Tasha, a female hip-hop artist and member of the Korean hip-hop trio MFBTY, which includes veteran Korean hip-hop artists Tiger JK and Bizzy. The soundtrack also features songs by pop vocalist K. Will, R&B vocalist Lyn, and rock band MC the Max.

A definition of K-pop based solely on "idols" also contributes to the tendency to describe K-pop's audience as only made up of teenagers. Fuhr (2016) describes K-pop as "teenager-oriented, star-centered, and mass-produced by multi-faceted entertainment conglomerates" (59). Kim Chang Nam (2012) notes that K-pop artists "have come to enjoy popularity among teens" (9). Mainstream media and online sources echo these sentiments by comparing male Korean pop groups to American boy bands who also boast large teenage female fan bases. The general consensus of comments in a K-pop subgroup on Reddit in response to the YouTube video, "What Koreans Think About Foreigners Who Love K-pop" confirms the belief that K-pop is only for teenagers: "I mean, if you're from America and in your mid-20s, don't you think it's strange among your coworkers if you tell them how much of a One Direction fan you are? That's the equivalent here. K-pop appeals mostly to the preteen-teen crowd." While teenagers may make up the most visible demographic of K-pop fans, they are not the only audience for the music. Several K-pop groups who have been active for decades have fans who started out as teenagers, grew up with the group and maintained their interest as adults, making them adult K-pop fans. Despite a four-year hiatus, first-generation K-pop group Shinhwa sold out a concert commemorating their fourteenth anniversary in Seoul in 2012 in a venue that seats twenty thousand with no new material released and little promotion before the concert. Jarryn Ha (2015) points to the emergence of "uncle fans," or "adult males, mostly in their 30s, openly following young female pop idols and actively engaging in fan groups and activities" (44). The 2017 KCON, a global Korean pop music convention, featured the panel "The Return of the Secret Life of K-pop Fans Over 30," the sequel to a similar panel the previous year.

Others characterize K-pop by the high level of extramusical activity by "idol" groups, which contributes to the perception of K-pop as a solely commercial venture lacking any creative merit. John Lie (2014) contrasts K-pop with high art: "K-pop, as a mercenary pursuit, does not stay true to its art (such as its art may be). In this sense, K-pop flatly contradicts the European Romantic ideal of the artist as a seeker after Beauty and Truth.... Nearly every aspect of K-pop is functional, intended to satisfy the market rather than fulfill some deep artistic or political urge" (176). Zoe Chace (2012) of *NPR* describes the K-pop music process as a factory, where "Korea decided to produce pop music like it produces cars.... So music moguls in the country created hit factories, turning young singers into pop stars and sending them on tour around Asia." Writing for *SPIN* magazine, David Bevan (2012) describes the producers of K-pop as "architects" and K-pop as "Korea's most useful export to U.S. and European labels." These metaphors focus on the constructed nature of K-pop, embodying the ideas of Theodor W. Adorno (2000), who also criticized popular music on similar grounds: "Popular music, however, is composed in such a way that the process of translation of the unique into the norm is already planned and, to a certain extent, achieved within the composition itself. The composition hears for the listener. This is how popular music divests the listener of his spontaneity and promotes conditioned reflexes." Adorno implies that the commercialization process strips pop music of any artistic merit, making it merely a shadow of "real" music made solely to appeal to the masses. Similarly, K-pop functions exclusively as a vehicle for profit in this view.

K-pop is also viewed as primarily commercial fare because it lacks the social relevance of other forms of popular music. Robert W. Stephens (1984) argues that 1960s soul "[responded] to changes in the social, political and philosophical views of the black community" (31). Punk music represents a rejection of the materialism and corporatization in mainstream music of the 1970s. Tricia Rose (1994) points out that rap music is "a direct extension of African-American oral, poetic, and protest traditions" (25). These radically different music genres of popular music share what Gracyk (2007) describes as the sociohistorical valuation of music, which suggests "that *every* evaluation of every piece of music (including 'aesthetic' evaluation) can and should attend to social and political values" (49). Because K-pop is not the soundtrack of a social or political movement, it lacks this kind of sociohistorical value, which contributes to its perception as creatively insignificant.

However, K-pop's commercial nature does not negate its creative value. Gracyk (2007) notes that comparisons between "high" and "low" art have particular implications: "Exploration of aesthetic value is so inescapably bound to the history of fine art that aesthetic values just *are* fine art values, which are, in turn, elite values" (34). Yet, Gracyk argues that popular music can also have aesthetics: "Most cultural products ... have an aesthetic dimension that can, is, and *should* be assessed. In some situations, other modes of value can and should take precedence" (Gracyk 2007, 33). Just because K-pop is not produced in the same way as fine art does not mean it does not have aesthetics and creative value. David Sanjek (1997) argues that music can be simultaneously commercial and possess creative and aesthetic value: "Separating the creators of musical forms from their marketers may satisfy for some of us a lingering predilection for the debatable notion that commerce inevitably sullies creativity. However, it enables us neither to construct a broad-minded analysis of national popular expression nor to understand the constraints within which all forms of culture, musical or otherwise, operate" (538). Viewing K-pop solely through a commercial lens overlooks the very aspects of the music that have contributed to its global success. Survey data reveals that music is the primary reason that fans outside of Korea like K-pop. In their quantitative study of K-pop fans in Latin America, Dani Madrid-Morales and Bruno Lovric (2015) found that 85 percent of respondents identified K-pop as their favorite music genre (33). K-pop fans' keen interest in the music itself is also demonstrated through their downloading and streaming habits. Some take to YouTube to make covers of their favorite songs, sometimes even rearranging the music itself. It is not just fans who find K-pop's music compelling. Claude Kelly, an American songwriter who has worked with Bruno Mars and Ledisi, is part of a cadre of American music songwriters and producers who sees K-pop as fertile, musical ground: "Some writers with bridges to spare have found an unexpected—though not unwelcome—refuge in South Korea, where K-pop artists still treasure the songcraft that persisted in R&B's mainstream until the early 2000s: Meaty chord changes, harmonic richness and a bridge that demands a singer demonstrate range and ad-libbing ability" (Leight 2018). K-pop's global reception suggests that people are drawn to K-pop because of its musical innovation, even as commercially produced music.

Definitions of K-pop focused on Korean pop groups, a teenaged audience, and its commercial nature fail to account for the wide variety of artists under the K-pop umbrella. But if this is the case, then how can we describe K-pop?

A New Definition of K-pop

In order to capture the diverse array of artists under the K-pop umbrella, I define K-pop as a kind of contemporary Korean popular music that first emerged in the 1990s, has global aspirations, and features a hybridity that combines Korean and foreign music elements.

K-pop has been linked to broad conceptions of Korean popular music. Keith Howard's (2006) edited collection, *Korean Pop Music: Riding the Wave*, the first monograph in English on K-pop, begins its analysis by tracing K-pop's roots back to the 1930s. *K-pop: Popular Music, Cultural Amnesia, and Economic Innovation in South Korea*, by John Lie (2014), begins its analysis with "traditional Korean music" and "the world of sound before the introduction of Western music towards the end of the Choson dynasty (1392–1897)" (16). In *K-pop: Roots and Blossoming of Korean Popular Music*, Kim Chang Nam (2012) prefaces the discussion of K-pop with an overview of the Korean popular music from the 1960s, 1970s, and 1980s.

However, the term K-pop began as an analogue to J-pop to describe popular music from Korea that began to make inroads in other, largely East Asian countries. K-pop emerged in the wake of specific economic and political changes in Korea that culminated in the 1990s to make the development of the K-pop music industry possible. In the decades following the Korean War, Korea experienced rapid modernization in a very short period of time. This swift transformation was grounded in what Charles Harvie and Hyun-hoon Lee (2003) describe as an outward-facing economic policy during the 1960s based on exports (260). At the same time, the government ruled through military regimes until the 1980s: "Military governments repressed creative freedom and strictly regulated the activities of those individuals and businesses that attempted to develop cultural products that did not support the government's economic objectives" (Kwon and Kim 2014, 425). Such regimes were particularly wary of the impact of foreign cultures, which they believed undermined Korean values, and sought to limit their influence. Jeff Chang (2008) recalls: "As early as the summer of 1971, U.S.-backed dictator Park Chung-hee ordered his police to round up longhaired Korean men and cut their hair. As the decade wore on, he escalated his 'social purification' campaign, detaining artists, intellectuals and church leaders. In the first six months of 1976 alone, police reported checking over 600,000 men on hair length and possession of 'obscene' T-shirts."

Korea became a democracy in the 1980s with an economy fueled by exports, but by 1997, the country faced a debilitating financial crisis. Hyun-chin Lim and Joon Han (2003) point to excessive borrowing as the chief cause: "Given the over-leveraged financial structure of the Korean corporate sector and overexposure to short-term external debt, the profitability shock triggered by a collapse of export prices such as semi-conductors incurred a series of *chaebol* bankruptcies" (200). The financial setback was severe enough to prompt a bailout by the International Monetary Fund. The crisis and subsequent request for aid revealed problems with the Korean economy and raised questions about Korea's ability to regulate its own economy. Previously seen as one of several East Asian "tiger" economies, "the crisis brought attention to the dark side of the Korean model, turning the Korean *miracle* into the Korean *mirage*" (Lim and Han 2003, 199). The economic crisis damaged Korea's global reputation, leading Eric Toussaint (2006) to declare, "I cannot see Korea as a model to be imitated.... The Korean way is neither commendable nor reproducible" (4211). The financial debacle motivated Korea to change its economic structure and rehabilitate its global reputation through the development and promotion of cultural industries, which included the music industry. Sung Sang-yeon (2010) links the self-perception of Asian nations and popular culture: "By consuming popular culture, people create a certain image in their minds.... Now that people can watch any music videos, movies and soap operas from the internet, the role of popular culture plays in constructing national image is greater" (28). One of the music industries to benefit is the K-pop industry, and the Korean government functioned as a key figure in its development. Seung-ho Kwon and Joseph Kim (2014) notes that the Korean government implemented initiatives designed to "facilitate the growth of firms within the domestic industry by providing cultural industry funding" between 1993 and 2012 (5). During this time, Korean entertainment agencies morphed from general business entities to sites that blended music production and profit. Before the crisis, music production was largely governed by broadcasting stations, but Solee I. Shin and Lanu Kim (2013) point to the repeal of the Basic Press Law in 1987 as a key factor in the expansion of the television market, which contributed to a diversification of musical types and provided the opportunity for Korean entertainment agencies to capitalize on the development of a musical market (262). Shin Hyun-joon (2009) argues that entertainment companies benefited from the government's focus on culture industries and diversified their offerings of music and television by using digital platforms while simple production companies remained dependent solely on record sales, taking "all the risky functions of the industry (similar to 'R&D' in other industries) and the winner takes all the profit" (511). These specific economic and political developments in Korea during the 1990s created the environment for the emergence of the K-pop music industry.

The subsequent rise of Korean entertainment agencies also had an impact on Korean youth, providing a new avenue where they could aspire to become artists. Korea's rapid modernization and economic upswing created a different experience for the *sinsaedae*, or new generation, identified as those born after 1970. Rebecca Y. Kim (2015) notes how they differed from their parents' generation: "The *sinsaedae* grew up without memories of war, poverty, and military dictatorships. They grew up as only children or with just one sibling in well-to-do middle-class families in the metropolis.... They grew up amid unprecedented economic growth and consumer individualism" (157). Part of this distinction involved being free of political concerns, in contrast to the "386 generation," which "spent most of their youth fighting for democracy under authoritarian rule" and "who will go down in history as a very active and passionate group of people who toppled a military dictatorship of more than three decades and built democracy in Korea" (S.-Y. Park n.d.). The *sinsaedae* was profoundly impacted by the 1997 financial crisis, which disrupted its economic sense of security: "Raised in an affluent society with full access to the Internet, this new generation witnessed their fathers being kicked out of jobs and their families collapsing" (S.-Y. Park n.d.). The generation following the *sinsaedae*, the *pal-ship-pal-man-won-sae-dae*, or 880,000 Korean Won Generation, was also affected by economic changes. 880,000 represents the average monetary accumulation of Koreans in their twenties. Unlike their *sinsaedae* counterparts, this sector of Korean youth had vastly different prospects: "Those born with a 'golden spoon' in their mouths get into the best universities and secure the plum jobs, while those born with a 'dirt spoon' work long hours in low-paying jobs without benefits" (Fifield 2016). Media have focused on how youth characterize Korea as "Hell Joseon," a term coined in 2015, "which harks back to the five-century-long, feudal Joseon dynasty's class system and lampoons a growing inequality between the haves and not-haves in Korean society" (Ock 2017). This perspective has developed despite Korea's economic promise. Against this backdrop, some Korean youth see the entertainment industry as a means of escape from such dismal prospects. Oh and Lee (2013) assert that Korean youth aspire to be like K-pop performers, as it gives them pride in being Korean. They define this as "Korean-style cosmopolitan striving," based on the notion "that Korean society, which suffers from *han*/melancholia, awards more social legitimacy to those who achieve economic gain and sports victories overseas than those who garner similar achievements in domestic competition" (Oh and Lee 2013, 115). Korean youth want to be like K-pop stars because they want to achieve success as Koreans in a global arena. The Korean identity of the K-pop performers is clearly significant.

Contextualized by specific historical and economic circumstances, K-pop also reflects global aspirations. When the Korean entertainment companies developed, they focused on the creation of domestic cultural production with a global destination and the government provided help. The Ministry of Culture, Sports and Tourism was established in 1990 by presidential decree, upgraded from a mere division. Its mission includes "establishing a brand as a cultural country" by "improving pride of the citizens through enhancing a national brand" and "expanding cultural territory through *Hallyu*" (MCST n.d.). The MCST formed partnerships with other agencies, including the Korea Creative Content Agency (KCCA). Established in 2009, KCCA (n.d.) describes part of its mission as supporting "the promotion of various overseas expansion projects to develop the content industry into an export industry." The Korean government has subsidized expos in Europe and Japan, organized international concerts, and subsidized concerts by the largest Korean entertainment companies (KCCA n.d.). Korean agencies receive subsidies from the Korean government, thereby tying K-pop to the country's efforts to rehabilitate its global image.

Moreover, such global aspirations impacted the promotion of K-pop. Technology helped promote K-pop's spread beyond Korea, a new feat considering that most popular music remained within national boundaries: "What digitized music and music video, which in turn could be disseminated with relatively low cost, did was to generate a condition of possibility of reaching a mass audience outside of national borders without a massive investment" (Lie 2012, 353). Ingyu Oh and Gil-sung Park (2012) argue that the advent of social media was also crucial: "YouTube has been pivotal in creating secondary users and future fans of K-pop, while maintaining the ongoing popularity of K-pop in Asia" (372). This resulted in increased attention to overseas audiences. K-pop concerts, initially limited to locales within East Asia, spread to locations within East Asia and then to Europe and North and South America. First-generation K-pop group H.O.T. held a concert in China in 2000, at a time when Asian music groups rarely toured beyond their home countries. Their Japanese counterparts, despite coming from an even more vibrant pop music culture, rarely toured outside of Japan. Later, Korean agencies would hold "family" concerts featuring many of the artists on their label in Japan, China, Taiwan, Indonesia, Thailand, France, and the United States. Some pop groups, like TVXQ, produce unique releases in Japanese solely for the Japanese market, while others, like Super Junior-M, release tracks in Korean and Chinese in order to cultivate fans in both countries. These global aspirations extend to the creation and maintenance of a global fan base by providing content in the form of interviews and video messages for fans in particular countries. Korean agencies make content available for global fans, using social media platforms such as Vryl and Navercast with various language options. These unique promotion strategies have paid off, making K-pop music a solid subculture in a wide variety of countries around the world.

K-pop's global reach has also sparked backlash in the form of critiques from other countries. In Japan, the backlash is tied to a fear of Korean cultural products supplanting native cultures against the backdrop of a long history of Korean-Japanese hostilities. Government officials have raised eyebrows at K-pop's spread, and some Japanese celebrities have articulated their fears about Korean popular culture squeezing out Japanese culture. Writing for the *Korea Times*, Park Si-soo (2014) notes that K-pop and K-drama "face grave challenges sparked by chauvinistic right-wing politicians and activists in Japan" and are subject to "anti-Korean rallies" where protesters march near businesses selling Korean pop culture merchandise, "waving Japanese flags and chanting hate messages in unison." In other instances, K-pop has become caught in political disputes, such as China's disapproval of South Korea's hosting of the US-produced Terminal High Altitude Area Defense (THAAD) missile system in early 2017: "China has in recent weeks begun alleging code violations against South Korean firms as an excuse to shut down some of South Korean company Lotte's retail facilities in China, and it has blocked online trade in South Korean goods. China has lashed out at high-profile Korean firms in entertainment, consumer goods, travel and the like" (Mody 2017). Despite such backlash, K-pop continues to target global destinations.

In addition to global aspirations, K-pop music features a hybridity that blends Korean and foreign music cultures. Some scholars, like Lie (2014), argue that K-pop contains no Korean culture: "K-pop is inauthentic in that it is neither Korean nor South Korean. Not only is it different from traditional Korean music, it also diverges from the long tradition of Korean popular music" (176). Lie defines K-pop's Korean identity by its proximity to traditional Korean culture. Furthermore, Lie (2014) relegates the Korean cultural presence in K-pop to a brand: "It may be faint praise to say that K-pop, as a product of Brand (South) Korea, is as good as a top-of-the-line Samsung cell phone: engineered to (near) perfection, reliable but affordable, stylish yet functional, and easy on the eye" (178). However, K-pop features several key elements of Korean culture made possible by Korea's specific cultural and economic changes. K-pop songs are sung largely in Korean, and language is one of the most significant markers of culture, even more so for Koreans; Sangjoon Lee and Abé Mark Nornes (2015) note that "the Korean language is, however, not widely spoken, and only ethnic Koreans can communicate with each other using it" (7). K-pop songs contain English phrases of varying lengths, but all-English versions of K-pop songs remain rare. The Korean language is part of K-pop's global appeal. In my blog post "The 'K' in K-pop" (2012), I observe that global fans identified the Korean language as a major reason for the appeal of K-pop and found the Korean language beautiful. Interest in K-pop music has also fueled the recent increased interest in the Korean language. Rosemary Feal, executive director of the Modern Language Association, attributes the large increase in enrollment in Korean language courses to Korean popular culture like K-pop music: "There's no doubt that Korean popular culture in film and music has captivated the minds of young people" (Gordon 2015). The presence of the Korean language in K-pop music links it to Korean culture.

In addition, most of the creative personnel involved in K-pop are Korean. Psy's Korean identity was inseparable from the popularity generated by his hit "Gangnam Style." His meteoric rise was unprecedented exactly because no other Korean performer had gained such a level of worldwide recognition. Such global attention elicited a certain level of pride from Koreans and Korean Americans who never thought they would see such a phenomenon in their lifetimes. Psy himself expressed the responsibility he felt as a Korean performer: "All the people in Korea are cheering me like I'm a gold medalist or something, so I have a responsibility to my country" (Rashid 2012). Psy's popularity in the United States drew on stereotypes of Asian men, another signal of the significance of his Korean identity. Psy's comedic performance and rotund appearance mirrored "racial stereotypes that Hollywood and the television media have long perpetuated: Think Long Duk Dong from *16 Candles* or Leslie Chow from *The Hangover*. Like Psy, they epitomize the 'comedic Asian male' troupe: buffoonish, desexualized, and emasculated" (Pan 2012). Psy's ethnicity also played a role in some of the inevitable backlash he experienced. Gil Asakawa (2012) reminds us that Psy's American Music Award performance was not without controversy: "Within minutes, blowback flew out over Twitter. Most of the messages were gut reactions to the irony of a song sung mostly in Korean being featured on the 'American' Music Awards. . . . Some of the tweets, though, were flat-out racist." The Korean identity of performers plays a role in the way they simultaneously challenge and engage in existing cultural dynamics.

K-pop music also engages in unique Korean production strategies that depend on and encourage audience participation. K-pop music artists often collaborate with foreign music personnel. Ingyu Oh (2013) notes that agencies "outsource original music scores to Western (notably Swedish, American and British) composers" (399). Pelle Lidell, a Swedish music producer at Universal Music Publishing, has written several top K-pop hits by "idol" groups, including TVXQ's "Mirotic" and Girls' Generation's "Tell Me Your Wish (Genie)." He has also organized music camps where European writers work with executives from SM Entertainment (Lindvall 2011). K-pop music has also engaged the services of American music producers and DJs. However, Korean producers are ultimately responsible for the sound of the music. Yoo Young-jin, SM Entertainment's veteran music producer, explains how he uses foreign music material: "I don't take a song from a foreign songwriter and just use it. Their songs are incredibly simple in terms of melody, lyrics and arrangement so I add certain parts to the song that I think are necessary to succeed in Korea" ("[Interview] Yoo Young Jin" 2010b).

At the same time, K-pop engages in unique promotional strategies that depend on and encourage audience participation. While other musical artists cultivate fan bases and may even coordinate fan activities, K-pop's promotional strategies uses the unprecedented access to fans that social media affords.

Korean agencies appeal directly to local and global audiences by inviting fans to interact with members of groups via Twitter, Instagram, and other social media platforms. Many K-pop groups maintain Twitter and Instagram accounts. In Korea, fan interest is parlayed through official fan clubs, which offer special perks for "fanmeets," concerts, and merchandise for a membership fee. While most official fan clubs are not open to them, global fans have established their own online fan clubs that range from the maintenance of a fan Twitter account or Facebook page to well-organized ventures where fan groups interact with the K-pop artists themselves. For example, when Girls' Generation traveled to New York as part of the 2011 SM Town in NYC family concert, Soshified, an unofficial US-based fan club not affiliated with SM Entertainment, also organized a fanmeet that SNSD attended (KisforKARENX3 2011). Korean companies also allow fans to post and remix material on platforms like YouTube and support other fan activities such as cover song and cover dance competitions judged by Korean artists. Such coordinated efforts to cultivate and maintain the relationship between K-pop artists and their fans is a distinguishing feature of K-pop.

While K-pop music blends Korean and foreign musical traditions, there is a particular brand of hybridization at play that involves Korean and African American music culture.

K-pop and African American Music Culture

While K-pop is influenced by several foreign music cultures, its hybridity is largely informed by African American popular music. Even though historical black–Korean interaction is limited, it acts as a precursor to K-pop's citational practices with black American music culture. K-pop's hybridity not only reflects the hybridity of African American popular music, but also drives its citation.

Black–Korean Interaction

Interpersonal interaction between Koreans and blacks includes the presence of African American soldiers in the Korean War, a small black community in Korea resulting in part from African immigration, and black mixed-race Koreans. Moreover, the media represents a site where race and ethnicity meet in the popularity of black mixed-race celebrities, the influx of African American culture in the 1970s and via Asian Americans in the 1980s and 1990s.

A limited history of black–Korean interaction in Korea acts as a precursor to the musical and performative citational practices we see in K-pop. The influx of African American culture into Korea is inseparable from the history of US–South Korean relations since the end of World War II. Allied nations, with the United States at the forefront, spurred the creation of the 38th parallel, which split the Korean peninsula into its current configuration of Democratic People's Republic of Korea (North Korea) and Republic of Korea (South Korea) without much input from Koreans themselves and little concern about the ramifications on the peninsula. Charles Holcombe (2011) notes that the parallel was "a mere line on a Pentagon office wall map, reflecting no particular preexisting cultural or geographic conditions" for the United States (295). The United States continued to influence domestic matters after the division. In South Korea, the United States supported anticommunist Korean leaders, some of whom were former exiled Korean nationalists (Holcombe 2011, 296). The United States also exercised influence at crucial points during the protracted fourteen-year negotiation of the 1965 Korea-Japan Normalization Treaty, acting as a mediator over Japanese fishing vessel seizures by Korea, massaging the removal of Kim Jong Pil, a politician who both sides agreed acted as an obstacle to the negotiation, and providing assurances and support for negotiations from the highest levels of American government, the White House (Cha 1996, 134, 138). Such interventions on the part of the United States did not always engender positive feelings from Koreans. Sometimes they viewed US actions as incursions on South Korean sovereignty and nursed anti-American sentiments. J. Mark Mobius (1966) notes that during the negotiations for the 1965 Korea-Japan Treaty, Koreans felt "that Americans have a lack of understanding of the feelings and aspirations of the Korean people" and that "the United States policy-makers do not understand 'Asian feelings'" (247). The student movements that help topple oppressive regimes in Korea also criticized the United States for its role in propping up those regimes. The student protests during Chun Doo-hwan's administration (1980–88) promoted the idea that US intervention was directly responsible for separation of North and South Korea. Anti-American sentiment during the administrations of Roh Tae-woo (1988–93) and Kim Young-Sam (1993–98) were linked to American stances on reunification and South Korea's relationship with North Korea (Oh and Arrington 2007, 336, 341).

Within the context of US-Korean relations, African Americans occupy a complex place. On one hand, African Americans are Americans, and as such are associated with the American military presence in Korea. As African American soldiers participated in the American military and diplomatic engagement with South Korea during and after the Korean War, some African Americans saw the conflict as an opportunity to bolster their standing in American society. Michael Cullen Green (2010) explains that "a larger (or at least more vocal) segment of the black public championed American intervention" and exhibited "a desire to appear patriotic in light of a crystallizing Cold War consensus on American foreign policy" (121). By aligning themselves with the United States in this way, some African American soldiers began to view Koreans through the racial lens of their white American counterparts. They believed North Koreans practiced "a distinctive, and utterly foreign and uncivilized, Asian way of war" and saw their South Korean allies as "barbaric, cunning, or ungrateful," routinely falling back upon imagery of the American West and Native Americans (Green 2010, 125). Black soldiers aligned themselves with the United States using the terms crafted within the context of American racial discourse. On the other hand, African Americans viewed South Koreans as victims of the same forces that perpetuated segregation in the United States. Greene (2010) notes that "private black citizens also labeled the war an imperialist, racist endeavor, especially during its first months. . . . [One editorial letter writer], observing that many South Koreans appeared reluctant to resist their northern countrymen, inquired if intervention might precipitate a global 'war of the color line'" (120).

The American military presence in South Korea, with soldiers that included African Americans, is one source of a small black population in South Korea that has developed. As a result of their presence, some of that population are black mixed-race. Ji-hyun Ahn (2014) notes that "in the Korean context, Amerasian symbolizes racial relations between America and Korea in modern-day Korea, particularly after the Korean War" and includes black mixed-race individuals (395). Such individuals represent a racial difference within the largely monoethnic Korean society. In some ways, their presence results in negative stereotypes and treatment toward African-descended people, which reflects American racial politics. Mary Lee (2008) notes this application during the 1970s in military camps: "Soldiers stationed in Korea admitted that 'Korean locals have been subjected to the attitudes of the white majority for so long that they practice discrimination without even being aware of what they're doing'" (69). Africans and African Americans in South Korea have noted such discriminatory treatment. Han Geon-soo (2003) notes the attitudes formed by African migrants in Korea: "These migrant workers point out that Korean people have a strong tendency toward racism. Most of them have experienced discrimination based on their skin color. Whenever they introduce themselves as African, Korean people relate Africa to poverty, famine and tribal war" (168). Such attitudes persist today for African Americans as well. Dave Hazzon (2014), writing for *Groove Korea*, notes that "experiences in Korea are tainted by the perception that blacks are lower than other races: Blacks are violent, unintelligent and poor. Black Americans are not really American, and are inappropriate teachers for Korean children." Such attitudes filter into media with recurrent instances of blackface on popular Korean television shows.

There has also been interaction between African Americans and Koreans in the United States. As a result of post-1965 changes in immigration law, the United States experienced an influx of immigrants from Asia, including Koreans, who settled in urban areas such as New York, Seattle, and Los Angeles as well as in locations in the American South and Midwest. One major flash point of the interaction between the groups occurred with the 1992 uprising in Los Angeles, which occurred in the wake of the acquittal of four white policemen in the brutal beating of motorist Rodney King. The ensuing destruction of property eventually made it to Korean businesses, many of which were also located in largely black neighborhoods. As a result, some see the uprising as indicative of tensions between African Americans and Korean immigrants, especially if they link the uprising to the Latasha Harlins case. While many characterize the relationship between African Americans and Koreans in the United States in negative terms, others point to major instances of solidarity and cooperation, especially in the wake of the LA uprising.

At the same time, media has opened an alternative site for cultural interaction informed by race and ethnicity. Ahn (2014) points to the significance of the media coverage surrounding Hines Ward, the American football player who is the son of a Korean mother and an African American father, who was named Most Valuable Player for the Pittsburgh Steelers when the team won the 2006 Super Bowl: "Because it was the first time ever in Korean television that the black body was represented with honour and respect, the Hines Ward moment is essential to understand racial reconfiguration in the Korean televisual landscape.... The moment in which the Korean media represented Hines Ward, a black mixed-race Korean, as a national hero was a monumental one not only in terms of media practice but also in terms of racial politics in popular culture" (397, 398).

Within the realm of K-pop, there are black and black mixed-race figures who have also attained a measure of fame, including singer Insooni and rapper Yoon Mi-rae. Sam Okyere, a television personality from Ghana, has been called "the most famous black man in Korea." Even though he has encountered racism, Okyere's learning the Korean language was linked with changing Korean perceptions, in the opinion of Benny Luo (2017): "He was offered a gig on a Korean reality show called 'Island Village Teachers,'... That was the first time he realized that language can break barriers. The fact that he was able to communicate with Koreans in their native tongue made him realize how powerful language is."

Such black–Korean interaction acts as a precursor to the hybridity at the heart of K-pop.

Hybridity in K-pop and African American Popular Music

K-pop and African American popular music are both hybrid musical forms, drawing on other sources to develop a different mode of music. While K-pop cites from a variety of sources, its citation of African American popular music is most influential and apparent, given the distinctive nature of black popular music and its hybridity.

While interaction between African Americans and Koreans is limited in Korea, the impact of African American culture is much more significant. During the 1960s, Korea experienced an influx of black popular culture as a result of the American military presence. Movement is at the heart of cultural mobility, what Stephen Greenblatt (2010) calls "the restless process through which texts, images, artifacts, and ideas are moved, disguised, translated, transformed, adapted, and reimagined in the ceaseless, resourceful work of culture" (4). Cultures are embedded not just in individuals but also in artifacts and ideas and undergo transformation, even as they transform other cultures they encounter. Yet, the effects of cultural mobility are also determined by the kinds of texts and ideas that flow into a country. The influx of American culture into Korea is unique because of the diverse nature of US culture. Noting the movement of American cultures, Emory Elliott (2007) recognizes that "many people of color lived in fluid transnational cultural borderlands developing political and cultural centers of contact and exchange that nourished their work" (10). This focus on particularly ethnic cultures in a global context results in "new worlds of previously ignored or erased diasporic interrelationships and remarkable cultural interpenetrations" (Elliott 2007, 13).

K-pop music is significantly impacted by African American musical culture, which is a part of American culture, making it an artifact of the very "cultural interpenetrations" that Elliott describes. When American culture travels, so does black American culture. The American military presence brought African American music through media sponsored by the US Armed Forces as well as Hollywood (Lie 2012, 343). During the 1960s, black American music dominated the American pop scene. *Billboard* discontinued its R&B chart between 1963 and 1965 because it replicated its Hot 100 chart, demonstrating the degree to which African American music dominated mainstream American popular music at the time. Given the prominence of African American music in American pop music since the 1950s and the spread of American culture in South Korea, elements of black American music found a place in the development of Korean popular music. While many remember the girl group the Korean Kittens for its 1964 appearance on the BBC show *Tonight*, the group also played songs like Ray Charles's "What'd I Say" for US troops. Kim Chang Nam (2012) singles out African American soul music as a distinctive influence on Korean popular music since the late 1960s: "It should be noted that their [African Americans'] impact indeed permeated the overall history of Korean popular music" (33). Such influence results from the influx of black popular music as well as its performances. Kennell Jackson (2005) notes that such performances are most successful when "they allow the audience to insert its own ideas into the performance.... They can end up in unlikely places, in contradictory alliances, can take on new and unintended forms, and can synthesize radically disparate materials" (5). Black performative culture invites others to participate without requiring them to give up their home culture. Cultural mobility encourages hybridization and explains the influx of African American music into South Korea and the subsequent outflow of K-pop to a global audience.

Moreover, African American music culture also enters into Korea via Asian Americans. Korean R&B groups like Solid, with its Asian American members, remind us that Asian Americans act as a conduit for black popular music in South Korea. Excluded from the popular music scene in the United States, some Asian Americans leave to pursue musical careers in East Asia. In the post "50 Most Influential K-pop Artists" (2010), Solid is credited as "the ones who started off the steady stream of Korean Americans who hit it big in Korean pop music scene—a major trend in K-pop in its own right." Korean Americans are also instrumental in bringing hip-hop to South Korea, as early hip-hop groups and members of first-generation "idol" groups were either born in the United States or spent significant time there: "Given the wide popularity of 'black music,' it is not a mere coincidence that Korean Americans who learned hip-hop music and allied dancing techniques in situ in turn brought them directly to South Korea" (Lie 2012, 357).

As a result, the hybridity at work in K-pop is one that recognizes that the individual cultures can mix and, at a certain level, remain distinct. In my book *Beyond the Chinese Connection: Contemporary Afro-Asian Cultural Production* (2013), I argue for the fluidity and changing nature of hybridization, because the cultures that come together form, not neat products, but messy and uneven results: "Cultural emulsion places cultures in a conversation with one another. The cultural difference that remains between them is important because it reinforces the reality that not all cultural interaction results in some kind of mixture, or the absorption of one culture into another" (34). This sentiment is echoed in other hybrid popular music like black popular music. Richard Ripani (2006) notes that twentieth-century African American music is based on the blues system, "a combination of factors of pitch, mode, rhythm, harmony, form and other elements of style and content that are nearly universal in American popular music, including genres such as blues, jazz, country, rock 'n' roll, gospel, and rhythm & blues" (4). At the same time, rhythm and blues also incorporates "the use of scales, harmony, formal elements, and stylistic features typical of European music. There is little doubt that rhythm & blues is neither strictly African nor European, but a blend of both musical traditions" (Ripani 2006, 4). It is also important to recognize the ways that ethnic musical cultures inform music, given the history of erasure of the influence of black popular music on other music traditions and the appropriation of black music forms. Joel Rudinow (1994) acknowledges while critics "unambiguously credit[] African-American culture as the authoritative source of the blues as musical genre and style . . . the dominant culture has by and large systematically neglected" to do so (127). Jack Hamilton (2016) echoes this perspective when he says that popular discourse has "generally accepted a view of popular music in the 1960s as split according to genre, and more tacitly, race: on one hand is rock music, which is white; on the other, soul music, which is black." He attributes this to the lack of acknowledgment of the way music is ethnically informed: "But by far the most common way that the whitening of rock-and-roll music has been discussed is simply not at all. The history of rock discourse is marked by a profound aversion toward discussions of race" (Hamilton 2016).

The African American popular music that enters Korea is distinct, emerging from a particular array of historical and cultural circumstances. Initially developed by African Americans, early genres were initially marketed under labels such as "race music" or "race records," terms used to describe music produced by and for African American audiences from the 1920s to the 1950s. The term rhythm and blues came into usage during the 1950s to describe a particular group of genres that initially appealed to black and other audiences but were gradually consumed by other audiences (R. W. Stephens 1984, 21). Rhythm and blues–based genres of black American popular music proliferated throughout the mid-twentieth century to include soul, R&B, funk, disco, urban contemporary, hip-hop, and myriads of permutations. Brian Ward (1998) includes R&B, black pop, soul, funk, and disco under the rhythm and blues designation (2). For Nelson George, R&B is "a synthesis of black musical genres" that would later be called soul, funk, disco, and rap (George 1988, x). Ripani (2006) declares that it is "more accurate to think of rhythm & blues as a collection of different, yet related styles and genres" (171). Ward, George, and Ripani all position the category of rhythm and blues as a catchall, but these genres also share certain musical elements. It is these musical aesthetics that shape what we mean when we describe R&B as "quintessentially black": "Rhythm and Blues absorbed changes in mass black consciousness and reflected them primarily by means of certain musical devices and performance techniques, rather than in the form of neat narrative expositions" (Ward 1998, 6, 14).

These elements inform other musical genres and remain unique, but also invite participation by practitioners who are not black. A graphic published by *Magnetic Magazine* illustrates what many popular music historians know: that variations of electronic dance music, or dance club music, can all be traced back to funk, disco, and hip-hop from the 1960s, 1970s, and 1980s, musical styles that emerged from African American musical scenes ("Stop Calling EDM EDM" 2015). When R&B is referred to as black popular music, the "black" refers to a culture rather than solely a racial designation. It does not restrict who can produce such music as long as they understand and embody the conventions well. Robin Kelley (1997) suggests that black concepts like *soul* can refer to "a discourse through which African Americans, at a particular historical moment, claimed ownership of the symbols and practices of their own imagined community" as well as "a way to talk about being black without reference to color, which is why people of other ethnic groups could have soul" (25–26). David Ritz (1970) argues that an integral element of soul music is the notion of positivity: "It seems to me that there is something intrinsic to the nature of black popular music which is open and positive; without diluting its own essential blackness it reaches out beyond itself; it wants to join rather than exclude; finally it wants *everyone* to feel all right" (46).

While African American popular music is produced in the West, it is also a distinctive form with different aesthetics. Guthrie Ramsey (2004) argues, "While African American music is certainly Western in most senses, it is Western with a distinct difference" (19). It would be a mistake to describe African American popular music as a Western mode of music, for while produced in the geographical West, it has a musical structure distinct from music from European traditions. Since the mid-twentieth century, black musical styles have utilized what Ripani (2006) describes as the blues scale, which should "be perceived not as simply an alteration of the Western system scale—*not* a major scale with a few notes changed, but as a very different configuration of pitches" (135).

Citational Practices and Intertextuality

As a result of this hybridity informed by African American music culture, K-pop's citational practices reflect intertextuality through emulation of the

R&B tradition and enhancement of that tradition. K-pop emulates distinct elements of the musical and performative R&B tradition. It enhances that tradition with Korean popular music aesthetics based on the mixing of genres.

Intertextuality and Emulation

K-pop emulates the R&B music tradition by citing its distinct vocals and instrumentation. R&B vocals are grounded in gospel and form the foundation of doo-wop, harmonization, and male and female vocal traditions. R&B instrumentation is rhythm-driven, characterized by syncopation and off-beat phrasing and manifested in genres including funk, soul, disco, and urban contemporary.

K-pop's citational practices are intertextual through the emulation of R&B tradition. Henry Louis Gates's (1998) African American literary theory of signification points to revision, or repetition with a difference, captured in the concept of "critical Signification," which reflects a relationship to tradition and its transmittal: "It also alters fundamentally the way we read the tradition, by defining the relation of the text at hand *to* the tradition. . . . If black writers read each other, they also revise each other's text. Thereby they become fluent in the language of tradition" (124). In order to improvise, one must know the tradition. A similar dynamic happens in music, which also has a tradition. Musical artists draw on their predecessors in a musical tradition. Their knowledge can be seen in the way they reference previous works.

K-pop exhibits the emulation of intertextuality through citational practices, drawing on vocal styles, instrumentation, visuals, and performance aesthetics of African American music culture. We commonly understand the practice of citing our sources when we reference someone else's ideas in texts. The same principle applies to cultural material. Steve Sherlock (2014) suggests: "Social actors routinely 'cite' cultural commodities in everyday life. . . . The words of others come to subjects with historically sedimented meanings and values, available as resources to incorporate into their own evaluative utterances" (3). As a result of encounters with other cultures, cultural material may be transferred with aesthetic and emotional meaning intact. The tempo of a song determines its mood. A vocal performance can signify joy or sadness. African American popular music codifies certain musical elements so that they mean the same thing no matter where one hears them. At the same time, use of cultural material by a different culture can result in a different significance. Constantine V. Nakassis (2013) calls this "a play of sameness and difference," where "citing something re-produces it in some manner and to some degree" but also "any citational act depends on inscribing a difference, or gap, between the very acts that are made iconic with each other" (56). When Korean artists and producers create music that engages in the African American popular music tradition, it takes on an additional cultural significance and can perform specific cultural work in a different context. Citational practices also represent an alternative to concepts like cultural appropriation that fail to capture the nuance of such cultural exchanges. Brittany Cooper (2014) asserts that there is a difference between citational practices and mere imitation, using artists like Michael McDonald and Bruno Mars as examples: "They are very intentionally citational, so you look at their music and you know exactly who they are invoking, you know how they are doing it, you know how they are remixing it, so they want you to see the direct link between their work and someone else's, and that's something different than appropriation." Intentionality underscores the link between the source material and the cited material in a new context and implies the same play with difference that Nakassis references. Cooper suggests by paying attention to what is happening with the music itself, we will be able to understand what is being cited and what the citation means. Because African American music is itself a hybrid music, it lends itself to such citation.

While K-pop cites from a variety of musical traditions, I argue that the African American popular music tradition most informs the music. Lee Soo-man, founder of SM Entertainment, one of the "Big Three" Korean entertainment agencies, has said: "We made K-pop based on black music" (quoted in Lie 2012, 357). Bang Shi-hyuk, Korean music producer and CEO of BigHit Entertainment, home of BTS, explains that "Black music is the base. Even when doing many genres like house, urban, and PBR&B, there's no change to the fact that it is Black music" (Do 2017). K-pop's engagement with black American music occurs at an aesthetic level. Some assume that popular music does not have aesthetics, reserving that term for more "artistic" forms of music. However, aesthetics includes the formal and structural elements attached to an object or a performance that we use to make meaning or to which we have an emotional response. In music, the formal or structural elements include melody, beat, tempo, and lyrics that may be associated with conventions of the musical style they reflect. These musical meanings are linked to the associations we make with melodies and hooks. Music and feelings associated with a particular note or vocal run can go beyond documentation by musicologists in notation. Leonard Meyer (1956) argues that music has meaning that is found in the way music refers "to the extramusical world of concepts, actions, emotional states, and character" (1). Like other forms of music, popular music contains these elements.

K-pop cites one of the most distinct aspects of R&B-based genres of black popular music: vocals informed by the gospel tradition. The gospel tradition incorporates techniques from African American sacred music, including percussion generated by handclaps, call-and-response and melodic repetition (R. W. Stephens 1984, 22–23, 27). According to Andrew Legg (2010), vocals in black popular music derive from "gospel singing practices and techniques ('gravel,' 'slides,' 'wails,' 'screams' and 'shouts')" (104). Emotional singing is often expressed through techniques like melisma, "the technique of singing many notes on one syllable," which "imparts a sense of individualism" and "can also be perceived as a form of improvisation" (Ripani 2006, 57). R&B-based genres of black popular music also incorporate the sentiment of gospel music, what Craig Werner (1999) calls the "gospel impulse," "the belief that life's burdens can be transformed into hope, salvation, the promise of redemption" (28). Jon Fitzgerald (1995) notes that Motown songs included "a swelling communal style 'sing-a-long' chorus, call-response vocals, 120 beat dance tempo with fingerclicks, a subtly shifting repetitive chordal backing featuring piano, expressive quasi-improvisatory lead vocals with blues inflections, and that H-D-H [Holland-Dozier-Holland, a Motown songwriting and production team] talent for dramatizing ordinary human emotions and experience—all these features make for a clearly black church-based sound" (4). These characteristics define black vocals, the very sound of which "conveyed rich, textured, and nuanced meanings that were primarily conveyed via tonal qualities as opposed to specific narrative content" (Neal 1999, 38). These types of vocals are not easy to perform, and as Ripani (2006) asserts, "it has remained difficult . . . for any person outside of the African-American community to produce an acceptable black vocal style" (190). K-pop's citation of black vocals is a conscious one that requires a degree of talent on the part of the singer, an ability that many K-pop artists possess.

These vocal elements can be seen in a variety of R&B music. David Goldblatt (2013) describes doo-wop, an a cappella group vocal style from the 1950s and 1960s, as "vocal rhythm and blues" and as "absolute vocality": "It is primarily, if not essentially, a vocal-centric song genre, songs voiced endless times a cappella in moods never before heard in vocalized popular music" (102). These vocals are not dependent on lyrical meaning, but on the deployment of "vocables," or "nonsense syllables" (Ripani 2006, 69). The structure of doo-wop mimics rhythm and blues instrumentation: "The background at the core of doo-wop was typically two tenors, a bass, and a baritone, with an additional tenor singing lead where a falsetto was commonly introduced to change the intensity of the vocalizing" (Goldblatt 2013, 102). Crooning is a solo style that conveys sentimentality through singing in a low, soft voice and depends on the quality of the singer, who must compete with the instrumentation that supports the song. In the black vocal tradition, harmonies can act to showcase a lead vocal, as with R&B vocal groups from the 1960s and 1990s that "often feature a lead vocalist singing the melody while the other voices provide harmonic support, often functioning more or less as a group of background singers whose parts harmonize the melody" (Ripani 2006, 159). Songs by "quiet storm" artists feature similarly slow tempos but more sophisticated, soulful vocals. The techniques in these vocal styles form an expressive repertoire distinctly linked to an African American tradition, drawing on "their power among singers and listeners precisely due to their African-American origins and the attendant affects, such as soulfulness, emotional depth, and sexual energy, which listeners associate with those origins" (Rischar 2004, 410). Vocals are not even confined to singing, for "the *sounds* of musicians (such as James Brown's whoops) are more important than the notes played" (Cloonan 2005, 79). While many focus on the lyrics of MCs in hip-hop, these performers also engage in distinct vocal expressions as well. William Jelani Cobb (2007) observes that "tonal adventurism was an inheritance from the fast-talking, pitch-varying pseudo-baritone couplets that radio dee-jays—another ancestor to the hip hop MC—had been practicing for decades" (45). Distinct vocals are a key element for a wide variety of R&B genres.

In addition to vocals, instrumentation represents another distinctive element of R&B-based genres of African American popular music cited by K-pop. Ripani (2006) notes that all R&B-based genres are informed in some way by the "blues system," whose elements include reliance on a unique set of pitches that revolve around the blues scale, melody that is distinct from harmony, the use of "offbeat phrasing" and the liberal use of improvisation (16). The incorporation of rhythm as a major element changed the sound of pop music in the 1960s. Fitzgerald (1995) notes that the Motown sound revolutionized pop music by centralizing rhythm: "[Holland, Dozier, Holland] elevated rhythm to a new structural status.... H-D-H would consistently derive catchy rhythmic or rhythmic/chordal motifs and use them as a foundation for either a complete song, or a particular section of a song" (5). Funk music represents a unique interplay of R&B vocals and rhythm-driven music. Rickey Vincent (1995) describes the musical aesthetics of the genre as one dependent on incorporation of musical structures: "Funk is a musical mixture. Its most popular form is dance-tempo rhythm and blues-style music with the rhythmic interplay of instruments stretched to a dramatic level of complexity" (13). Within this structure, the bass guitar guides the rhythm, but horns function as melody and percussion and keyboards function as both a rhythm and lead instrument (Vincent 1995, 17). Because of the dynamic nature of the complex rhythms and melodies, funk music also functions as dance music. Vincent notes: "Funk music, with its nonstop, sweaty dance appeal, is also the no-nonsense form of dance entertainment most directly related to the rhythm and blues tradition" (19).

Within funk, rhythm is deployed in different ways. Portia K. Maultsby (2006) notes that the foundation of funk music lay in its innovative use of rhythms, exemplified by one of its pioneers, James Brown, who introduced a musical aesthetic "characterized by the interlocking of the drum pattern and a two-bar bass line, counter or contrasting guitar, keyboard and horn riffs, and a vocalist singing in a gospel style" (297). Larry Graham, the bassist for Sly and the Family Stone, innovated that rhythm: "Exploiting the instrument's rhythmic and timbral capabilities, he transformed the bass into a percussive instrument by pulling, plucking, thumping, and slapping the strings" (Maultsby 2006, 297–98).

Other modes of R&B instrumentation also focus on improvising rhythm. While the triplet swing appears in the 1970s in Parliament's "Flashlight," Ripani (2006) credits singer Janet Jackson and producers Jimmy Jam and Terry Lewis with popularizing a similarly innovative rhythm in the 1980s, "a new sound that fuses the rhythmic elements of funk and disco, along with heavy doses of synthesizers, percussion, sound effects and a rap music sensibility" (130). This mode of instrumentation also finds its way into hip-hop through the use of sampling, the use of a repeated section of music from a piece of recorded music in a completely new, transformative way. Such repetition is a characteristic of the blues system where the sample functions as the repeated musical figure in blues (Ripani 2006, 139, 140). Disco combines rhythm with other elements to create a distinctive sound. Many associate disco with its later watered-down incarnation where "the rhythmic complexity of black dance music was reduced to a brisk procession of dehumanized beats, swathed in syrupy synthesizers or sub-Philly strings to give it a sheen of pseudo-sophistication, and topped with a few cursory chanted phrases" (Ward 1998, 426). However, George (1988) identifies disco as legitimate black cultural expression: "Disco began as an extension of black dance music. First in Europe and then in the U.S., discotheques became popular as places you danced to recorded music, just like at a house party. And most of the music initially played at discos was supplied by black artists" (153). Peter Shapiro (2005) marks the beginning of disco as a musical genre with the release of Melvin and the Blue Notes' "The Love I Lost": "It was just that they [Gamble, Huff, and Melvin] had hit upon the epitome of dance music: the hissing hi-hats, the thumping bass sound, the surging momentum, the uplifting horns, the strings taking flight, lead singer Teddy Pendergrass's over-the-top gospel passion working as sandpaper against the honeyed backing vocals" (145). Kai Fikentscher (2006) points to MFSB's "Love Is the Message" (1973) as one of the most influential disco records, with its "veritable orchestra of soul and funk musicians," "the lush sound that became known as The Sound of Philadelphia," and "disco beat" (321). The distinctive musical style of Philadelphia International Records (PIR) also informs disco.

Founded by Kenny Gamble and Leon Huff, PIR developed what has become known as the Philly sound, "a sort of velvet-cased soul-funk amalgam which was characterized by rich string and horn arrangements, taut rhythm tracks, and dramatic gospel vocals delivering thoughtful, storyline lyrics" (Ward 1998, 418). Artists such as the O'Jays, Harold Melvin and the Blue Notes, the Spinners, and Barry White exemplify the sound.

While many decry it for lacking artistic qualities, hip-hop also has distinct musical elements and brought innovations to the R&B genres of black popular music. In the documentary *Hip-Hop Evolution* (2016a), Kurtis Blow explains that early hip-hop diverged from the prevalent, Eurodisco-derived music of the 1970s by gravitating toward the soul and funk records of the 1960s. MCs who rapped over the best parts of early rhythm and blues-based R&B songs reinscribed that musicality into their new music. Technology allowed hip-hop artists to make such musical innovations. Cobb (2007) credits the introduction of the E-mu SP12 drum machine as a game changer because "it allowed the user not only to create electronic drum tracks, but also to *sample*, or reproduce previously recorded sounds . . . At its best, the new generation of producers did for music what Romare Bearden's collages had done for art: to take pre-existing scraps of sound or color and compose them into an entirely new piece of art" (52). Cobb's reference to Bearden's collages is apt. Rather than thoughtless pastiche, sampling by hip-hop artists exhibited a high degree of musicality and intention. Different MCs would make different use of instrumentation. West Coast rap distinguished itself from its East Coast counterpart by developing an entirely different sound. Groups like Cypress Hill "favored dark, dense sounds that bubbled up from the haunted corners of the psyche. . . . The beats warbled up from the bottom of the register and consistently sounded like a bass drum being played at the bottom of the San Francisco Bay" (Cobb 2007, 58). Rapper Cold187um explains that the slow-tempo hip-hop of Snoop Dogg and Dr. Dre brought groove derived from funk music to the fore (*Hip-Hop Evolution* 2016b). Like other R&B genres, hip-hop features distinct instrumentation.

Intertextuality and Improvisation

In addition to emulating the R&B tradition, K-pop's citational practices enhance the R&B tradition. Distinct Korean musical aesthetics, characterized by the mixing of genres, broaden R&B by bringing its elements into new contexts. The intertextuality in play in K-pop also involves improvisation. Gates (1999) argues that signification also involves difference: "Writers Signify upon each other's texts by rewriting the received textual tradition. . . . This sort of Signifying revision serves, if successful, to create a space for the revising text" (124). In musical styles like jazz, such revision comes off as riffing or improvisation, taking what is established and rendering it in a new way or taking it in a completely new direction. Craig Werner (1994) calls this the jazz impulse, which "focuses on realizing the relational possibilities of the self, of expanding consciousness through a process of continual improvisation" (219). K-pop engages in a similar enhancement by incorporating Korean music aesthetics characterized by the mixing of genres and styles with elements of R&B genres. There are elements of K-pop that are distinctly Korean, drawing from the legacy of Korean popular music. Min-jung Son (2006) notes how Korean female singers "performed the new songs using traditional Korean performance practice" that "eventually evolved into the very trademark of the song style t'ûrot'û" (55). Even as Korean popular music incorporated the rhythms of trot from Japanese music, it retained a distinct singing style. Similarly, K-pop possesses unique musical attributes derived from Korean musical culture. Fuhr (2016) points to *ppong*, "a specific understanding of the melodic-harmonic structure in many K-pop songs . . . characterized by the paramount role of vocal melody" (103). Jamie Shinhee Lee (2004) observes that K-pop songs often feature "Koreanized English which only Koreans can understand" (434).

Moreover, music critics describe K-pop's tendency to combine multiple music genres as a unique trait. Robert Barry (2012) points to the hit song "Nan Arayo" by K-pop pioneer Seo Taiji and Boys, often cited as the first K-pop group, as exemplary: "You hear at first something like the Beastie Boys' fusion of hip hop, rock and punk attitude, with a little of the laid back beats of British groups like Soul 2 Soul thrown in and a bit of a daisy age cherry on top. . . . This kind of hybridity is often remarked as a predominant feature of contemporary K-pop." What makes this unique to K-pop is "a specific reference to all the most self-consciously, futuristic Western styles of the last decade or so" (Barry 2012). Joseph L. Flatley (2012) observes the multiple kinds of dance music in K-pop: "[K-pop] somehow manages to simultaneously sound like just about every contemporary musical genre, a conflation of the various strains of electronic dance music—mostly trance, electro, and dubstep—arranged in conventional pop song structure." Seabrook (2012) points to several different influences on K-pop, including "hip-hop verses, Euro-pop choruses, rapping, and dubstep breaks." The ease with which K-pop incorporates genres may be attributed to its Korean nature. For example, songs that blend genres are one of the hallmarks of SM Music Performance sound. Using SNSD's "I Got a Boy" as an example, Joe Palmer (2015) describes it this way: "They play with structure in strange ways and swap genre without any notice. Pop songs were designed to lull you into security, make you feel at ease so you won't go against the system. SM does the opposite and it makes for an interesting case." Park Gil-sung (2013) notes that this mode of K-pop production brings Korean cultural values to the creative process: "K-pop represents a unique system of global division of labor, geared towards the creation of a new Korea-led system of 'manufacturing creativity,' which encourages and mass produces innovative music and musical performances" (16). Thus, Korean music production introduces unique elements into the music even while drawing on the R&B tradition.

Representation and Citation of Performance

In addition to musical elements, K-pop cites African American performance elements in music videos, providing additional options in terms of representation for Asians. K-pop music videos draw on distinct choreography, staging, and styling of African American popular music culture.

Black American popular music has often blended music and choreography in distinct ways. Marion Leonard and Robert Strachan (2003) describe the deliberate link between dance and music in the 1950s, where "doo-wop vocal groups such as the Cadillacs and the Orioles developed well-honed stage acts involving synchronized dancing that echoed the closeness of their vocal harmonies" (657). Such performances focused more on sophisticated expression with what Jacqui Malone (1988) calls "vocal choreography," revolutionized in the mid-twentieth century by Cholly Atkins, best known as one of the chief choreographers at Motown during its heyday: "The body is always doing something that is rhythmically different from the voice.... The movement is continuous: even when the back-up singers are not in the mike area, they are still performing interesting steps derived from authentic jazz movements.... Atkins sees the choreographic process as a mathematical one in which the singers have to move away from their mikes to dance, then get back by a certain time to sing" (16). Unlike choreography for dancing only, Atkins's choreography was designed for vocal groups and attuned to the music. He was concerned with dance routines that "worked their magic not by retelling a song's storyline in predictable pantomime but by punctuating it with rhythmical dance steps, turns, and gestures—drawn by the rich bedrock of American vernacular dance" (Malone 1988, 17). Such choreography complements the music and fits the personality of the group. While Atkins's choreography for the Supremes, Motown's signature girl group, was a "demure style" consisting of "stylized swaying hands, half-turns, and across-the-shoulder glances," the choreography for Gladys Knight and the Pips, a mixed-gender group where the male members serve as backup for Knight as the female lead, involved "elements of the class act tradition, minus the taps: precision, detached coolness, elegance, flawless execution, and dignity" (Malone 1988, 15–16).

While Atkins's work with groups was unique, no single artist has had more of an impact on African American popular music and choreography than Michael Jackson, a onetime Motown artist who went on to become a pop icon. Judith Hamera (2012) attributes virtuosity to Jackson's dance performance: "He combines exceptional musicality, precise execution, and a repertoire that draws from so many genres it is best described as 'polycorporeal' with recurring invocations of hard work belied by the apparent effortlessness of his performances.... His virtuosity is a function of his execution of these moves, not any inherent complexity of the moves themselves" (754). Moreover, other black dancers inform Jackson's performance: "His moves quote Josephine Baker, Cab Callaway, Fred Astaire, Gene Kelly, James Brown, Jackie Wilson and anonymous street dancers, to name only a few sources" (Hamera 2012, 762).

Likewise, choreography carefully attuned to the music is a hallmark of Korean "idol" groups. Yoo Young-jin, who was a dancer prior to becoming a music producer for SM Entertainment, illustrates the centrality of choreography to the music-making process: "From the H.O.T. years, I would have some of my own ideas about the choreography. If there is a specific choreography that I had imagined, I would make it and give it to the choreographer. For me, songwriting is something that makes the stage performance and music become one" ("[Interview] Yoo Young Jin" 2010a). Some describe "idol" choreography as mechanistic, but this overlooks the clear influence of African American popular dance. The choreography of K-pop groups often invokes elements of the latest dances from African American expressive culture as well as moves from hip-hop. Several K-pop "idols" with long careers, including Taemin of SHINee and Yunho of TVXQ, cite Michael Jackson as an influence.

In addition to choreography, K-pop also cites the fashion style of African American music videos. Shane White and Graham White (1998) describe clothing as part of a distinct expressive culture of African Americans, "the public presentation of the black body" and "the cultural imperatives that have influenced the ways in which African Americans have clothed themselves, styled their hair, and communicated meaning through gestures, dance, and other forms of bodily display" (2). Such visual choices appear in what Roopali Mukherjee (2006) describes as the "ghetto fabulous aesthetic," relying on "bling," which "encapsulates designer labels, fur coats, gold and diamond jewelry" and is promoted by ethnic fashion labels run by Sean "Puffy" Combs and Kimora Lee Simmons as well as media platforms like MTV (600–601). The fashion in African American music videos also reflects a tradition of sartorial style, which Monica Miller (2009) identifies with blacks throughout the diaspora: "Black people are known for 'stylin' out,' dressing to the nines, showing their sartorial stuff, especially when the occasion calls for it, and more telling, often when it does not. In contemporary culture, stylin' out takes a number of forms and happens in multiple locations, from the high style seen at the famous White Parties in the Hamptons given by the hip-hop fashion mogul Sean 'Diddy' Combs to any black church on Easter Sunday, to the locker room after the Super Bowl championship" (1–2). This variety of styling drawn from African American culture appears throughout K-pop music videos by Korean pop, R&B, and hip-hop artists.

However, K-pop's citational practices do not go unnoticed. K-pop music has an audience that consistently recognizes these practices.

K-pop Music Press

Global fans, or fans outside of Korea, deem K-pop's citational practices authentic. Their presence outside of Korea makes them part of a transcultural fandom, one whose reviews serve as critical content, making them part of K-pop's music press. While some question K-pop's authentic engagement with African American popular music culture, these online reviewers document the consistent way K-pop artists participate in the African American popular music tradition.

K-pop Fans as Music Press

While fans have carried a negative reputation as passive consumers, K-pop fans function as producers of critical content. As members of a transcultural fandom, they use technology to access and provide critical commentary about K-pop, positioning themselves as members of K-pop's music press.

Fans tend to be overlooked as critical appraisers of music, passed over in favor of mainstream music publications and professional music critics as K-pop rises in popularity. From 2011 to 2014, *Billboard* maintained a Korea K-pop Hot 100 chart, which featured songs popular in the United States and Korea. It was reinstated in 2017. *Billboard* also maintains a column devoted to K-pop on its website, focusing on the trends of its most popular artists. *SPIN* publishes features on a wider array of K-pop and its lesser-known artists. Even *Vibe*, known for its coverage of American hip-hop and R&B, has featured stories on Korean R&B and hip-hop artists like Dean, Chanyeol of pop group EXO, and Korean American rapper Dumbfoundead. Because of such coverage, some do not see fans as serious critics. Mark Duffett (2013) notes the tendency to define fans solely as consumers, which "indicates participation in a commercial process, but since 'to consume' means to digest and to exhaust it also implies a kind of using up" (20). Others see fans as passive; Lawrence Grossberg (1992) notes that for some, fans represent "the lowest and least critical segments of the population" who are "easily manipulated and distracted (not only from 'serious' culture but also from real social concerns)" and "are simply incapable of recognizing that the culture they enjoy is actually being used to dupe and exploit them" (51). Because of the marginalized nature of fandom, fans "are sometimes represented as an eccentric faction with interests beyond the comprehension of the ordinary media audience" (Duffett 2013, 45). Moreover, many see K-pop exclusively as music for teenagers, most of whom are young women whose behavior is frequently described as obsessive, crazy, extreme, emotional, and unacceptable. While emotional expressiveness is common, encouraged, and embraced within the fandom, "desire for emotional intimacy has traditionally been socially coded as feminine" and seen as "the taint of overzealous enthusiasm" (Duffet 2013, 46). All of these characterizations culminate in a picture of a K-pop fan as an obsessive consumer caught up in larger forces. Koichi Iwabuchi (2010) argues that fans must be considered "in terms of marginalized identity politics (gender, sexuality, race, ethnicity, class, nation, and so on), coping with the tyranny of everyday life in the neoliberal world, the manifestation of a more participatory media culture, and the transnational audience/fan alliance against the control of media culture production and distribution by global media culture industries" (88).

However, Bertha Chin and Lori Morimoto (2013) argue that characterizations of fans as consumers, overemotional participants, or victims of capitalism "ultimately tell[] us little about what actually attracts and motivates fans" which "is absolutely critical to any nuanced discussion of how fandom works across borders" (97). K-pop fans outside of Korea participate in a transcultural fandom made possible by technological advances, including the digitizing of music and online platforms like YouTube. Michael Emmison (2003) notes that these audiences tend "to consume culturally or to participate in divergent cultural fields" and have "the capacity to navigate between or across cultural realms, a freedom to choose or select one's position in the cultural landscape" (213). Chin and Morimoto (2013) emphasize the unique nature of cross-cultural fandom: "Transcultural fans become fans because of affinities of affect between the fan, in his/her various contexts, and the border-crossing object" (93). While K-pop is a subculture in many countries, it is a diverse one that actively creates content. K-pop fans are mostly female, range in age, and include a variety of races and ethnicities. Their fan activity can be found on websites, in forums, on social media, and on YouTube videos and rises to the level of archive-building. While they do not have the same level of access to K-pop artists as their Korean counterparts, they are prolific in their creation of commentary that ranges from appreciation to critique. Much of what we know about K-pop comes from the collecting activities of fans.

Some fan reviewers write on their own websites and blogs for pleasure and are more motivated by a desire to share their opinion and, in some cases, promote their favorite acts. Whether they are fans of K-pop music in general or individual K-pop artists, these fans are in a good position to view a wide swath of music. Given that the emergence of the first Korean pop groups date back to the early 1990s, there are fans with a kind of memory that stretches back that far. These fans are well-versed in the history of the individual groups they follow. For example, *All About Cassiopeia* is a fan site for fans of the male "idol" group TVXQ. Dating back to 2008, it began on the digital platform Crunchyroll, but developed into a full-fledged, staffed site with the mission to provide "the hottest and latest news updates, breaking language barriers by translating information into the universal language and organizing projects to spice up your fandom life" (*All About Cassiopeia*, n.d.). *All About Cassiopeia*'s entry on TVXQ's Second Asia Tour Concert "O" resembles the layout of a Wikipedia page, providing context for the concert and details about the show, including setlists, description of the stage setup, and media coverage. Similarly, *Soshified*, a fan site dedicated to the girl group Girls' Generation, includes not only information, updated news, and pictures but also fan commentary through editorials written about the group and music reviews. Because the staff of the site are focused on one group, they can provide an overview of the group's music over time. A review of Girls' Generation's repackages on *Soshified* compares new releases to previously released material: "If the first Japanese album had an electronic sound, the repackage remixes double down on it. 'THE GREAT ESCAPE' remix is solid. It takes the original song and tweaks it to be more gritty" (MoonSoshi9 2012). Other fan sites evaluate K-pop in other ways. The website *K-pop Vocalists' Vocal Analyses* (n.d.) touts the credentials of its writers: "Pandayeu has taken vocal lessons for years. Ahmin has taken vocal lessons for years in Bel Canto and Speech Level Singing, while earning also a higher diploma in vocal performance from ACM in Guildford, UK, and an Associate of Arts Degree from M.I. in Los Angeles, CA. Papers however don't mean much if the instructor doesn't have experience in hearing and targeting issues in singing. Credentials can be found within the actual content of the analyses as well." These well-organized fan ventures reveal the knowledge that fans have about K-pop music, positioning them to recognize K-pop's citational practices.

Fan reviewers who publish blog posts, articles, and reviews represent a subset of global K-pop fans and function as key content producers of critical material about K-pop. Speaking of fans as a "vital force *interior* to the workings of Hallyu, though *exterior* to the productive site of Hallyu content," JungBong Choi (2015) observes that global fans "shoulder the role not just of information provider/mediator/distributor but also of cultural designer/administrator" (42, 43). They are active participants in the creation and dissemination of K-pop culture. As a result, K-pop fans deserve to be characterized as "cultural curators" who indeed "curate, manage and catalyze" cultural production of Hallyu, including K-pop (Choi 2015, 42). Other K-pop fans maintain fan sites and Facebook pages and groups that feature profiles, pictures, and updated information and engage in fan projects that celebrate comebacks and anniversaries. This curation activity includes writing music reviews. Many of these fans develop the ability to discern the various influences on K-pop music derived from listening to entire albums, not just the promoted tracks that gain the most attention, and to contextualize them within an artist's entire discography. Such musical knowledge is supplemented by hours spent reading and watching countless interviews, appearances, and impromptu performances. Global fans access appearances on Korean radio on YouTube that are video-recorded and subtitled. More casual than scripted television appearances, these appearances allow K-pop artists to perform their own music live as well as covers of their favorite Korean and non-Korean artists. K-pop artists will often use the opportunity to talk about their music and their influences.

Other fans write online reviews and articles for Korean entertainment outlets. These media outlets are revue-generating venues through the advertising promoted on the sites. They maintain staff and regularly produce content, making them different from individual fan sites operated by many fans. Founded in 1998, *soompi* originated as an English-language fan site for H.O.T., the first successful "idol" group, and developed into a media site with staff in San Francisco and Seoul. In 2015 it was acquired by Viki, a global video streaming site. Other K-pop media sites, such as *allkpop*, *hellokpop*, and *seoulbeats*, distribute news about K-pop and maintain staff writers who write features, opinion pieces, and reviews. These reviews often contextualize a song or a group's music within an artist's body of work. These fan reviewers are more consistently engaged with K-pop music and its culture than mainstream outlets that occasionally cover K-pop or only focus on the most popular acts. The reviews differ from other modes where fans express an opinion, like reaction videos, but these lack the evaluative function of a track-by-track album review, where the individual considers the merit of each song. Fan reviewers utilize what David Brackett (2000) calls musical rhetoric, which "permits us to consider the connection between an individual piece and the conventions of genre. . . . If pieces are 'understood' by their references to genre, then this occurs through activating codes in certain ways" (26). This strategy foregrounds the aesthetic elements of songs as experienced by an average listener, a listener who may connect K-pop songs to genres of black popular music that they may know. In order to utilize musical rhetoric, they demonstrate a simultaneous knowledge of the conventions of black popular music and also the ways that K-pop artists deploy them. Because these fan reviewers write for a media outlet, their reviews carry a sense of authority, an assessment meant to be shared with others as a critical assessment.

These reviews may reflect their emotional reaction to the music. Meyer (1956) notes that the nexus of emotion and music occurs between emotional meaning embedded in the music itself and the context that surrounds the music that is filtered through an emotional lens (3). In their reviews, K-pop fans often comment on the ways the music makes them feel or the emotions that performances convey. While they are not professional critics, their critical appraisals are nevertheless significant. As Guthrie Ramsey (2004) notes, "Real people negotiate and eventually agree on what cultural expressions such as a musical gesture mean. They collectively describe what associations are conjured by a well-placed blue note, a familiar harmonic pattern, the soulful virtuoso sweep of a jazz solo run, a social dancer's imaginative twist on an old dance step, or the raspy grain of a church mother's vocal declamation on Sunday morning" (25). General audiences and fans are equally capable of making critical appraisals of K-pop.

While lyrical knowledge may vary, these global fans can access musical meaning, especially for K-pop informed by African American popular music, a tradition with which they may know well, given its influence on a plethora of Western musical genres. Brian Ward (1998) gives weight to this kind of musical knowledge, especially in relation to R&B: "The actual sound of a record or performance—the grain of a voice, the tone of an instrument, the manipulation of harmonies and rhythms—contributed to at least as much to its meaning as any lyric" (81). Fan reviewers of all stripes reveal their knowledge through reviews that frequently recognize the way K-pop music draws on the African American popular music tradition.

K-pop Critics and Authenticity

Fans' critical appraisal of K-pop is not uniform. K-pop's authenticity remains a highly debatable topic. Some fan critics negatively characterize K-pop's citational practices, calling them a pale imitation of African American popular music and questioning Korean artists' experience with the socioeconomic realities that inform the music. However, citational practices better capture K-pop's engagement with black American popular music. Ultimately, K-pop fan reviews, in recognizing such practices, confer authenticity.

Some fan critics question K-pop's authenticity when it engages in citational practices. They suggest that because K-pop artists are not African American, they can only imitate black popular music. These fans insist on what Rudinow (1994) calls "experiential access": "One cannot understand the blues or authentically express oneself in the blues unless one knows what it's like to live as a black person in America, and one cannot know this without being one" (132). In a recent roundtable on black K-pop fans on the K-pop media site *seoulbeats*, one member echoes this opinion: "The idea that 'acting Black' somehow makes them cool or more authentic and will appeal to the masses is systematic of a culture steeped in a lot of isolationism and refusing to show even a modicum of respect for other cultures" ("Roundtable: Thoughts and Experiences of Black K-pop Fans 2015"). Such fans argue that K-pop artists do not give credit to the influences on that music, thereby getting the credit for the music and erasing the black originators, both artistically and financially. Mark Anthony Neal (2005) notes that "*someone* benefits financially from the production, distribution, consumption and critical gatekeeping of the music, and too often it is not the black folks whose minds and spirits loom large in the creation of the music" (370). Such comments reflect what Paul C. Taylor (1997) dubs "the Elvis Effect," where non-black "participation in traditionally black avenues of cultural production produces feelings of unease." Such feelings emerge from previous instances where some non-black artists forayed into the tradition, oblivious to its sociohistorical context and meaning. These critiques reiterate descriptions of Asian popular culture as capable only of imitation. Some critics reduce "the entire Korean music industry to a mimetic machine that assiduously copies Western or Japanese pop culture" (Park G.-S. 2013, 16). Shin Hyun-joon, Mori Yoshitaka, and Ho Tung-hung (2013) note that East Asian popular music is often perceived as "merely an imitation of Euro-American music" and "is considered as an area of consumption rather than creative production" (2). This notion of imitation takes away the ability of East Asian countries to be innovative and historically serves "to recognize the superiority of Western ways, to show a flexibility and intelligence not shared by all 'backward' nations" (Rosenstone 1980, 575). As a result, critiques of K-pop artists that assert they cannot produce authentic African American popular come dangerously close to anti-Asian discourse.

Other fan reviewers argue that Koreans cannot authentically engage the black American popular music tradition because they have not experienced the socioeconomic realities in the United States in the twentieth century that shaped black music. They critique K-pop artists for failing to acknowledge the culture from which black popular music emerges. In the piece "Aegyo Hip Hop:

Cultural Appropriation at Its Messiest," *seoulbeats* writer Mark (2013) criticizes K-pop groups for appropriating hip-hop: "However, this becomes problematic when certain elements are added simply for the sake of upping and artist's 'cool' factor while it's being culturally appropriated in a way that is disrespectful (not to mention laughable) to the original product. We've discussed before on this site, K-pop's disconnect with the authentic culture of hip hop, and the lack of sensitivity shown towards the context from which hip hop originates" (n.p.). Such critiques define authenticity using a sociohistorical context, which is a common critical lens applied to black popular music. Similarly, Nelson George (1988) asserts that rhythm and blues originally had a socioeconomic meaning as "an integral part of . . . a black community forged by common political, economic and geographic conditions" (x, xii). As black popular music became popular with mainstream audiences, it was "divorced from many of its organic sources, sources that often sought to invest the tradition with a highly politicized and critical consciousness" (Neal 1999, 86). K-pop becomes another iteration of mainstreaming in this view.

However, citational practices represent an alternative to negative cultural appropriation, one that allows fan reviewers to determine authenticity based on engagement with a range of K-pop. Rudinow (1994) explains that authenticity represents "a kind of credibility that comes from having the appropriate relationship to an original source.... In such applications authenticity admits of degrees. A given piece of work may be more or less authentic than another" (129). Authenticity resides on a continuum where a range of "appropriate" relationships are possible that are not based solely on identity. The history of African American popular music shows that non-blacks can achieve such authenticity. David Brackett (2000) reminds us that black popular music is "hybrid at the root, resisting closure as a concept in the vigorous enunciating practices that perform its identity in ever new guises" (88). Unlike the segregated mainstream music industry of the 1950s and 1960s, early R&B music production involved non-black artists, who tutored themselves in black music aesthetics: "The songs are not only expressive in themselves, but in their use of prolific vocal ornamentation within typical song forms, they also teach (black and nonblack) audiences *how* to be expressive in a way that is, however slippery to define, presented as African-American" (Rischar 2004, 411). Collaborations between black and white American musicians that produced iconic African American popular music show that non-blacks can authentically engage with black music. The documentary *Muscle Shoals* reveals how studio musicians in Alabama, many of them white, were responsible for some of the most soulful records by Aretha Franklin, Clarence Carter, Wilson Pickett, Percy Sledge, and others. Such collaborations between black performers and white musicians suggests that black music has democratic impulses, that is, it *invites* those who are outside of its tradition into the tradition rather than being exclusionary. Such impulses are related to the worldwide appeal and spread of black American popular music: "It was untrammeled, emotional, *different* music, and it fit the times. Soul played at black activist centers and white fraternity bacchanals; soul cassettes went to Saigon in rucksacks; soul singers, particularly James Brown, drew the twenty-two-year-old Mick Jagger to the Apollo night after night" (Hirshey 1984, xii). This is not to say that there are not instances of negative cultural appropriation in K-pop. Rather, the history of African American music shows that cultural appropriation is not the only way to describe non-black engagement with black music.

When K-pop fan critics recognize the way that black American popular music informs K-pop, they recognize K-pop's "appropriate" relationship and knowledge of the African American popular music tradition. When they do so, these fans grant authenticity to K-pop's citational practices. Audiences are key in conferring value and determining authenticity, for, as Allan Moore (2002) argues, "It is the *success* with which a particular performance conveys its impression that counts" (220). An audience determines the difference between a mimetic performance that goes through the motions and one that reflects a true understanding of genre. It arrives at a conclusion about authenticity through listening: "We should observe how (if at all) a track expresses authenticity, and for what particular audience. . . . 'authenticity' is a matter of interpretation" (Moore 2012, 266). As a result, authenticity links the expression of a music's elements and audience reception. What members of an audience hear depends on the background they bring and their knowledge of genre conventions. Audiences that base their conclusions about authenticity on understanding the conventions of the genre will generate different conclusions than those who have no knowledge of the musical tradition and genres from which the artist draws.

Indeed, global fans propelled Psy to worldwide recognition and raised the profile of K-pop. While K-pop is a hybridized mode of popular music, it is most influenced by the black American popular music tradition. That influence can be seen if we view K-pop as a mode of Korean popular music that, since the 1990s, has combined Korean personnel, language, and production and promotion strategies with foreign, most notably African American, musical styles and sought a global audience. The hybridity that defines K-pop reflects an intertextuality that simultaneously emulates and enhances the R&B tradition.

2

"A SONG CALLING FOR YOU"
Korean Pop Groups

While Psy transfixed the world with "Gangnam Style" in 2012, another equally unprecedented event occurred in the K-pop music world. Shinhwa, the oldest male Korean pop group with an original lineup, announced a comeback after a four-year hiatus. The group released its last album, *Volume 9*, in 2008, prior to the military service of its members. Before the comeback, Korea's mandatory military service for males virtually ensured the disbandment of male pop groups created by large Korean agencies. Shinhwa had already beaten the odds by staying together more than ten years, but many believed it was unlikely that the group would ever reunite. Yet, in 2012 Shinhwa released *The Return*, their tenth studio album, after holding two sold-out concerts in Seoul. Shinhwa's reunion sparked a series of reunions of other veteran pop groups. Two years later, g.o.d (Groove Overdose), another first-generation male pop group, announced its comeback, released the album *Chapter 8* (2014) nine years after its last album *Into the Sky* (2005), and embarked on a tour that included two dates in the United States. Popular female group S.E.S reunited for its twentieth anniversary with the album *Remember* in 2016. H.O.T., the male pop group that started it all, reunited for a performance on the television show *Infinite Challenge* in 2018. These reunions not only point to the longevity of Korean pop groups but also reveal a continued intertextuality common to Korean "idol" groups. Korean pop groups exhibit intertextuality by citing R&B musical and vocal elements in catchy pop songs and enhancing the tradition by infusing multiple genres with R&B elements. In music videos, they cite the choreography and styles of African American performance in ways that provide alternatives to Asian stereotypes. Driven by promotions that focus on image and music quality, K-pop "idols" mirror strategies employed by black American music producers. In doing so, they participate in cultural work that makes them part of a global R&B tradition.

Citation of the R&B Tradition: Funk, Club, and Urban Contemporary

From the earliest acts to the most recent cohort, "idols" have produced catchy pop songs that incorporate musical and vocal elements from R&B. An examination of pop acts on the Korean label YG Entertainment reveals that even though they all draw on the R&B tradition, they do so in different ways. They cite such disparate styles as funk, club, and urban R&B in catchy songs that have broad appeal. Moreover, K-pop "idol" groups also perform R&B ballads and benefit from music production by African American producers with much experience in R&B genres.

R&B Foundations of K-pop

Since K-pop's beginning, contemporary Korean pop groups have drawn on black American popular music. All K-pop music roads lead to Seo Taiji (Jung Hyun-chul), who with his group Seo Taiji and Boys and as a solo artist changed the face of Korean popular music. Seo Taiji and Boys debuted in 1992, with Seo Taiji, Yang Hyun-suk (who would go on to found YG Entertainment, one of the "Big Three" Korean entertainment agencies), and Lee Juno. Seo Taiji popularized elements of African American music culture in Korean popular music, including choreography and hip-hop culture, and sparked a new mode of pop music that achieved a significant measure of success with Korean youth. This new music differed from their parents' music. Doobo Shim (2006) notes that the group's first hit, "Nan Arayo" [I Know]" "excited local music listeners, who were fed up with the ballads and *ppongjjak* [a musical style informed by Japanese *enka*] that lacked dynamism and musical experimentation" (36). Seo Taiji and Boys also drew from hip-hop, using the breakbeat, sampling, and rapping to complement the choreography that accompanied their songs. These elements complemented performers that differed from ones Koreans were used to seeing: "Until Seo exploded onto the scene, the normal presentation of self in a performer had meant standing up straight and virtually motionless, but the new norm soon came to embrace gesticulation and dance as essential elements of performance. And the group did not merely sway or move in the way that most South Koreans then thought of as dancing (fox-trot, go-go, hustle); the group engaged in the acrobatics of break dancing" (Lie 2014, 78). Such performances were accompanied by the signature fashion style of hip-hop practitioners: "The neo-Confucian ethos of seriousness and sincerity, along with conservative attire and a demure posture, gave way to a new urbanity and pizzazz. The sartorial semiotic turned away from diligent, obedient businesspeople and toward urban youths (presumably unemployed and underemployed) with attitude. Seo Taiji became the face of hip-hop's aesthetic of bling and baggy clothes" (Lie 2014, 78). Much of this style can be traced to the unique expressive strategies of African Americans in the 1990s.

The adoption of musical and expressive elements of African Americans helped Seo Taiji pioneer a foundation for modern Korean pop groups, or "idols." As we will see with modern Korean pop groups that formed in his wake, Seo Taiji was not limited to genre: "The band creatively mixed genres like rap, soul, rock and roll, techno, punk, hardcore and even *ppongjjak*," (Shim 2006, 36). Sarah Morelli (2001) observes that Seo Taiji introduced the staple song structure of K-pop "idol" groups, which "employs rap only during the verses, singing choruses in a pop style" (250). In addition to creating lyrics that spoke to the concerns of Korean youth, Seo Taiji inspired the generation of youth that would become "idols": "The fact that Seo Taiji was a high school dropout but managed to earn social respect and succeed financially influenced parents' ideas about stardom. In a country where the average family viewed university entrance examinations for children as being of the utmost importance, stardom came to be considered a new option for success" (Shim 2006, 37). Many K-pop "idols" subsequently recognized Seo Taiji as an important model.

Korean pop groups that followed Seo Taiji retained his emphasis on the rhythm-centric music developed by African Americans. Michael Fuhr (2016) notes that the "song dramaturgy" of "idol" groups, which "governs the way songs develop," is grounded in the use of rhythm, including repeating the rhythm, changing the rhythm or blending rhythms together (91). The rhythmic work at play in Korean pop songs echoes the emphasis on rhythm in songs pioneered at Motown Records: "The concentration of session players and writers on details of the 'groove' made these Motown songs very different from other pop songs of the day. . . . It also meant that many more listeners and future songwriters were being influenced by a reorienting of musical priorities, with structural emphasis shifting from harmonic progression to 'grooves,' and a steady progression . . . towards the increasingly complex rhythmic textures of many subsequent styles" (Fitzgerald 1995, 8). Moreover, vocalists and rappers in Korean pop groups also cite black American popular music. In "idol" songs, "rap vocals . . . define the song's flow and dynamic" (Fuhr 2016, 91). R&B vocals as well as instrumentation can be found in a large number of Korean pop songs, and at least one member of most Korean pop groups has the ability to emulate such vocals. For example, while Girls' Generation (also known as SNSD) is a Korean girl group best known for its appearance, its three strongest vocalists formed the sub-unit TaeTiSeo, whose sound showcases vocal talents that follow the R&B style of black American female vocalists. In a *Billboard* interview, member Tiffany says, "Our main goal was to not be visually entertaining but be vocally entertaining," and goes on to reference African American singers Ciara and Rihanna as inspiration (Benjamin 2014). While some question their vocal talent, live Korean pop vocals showcased on Korean radio shows such as *Kiss the Radio, Young Street, Shimshimtapa,* and *Blue Night Radio* demonstrate that vocal talent is crucial for successful K-pop "idol" groups.

The first successful male "idol" group, H.O.T., drew on Seo Taiji's citation of African American choreography and styling. H.O.T. debuted in 1996 with members Moon Hee-joon, Jang Woo-hyuk, Tony An, Kangta (Ahn Chil-hyun), and Lee Jae-won. Lee Soo-man, founder of SM Entertainment, another "Big Three" Korean entertainment agency, formed the group. Shim (2006) notes that Lee was able to take advantage of the weakening influence of networks and the expanded influence of record and entertainment companies to recruit members of "idol" groups in the wake of Seo Taiji's success (37). Lee introduced fans to the pop star formula, surveying teenaged girls "to find out what they wanted from their idols" and selecting "aspiring idols based on their looks as well as on their dancing and singing abilities" (Shim 2006, 38). Like Seo Taiji, H.O.T. covered a variety of music styles. The group debuted with the pop song "Candy" (1996) and a music video featuring the members in oversized, colorful outfits at an amusement park, a style that hearkens to the urban style of African Americans in the 1990s. By the time the group released its last album, *Outside Castle* (2000), its tone turned significantly darker. The title track features a classical orchestration and a video where the members are dramatically dressed in black against the backdrop of towering marble columns. The success of H.O.T. led to the formation of several more male "idol" groups. While Lee pioneered the casting and training system for Korean pop groups, others tweaked that formula to produce a plethora of groups who differed from each other in their music, performance, and personality. Nevertheless, they all continued to cite elements of African American popular music.

Funk Instrumentation and Gospel Vocals: g.o.d (Groove Overdose)

Frequently characterized as trendy, Korean pop groups reach back to older R&B genres of black American popular music. The citation of funk instrumentation and gospel vocals by first-generation male "idol" group g.o.d (Groove Overdose) is fundamental to the group's distinct style.

One of the first male pop groups to emerge in the wake of H.O.T.'s success, g.o.d also deviated from its model. Instead of coming together through a casting process, member Park Joon-hyung spearheaded g.o.d's creation, recruiting Danny Ahn, his cousin, and Son Ho-young, Ahn's friend. Both Park and Ahn were Korean American, and traveled to Korea to become artists. Yoon Kye-sang was added through an audition and Kim Tae-woo joined when he was a high school student. Park Joon-hyung explains he sought to form "not a 'boy boy group' but people like little kid adults can look up and listen to without thinking these are like kids" ("Interview with Korea's g.o.d" 2001). Under the tutelage of Park Jin-young, founder of JYP Entertainment, g.o.d debuted in 1999 with their album *Chapter 1*, and two hit songs. "To Mother" was a ballad, and the accompanying video featured Jang Hyuk, a popular actor, as the video's protagonist ("[HD] GOD—Dear Mother" 2013). It opens with Jang in a rowboat with a harmonica in the middle of a fog-filled lake, reminiscing about his mother. Flashbacks filmed in black and white show his mother working menial jobs and Jang's harassment by classmates for their poverty. They also show the love the mother has for her son, for she gifts him the very harmonica seen in the opening scene. The mother dies, and it turns out that Jang is at the lake to scatter her ashes. Instead of being the center of the video, the members of the group appear only briefly. By contrast, "Observation," the second song from the debut album, looks more like a pop video and establishes the group's playful reputation ("G.O.D—Observation" 2012). Here, they are aliens who come to observe life on earth. Wearing shiny outfits on their spaceship, they later don the oversized clothing of the youth of the time. The video features their "car driving" choreography, the kind of synchronized dancing that H.O.T. popularized. In 2001, g.o.d strengthened the trend of "idols" on television as the first idol group to parley their personalities into their own reality show, *g.o.d's Baby Diaries*, where the members took care of a baby. Such appearances bolstered their popularity as they embarked on a domestic tour that same year, including a performance at Seoul Olympic Stadium, making g.o.d only the second Korean pop group at the time after H.O.T. to play the 69,000-seat venue. It was also the same venue played by Michael Jackson on his HIStory tour in 1996. Attendance at such concerts were important because, as Kim Tae-woo notes, "Since SNS [social networking services] and the Internet weren't prevalent back then, fans also made a bigger effort to come and watch their artists. Otherwise, you wouldn't have any opportunities to see them" (Yoo 2015).

The group remained with JYP Entertainment for their next five albums: *Chapter 2* (1999), *Chapter 3* (2000), *Chapter 4* (2001), and *Chapter 5: Letter*

(2002). With Yoon pursuing an acting career, the remaining members released two albums, *An Ordinary Day* (2004) and *Into the Sky* (2005). The group went on hiatus after 2005 and reunited in 2014 for the release of *Chapter 8* with all five original members. The video for the track "Saturday Night" continues to reflect the group's playful nature ("[MV]god_Saturday Night" 2018). It opens with four of the noticeably older members sitting on a curb at night in a city, when the fifth hobbles up on a pair of crutches. The video recounts what happened earlier in the day. Each of them engaged in hijinks in their less than glamorous jobs as an office worker, a street entertainer, a chauffeur, a manual laborer at a car salvage, and a DJ at a small club that caters to older patrons. In the final sequence of the video, the guys decide to go to the small club, but when g.o.d songs are played, they shove their dates to the side, yell and jump up and down excitedly, and take over the dance floor to nostalgically perform their old choreography.

While g.o.d has a playful group persona, the group's music has consistently drawn from instrumentation of funk music since their debut. Park Joon-hyung explained his musical vision for the group when it was formed: "The rule of our music, the way I wanted to make our music was . . . I want it like the sounds from like the 70s to 60s, kind of like disco music, funk era, bring it to the 90s and 21st century, and put in beats that would be easily digestible to the people nowadays" ("Interview with Korea's g.o.d" 2001). "Intro" (1999), the first track on their first album, includes a sample of the Gap Band's "Outstanding" from the 1982 album *The Gap Band IV*. The Gap Band's original song is an upbeat funk track. g.o.d's track incorporates the most recognized musical fragment from "Outstanding" to set a funky tone for "Intro" as well as the album. The languorous rhythm, the epitome of an African American cookout, repeats until the introduction of the rap in Korean. The sample lends a laid-back, funky feel to the track that complements the casual rap. The music video for "Observation" incorporates a sample from "Love Rollercoaster" (1975) from the 1975 album *Honey* by the Ohio Players, another key figure in funk music, during the breakdown in the middle of the song. The group continues to use musical phrase in live performances of the track, often using a live band to do so. The sample of the chorus of "Love Rollercoaster" changes the electronic rhythm of g.o.d's track by introducing the infectious guitar that establishes the dance rhythm as well as the denser instrumentation that supplements the rhythm with significant bass guitar, drums, and whistles in the original. The sample lends "Observation" the Ohio Players' brand of funk, which is reminiscent of Sly and the Family Stone, who "introduced to funk a unique bass technique, the technology of rock (wah-wah pedal, fuzz box, echo chamber, vocal distortion, and so on) and blues-rock flavored guitar" (Maultsby 2006, 297). While funk is often associated with guitar, it also innovated the sound of electronic instruments. By the 1970s, "funk became the medium by which electronic sound effects never before heard on synthesizers of the future could be channeled through a black aesthetic" (Vincent 1996, 19). Funk of the 1980s incorporated bass parts that were performed on synthesizer but retained the complex rhythm patterns that are the hallmark of earlier funk music (Ripani 2006, 135). The sample from "Love Rollercoaster" is sandwiched between another sample featuring heavier synth instrumentation in electronic sequences drawn from the British new wave duo Yaz's 1982 hit "Don't Go." Yaz's music "drew on the dance rhythms of disco and funk" (Cateforis 2004, 569).

g.o.d also cites the gospel-inflected vocals of R&B through the powerhouse vocals of Kim Tae-woo. The group's primary vocalist, Kim names Stevie Wonder, James Ingram, and Brian McKnight as inspirations (Yoo 2015). Kim is particularly influenced by McKnight. Coming from a musical family and having studied jazz and gospel, McKnight performed with the band Revelation Funk in the 1970s, and provided backup vocals for Ray Charles before being tapped by Quincy Jones for the 1980 hit "Just Once," which began a slew of hits for him in the 1980s and 1990s. Kim's vocal style complements g.o.d's funk-inflected instrumentation, for a central element of funk is "a vocalist singing in a gospel style" (Maultsby 2006, 297). "One Candle," from g.o.d's 2000 album *Chapter 3*, features harmony against gospel-inspired instrumentation. The song begins sparsely: gospel organ accompanied by a walking bassline and accentuated with handclaps and cymbal percussion. As the song continues, the instrumentation becomes more lush and Kim Tae-woo's gospel vocals, backed by a throng of female voices, increases in intensity and improvisation. g.o.d's "Sky Blue Promise," from the 2014 album *Chapter 8*, is a rearrangement of "One Candle" fourteen years later. It begins with a lively guitar and fingersnaps that supplement the spoken intro. The gospel backing vocals for Kim are replaced with more buoyant vocals, but Kim's vocals continue to build in intensity and ornamentation throughout the song. The gospel choir feel returns in a bridge with Kim's vocals, accompanied only by a light organ, followed by group harmony and handclaps. This combination of funk and gospel-inflected vocals is a hallmark of R&B genres.

Club Music and Urban R&B: 2PM and Wonder Girls

Even though "idol" groups undergo a similar casting and/or training process, they deploy the musical talents of their members in different ways by citing different musical elements from R&B-based genres of black popular music. While 2PM and Wonder Girls were labelmates with g.o.d at JYP Entertainment, they engage different styles of R&B music. 2PM uses its vocal variety in high-energy club tracks, while Wonder Girls cite 1990s black female R&B groups.

After several first-generation K-pop groups disbanded, the next generations of "idol" groups became more active outside of Korea. Some included more non-Korean members while others used more foreign creative personnel to produce "hook"-centered tracks (Kim C.-N. 2012, 107–10). Emerging with the next generation of K-pop "idol" groups, 2PM originally consisted of five vocalists, Jun.K (Kim Min-jun), Nichkhun (Nichkhun Buck Horvejkul), Woo-young (Jang Woo-young), Junho (Lee Jun-ho), and Chansung (Hwang Chansung), and two rappers, Taec-yeon (Ok Taec-yeon) and Jay Park. They were not novices. Jun.K had previously won singing competitions, while Taec-yeon, Junho, and Chansung had previously participated in a survival show. Some of the members had lived in the United States and Jay Park, the group's former leader, is Korean American. 2PM was originally part of a larger group called One Day with 2AM, a vocal group also under JYP Entertainment. Originally billed as the hip-hop counterpart to 2AM, 2PM, whose name references the hottest time of the day, became known for its "beast" image, which included the display of "dynamic acrobatic and b-boy dance styles, maximizing their tough manly images" (Jung S. 2011, 162). This "beastly" image disrupted the pretty-boy image of other male groups in K-pop at the time: "2PM's stage performances demonstrate sexy and tough masculinity by often showing off their well-toned muscular bodies" (Jung S. 2011, 165). Their debut single in 2008, "10 Out of 10," features choreography and scenes with backflips and breakdancing intercut with scenes where members fantasize about attempting to seduce the female protagonist. This represents a shift from other K-pop music videos of the time, which rarely showed members of male groups interacting with women. The track was included on the group's first album, *01:59PM* (2009). With *Hands Up* (2011), the members began to contribute to the production of their own music, with Jun.K writing "HOT" and Junho writing "Give It to Me" on the album. The members would go on to write and arrange their own music as well as tracks for their labelmates at JYP, including GOT7 and Kim Tae-woo of g.o.d. 2PM debuted in Japan with sales just behind Kis-My-FT2, a top group produced by Johnny's Entertainment. Individual members made solo debuts, with Jun.K releasing three mini-albums, Wooyoung releasing two mini-albums, and Junho releasing a full album and a mini-album. The group went on to release additional albums, including *Grown* (2013), *Go Crazy* (2014), *No. 5* (2015), and *Gentleman's Game* (2016).

2PM is known for highly produced, high-energy club tracks that draw on the group's deep bank of vocalists. Unlike g.o.d's consistent use of funk rhythm, 2PM's tracks focus on powerful rhythmic diversity. Mark Jonathan

Butler (2006) simply says that rhythm "is the raison d'etre of electronic dance music—one of its most prominent and interesting characteristics" (4). "Jump," from the group's 2015 album *No.5*, would fit in well in any rotation designed to get people on the dance floor at a club, with its overwhelming electronica intro and a driving club beat. Eric_r_wirsing (2015) calls "Jump" a "club-banger, unapologetically laced with raps and a flurry of synth beats, as well as a belted chorus and repeated 'jump jump jump's' and 'dance dance dance's' that give the thing easy and earwormy hooks." 2PM also has rhythmically driven tracks like "Magic," also from *No.5* (2015), which explodes with horns and the rhythm that proves to be most noticeable to listeners. Jara (2015) notes the track "is attention grabbing from the start with a funky swing rhythm that is full of bursting brass instruments." Jeff Benjamin (2015) observes that "the tempo gets picked up with this swing-y, throwback track with blasting brass." The more assertive nature of the song makes a place for a rap style that has more swagger and includes English phrases.

In other songs, 2PM utilizes its vocalists. Fan reviewers connect 2PM's sound to the polished production that defines 1990s R&B. Referring to 2PM's "All Night Long" from the *01:59PM* (2009), fan reviewer Random J (2010) links the track's use of Autotune to 90s R&B singers: "Vocoded, auto-tuned and talk box vocals in a slow jam are fine. There was a time when they were staples. Blackstreet and Teddy Riley popularized it back when and K-Ci and JoJo ran with it for their songs." At the same time, the group is praised for its maturing vocals. Eric_r_wirsing (2015) calls "Wanna Love You Again" from *No. 5* "a lush ballad" with "buttery-smooth backing vocals" and "vocals that nicely defy the metronome and give it a very soulful feel." Jara (2015a) agrees: "This time 2PM presents a dreamy slow tempo R&B track where the members show off their vocal abilities by singing in falsetto, which is later contrasted with yet another baritone rap. What I like the most about 'Wanna Love You Again' is that you can hear and feel the sincerity in the boys' soulful voices." However, 2PM represents one of several ways later generations of "idol" groups engage in the aesthetics of R&B.

While most K-pop "idol" groups tend to be male, girl groups contribute significantly to the Korean pop music landscape. A year after the debut of H.O.T., SM Entertainment debuted its first all-female group: S.E.S, made up of Bada (Choi Sung-hee), Eugene (Kim Yoo-jin), and Shoo (Yoo Soo-young). Along with other female groups like Fin.K.L and Baby Vox, these first-generation girl groups combined a cute aesthetic with the urban style and assertiveness found in black American female groups of the 1990s like TLC. TLC blended its members' voices, deftly utilizing the accessible rap style of Lisa "Left Eye" Lopes with the vocals of Tionne "T-Boz" Watkins and Rozonda "Chili" Thomas against the backdrop of urban contemporary beats. Their sound defined a particular kind of girl group that was different from other pop-oriented acts of the 1990s like the Spice Girls. Elias Leight (2018) notes that "hip-hop's DNA was readily apparent in their sample-heavy beats, often created by producer Dallas Austin, and Lopes' raps; their R&B element came from group backing vocals and Watkins' surprisingly low, melismatic leads. The resulting combination was shiny and supple, showing facility with decades of R&B history." TLC represented an urban girl group sound that blended vocals with rap, creating a model followed by K-pop female "idol" girl groups. Nataki Goodall (1994) points to TLC as a model of female assertiveness: "[TLC] are able to emphasize their femaleness and at the same time declare their mastery of the microphone" (86). Rana Emerson (2002) places TLC with other 1990s black female performers who express an independent perspective: "Black women performers are frequently depicted as active, vocal, and independent. . . . Speaking out and speaking one's mind are a constant theme. Through the songs and videos, Black women are able to achieve voice and a space for spoken expression of social and interpersonal commentary" (126). Goodall (1994) traces independence to song lyrics and Emerson to music videos, yet I argue that such female assertiveness also emerges in the music aesthetics, aesthetics that are echoed by K-pop girl groups.

Wonder Girls debuted in 2007 with JYP Entertainment, making them labelmates with male artists 2PM, Rain (Bi), and g.o.d. Over the course of ten years, the group changed its lineup, which included Sunye (Min Sun-ye), Yeeun (Park Ye-eun), Sunmi (Lee Sun-min), Sohee (Ahn So-hee), Yubin (Kim Yu-bin), Hyuna (Kim Hyun-ah), and Hyelim (Woo Hye-rim). Hyuna left the group in 2007, going on to become a member of the female group 4Minute, and later launching a solo career where she collaborated with male idols in groups like Trouble Maker (with Jang Hyun-seung, formerly of BEAST) and Triple H (with Hui and E-Dawn of Pentagon). Sunye and Sohee left the group in 2015. The first girl group produced by JYP Entertainment, the Wonder Girls were introduced through the television show *MTV Wonder Girls*. The group's debut single "Irony" utilized elements of hip-hop. In a retrospective of the Wonder Girls' career, Tamar Herman (2017a) describes the track as "pretty dated with its R&B-pop styling and redundant beat, but the sleek, hook-filled chorus was filled with promise." The group released its first full-length album, *The Wonder Years* (2007), which features "Tell Me," a synthesizer-filled track. In 2008 the group released what would become one of their most popular tracks, "Nobody," which ended up on *The Wonder Years: Trilogy* EP. "Nobody" "revived the industry with a modern update to old school sounds that drew on Motown and the disco era for inspiration, which resulted in the single becoming one of the most popular Korean songs ever" (Herman 2017a). The group would go on to release two additional full albums, *Wonder World* (2011) and *Reboot* (2015), along with four mini-albums, *The Wonder Years: Trilogy* (2008), *2 Different Tears* (2010), *Wonder Party* (2012), and *Nobody for Everybody* (2012). Wonder Girls disbanded in 2017.

Wonder Girls are heirs to the urban contemporary black female groups of the 1990s, which distinguishes them from their Korean male group counterparts. Wonder Girls' "Ee Babo [That Fool]" from the 2007 album *The Wonder Years* opens with a synthesizer riff coupled with an earth-shaking bassline designed to be blasted from a car while driving. The verses feature light and bubbly vocals with some well-placed harmonies on the chorus. Rather than drowning out the vocals, the rhythm complements the sung verses as well as the confident rap verse that contrasts with the sweeter vocals of the verses. "Hey Boy," from the 2012 release *Wonder Party*, has a similar urban vibe, opening with actual car sounds and horns, which contrasts with a lone vocal and well-placed guitar licks. When the beat finally drops, its syncopation provides the backdrop for a very deliberate vocal run countered with a rap interjection of "baby." The song later develops into a bridge dominated by falling scale harmonies with no musical accompaniment. Wonder Girls make use of the higher pitch of women's voices often juxtaposed with the forthright rapping style of Yubin in ways that are reminiscent of black female groups that crossed over into pop in the 1990s. Yet, "idols" would continue to emulate other styles of R&B.

While g.o.d, 2PM, and Wonder Girls are all with the same Korean agency, they show how consistently "idol" groups cite a variety of elements of R&B. However, the use of R&B producers is common throughout the K-pop music industry.

K-pop Producers and R&B: Teddy, Harvey Mason Jr., Teddy Riley

Critics frequently describe "idols" as manufactured, giving little serious attention to the music producers who are critical in developing their sound. Korean music producer Teddy infuses electronic dance music with hip-hop, while African American producers Harvey Mason Jr. and Teddy Riley bring their distinctive R&B sound to K-pop.

More so than other kinds of Korean pop music, "idol" groups rely on music producers and agencies to craft their music. The advent of pop music necessitates the creation of new ideas of creative personnel and the shifting responsibilities of existing ones. Unlike music produced before the advent of recording, the use of magnetic tape "enabled musical parameters that were difficult to notate . . . to be more easily handled on a trial-and-error basis during the recording and mixing process. Within this, the function of the composer became integrated into the recording process, which was carried out much more as teamwork" (Wicke, Liang, and Horn 2003, 186). As a result, we see the proliferation of creative personnel, especially in contemporary popular music. More individuals are credited with lyrics, composition, music, and arrangement, even more so with Korean pop, which is part of a larger culture industry in Korea. K-pop creative personnel embody Antoine Hennion's (1989) characterization of contemporary music production, which represents "the collective work of recording professionals: artists, lyricists, composers, arrangers, artistic directors, producers, sound engineers. Whether it is a matter of sound, of language, or music, or of the search for singing talent, the same operation takes place: the fragments need to be pried from their context so that they can be inserted into the song" (409). It is the producer's vision that determines how a song sounds by working with engineers, vocalists, musicians and beatmakers. Initially, record producers were considered to be engineers of sound. However, ever since the 1960s, music producers have evolved into artists in their own right. Virgil Moorefield (2005) explains that music producers like Phil Spector, responsible for the sonically distinctive Wall of Sound, and George Martin, music producer for the Beatles, used "the juxtaposition of tape loops with string quartets" and "the manipulation of figure and ground through placement in the mix," to create something new: "Their interest lay not in replicating the natural world, but rather in transforming it into something else: by embracing subjectivity, they made a potent argument for viewing the producer as auteur" (xv). The activities of the music producer rise to the level of artist when the producer becomes involved in activities traditionally assigned to arrangers and composers, such as style and musical form (Moorefield 2005, xv).

K-pop music producers also may surprise listeners by bringing African American popular music aesthetics into electronic dance music. Just as Yoo Young-jin created the distinctive SM Performance Sound inflected by R&B, Teddy Park (Park Hong-jun), also known by his stage name Teddy, developed a reputation for hip-hop–infused tracks for YG Entertainment. He began his career as a member of the Korean hip-hop group 1TYM with YG Entertainment in 1998. Along with fellow members Danny (Im Tae-bin), Jin Hwan (Oh Jin-hwan), and Baek Kyoung (Song Baek-kyoung), 1TYM debuted with the 1998 single "One Time for Your Mind" from the debut album of the name. The mid-tempo song opens with heavy but simple synthesizer riff, interrupted by bold rapping style for the verses and complemented by sing-song vocals on the chorus. The video for the song shows the members of the group with oversized clothes performing b-boy inspired choreography. 1TYM went on to produce five albums in total in a career that spanned eight years, making them pioneers in Korean hip-hop. Two years after his debut, Teddy began to be involved in the music production for 1TYM, arranging and writing lyrics and cocomposing "One Love" from 1TYM's 2000 album, *2nd Round*. While a member of 1TYM, Teddy also produced for his fellow YG Entertainment hip-hop labelmates, cowriting lyrics for "Hip Hop Seoul Ja," a rare all-English track from Jinusean's 2001 *The Reign* album. Jinusean, a duo made up of Kim Jin-woo and Noh Seung-hwan, debuted a year before 1TYM. Both members of Jinusean moved to the United States at the age of twelve and point to the impact of this direct experience on their music: "Not too many people get to listen to the original rap artists, who are from the States, like Cypress Hill, not too many people in Korea get to hear them. . . . We're working with the same original rap artists from the States, and that means three hundred, four hundred thousand Korean people listening to the original, real thing. That's what I wanted to show them, to let them listen to" (Johnson 2003, 85). Teddy was able to work with a form of hip-hop that drew directly from the aesthetics emerging from the United States.

While a frequent collaborator with YG Entertainment's hip-hop acts, Teddy also works with YG Entertainment's "idol" artists, bringing a hip-hop sensibility to electronic dance music. While some may perceive EDM as completely unrelated to African American popular music, many of its genres have roots in black American popular music. EDM genres can be traced to the 1970s American music scene. Ricky Vincent (1996) acknowledges that, while a genre of its own, funk music has a tremendous impact as a dance genre: "Funk music, with its nonstop, sweaty dance appeal, is also the no-nonsense form of dance entertainment most directly related to the rhythm and blues tradition" (19). Disco, which grew out of the 1970s funk, "emphasized the beat above anything else" and "mutated into a variety of different dance-based genres, ranging from dance-pop and hip hop to house and techno" (Bogdanov 2003, ix). Today, a myriad of dance genres described as electronic dance music continue to foreground rhythm just like other R&B genres. EDM genres like techno are forms of hybrid music designed to get people to dance and have their origins as African American music as well. Rather than the monotonous music that comes to some people's mind, it features a focus on rhythm: "At that nascent state, Detroit techno (and Chicago house) was being packaged and presented as the smiley-face music of Berlin, Madchester and Belgium, the sound of Europeans and Ecstasy" (Beta 2015).

Techno is often characterized as a European music form, but C. Vecchiola (2011) notes that "Detroit techno is known for its use of layered rhythms and the influence of funk music" (100). Black music genres feature prominently in the development of techno. Eddie "Flashin" Fowlkes, pioneer techno producer and DJ, was inspired by DJ Frankie Knuckles's use of multiple musical genres:

"Frankie has his own edits of Philly International tracks and others on a reel-to-reel tape which he played" (Hoffman 2005). Philly International was a record label that pioneered the "Philly sound," reflected by the production duo Leon Huff and Kenneth Gamble as well as Gene McFadden and John Whitehead, and music marked by lush strings and power horns. Kevin Saunderson echoes the eclectic mix from which they drew: "We all had the same music—stuff like Kraftwerk, B-52s, New Order, Depeche Mode, Alexander Robotnik, some Funkadelic, even some Prince, some disco records, Eddy Grant" (Hoffman 2005). Detroit not only pioneered the incorporation of rhythms from black music genres, but also the practice of mixing disparate elements into something new. More significantly for "idol" acts, techno also had a transnational impulse. American EDM artists traveled to places like Europe to perform, and in doing so, took advantage of the growing fan base for the music and developed a transnational fan base for the music they created. *Exhibit 3000*, a collection housed at Submerge, maker of vinyl records for global distribution since 1992, shows the global presence of Detroit-based techno: "The combination of the density of the pushpins representing mail-order customers and the breadth of the pushpins representing artist appearances and retail distribution conveys a visual representation of Submerge's, and by extension EDM's, global reach" (Vecchiola 2011, 108). The African American foundations for EDM also inform some of its social meaning. Andy Beta (2015) notes: "Hearing about techno as it was originally conceived—as a reaction to inner-city decay, as byproduct of African-American struggle, as a form of protest—served as a crucial reminder of the roots of this dance music, and that the name Underground Resistance was in no way a euphemism, but a reality."

Such permutations of EDM represent the emulation of the R&B tradition. Teddy brings his experience with hip-hop and EDM tracks to several electronic dance hits by the female group 2NE1, including the 2011 global hit "I Am the Best." A reviewer says that that the track has a "beat so high-energy that it could survive in the busiest clubs without a trace of vocal add-ons" ("[Review] "I Am the Best," 2011). Teddy also worked on BigBang's "Fantastic Baby" (2012), which blends rap and techno: "That techno sound they were going for this year was intensified, but also allowed to mature. The hook is more effective, the synths more cohesive, the dynamics present, and the melody only second to everything else" (Nicola Rivera 2012). At the same time, the track features raps and the kind of musical manipulation one hears in sampled hip-hop.

In addition to Korean producers, African American producers working with "idol" groups cite R&B elements. Harvey Mason Jr., veteran producer for a range of American R&B artists, draws on his childhood growing up in a musical household with his father, jazz drummer and founding member of FourPlay, Harvey Mason Sr. Mason Jr. encountered musical legends like Quincy Jones, the Brothers Johnson, and Herbie Hancock at an early age. His first successful song was Brandy's 1998 hit "Truthfully," and he worked with Destiny's Child, Whitney Houston, and Michael Jackson. In 2000 Mason Jr. formed the Underdogs, a music production company with Damon Thomas, who was a production partner with Kenneth "Babyface" Edmonds in the 1990s. As the Underdogs, they worked on songs for several SM Entertainment artists, including BoA, SHINee, EXO, and Girls' Generation. Jeff Benjamin (2013) of *Billboard* credits the Underdogs with giving SHINee's "Symptoms" "a woozy, electronic production over a snappy R&B beat" and the "aural shift at just 18 seconds in, leading up to a sweeping chorus allowing Onew, Jonghyun, Key, Minho and Taemin to showcase their signature harmonies over a banging piano production." Zander Stachniak (2015) calls another Mason Jr. production, EXO's "What If" (2015), "a beautiful, old-school R&B song. . . . If you care for R&B, this song is a must for your slow-jam playlist." Mason Jr.'s work on EXO's "Overdose" from the 2014 EP of the same name blends electronic music with more dynamic rhythms found in hip-hop. Overwhelming the listener with a heavy beat accentuated with handclaps from the beginning of the song, the rhythm continues to underscore the rap-dominant verses, which are laid-back yet punctuated, and the vocals, which provide sonic contrast. The song gains further interest in the pre-chorus, where a snare drum and minor electronic effects highlight the vocals, providing an organic sound in the midst of a largely electronic soundscape. The chorus brings back the heavy bass-inflected instrumentation to support the vocals that are sung in unison. The latter half of the song introduces orchestral effects that contribute to the building of sound that culminates right before the final chorus. Writing for *allkpop*, eric_r_wisring (2014) calls "Overdose" "an ace, danceable song, electronically reinforced and bombastic, the chorus is grand and dramatic. A club classic if I've ever heard one." Jessica Oak (2014) calls it "a heavy-hitting urban-pop banger with hard rhythms of hip-hop, R&B hooks and electronic beats." These fan reviewers tend to reference rhythm accentuated by elements of electronic pop provided by the expertise of Mason Jr.

Teddy Riley, another African American R&B producer, brings his experience as a pioneer of new jack swing to the electronic sound of Korean pop groups. As a member of the American R&B group Guy that debuted in 1989, Riley is credited as the creator of new jack swing, which "uses a triplet-swing rhythm in the sixteenth notes; good examples of this effect can be heard in the songs "My Prerogative" (1988), which he composed for Bobby Brown's album *Don't Be Cruel*, and "Off on Your Own" (1988) from the Al B. Sure album *In Effect Mode*" (Ripani 2006, 131). Riley developed even more R&B credentials as a member of the 1990s R&B group Blackstreet. While Riley formed the girl "idol" group BP RaNia (formerly known as RaNia) and produced their 2011 song, "Dr. Feel Good," he also brings an R&B sensibility to Korean male pop groups. Riley admits: "What I did with K-pop, I brought my genre to it—I just merged New Jack Swing with K-pop, because they were following the New Jack Swing style anyway" (Shephard 2017). That influence is seen in tracks ranging from Girl's Generation's "The Boys," which "has the hip-hop background beat and sexy R&B vocals that are essential to new jack swing," to male group BTOB's "WOW," which garnered praise from Riley on Twitter (Lindsay 2012). While some "idol" groups reflect intertextuality through the emulation of the R&B tradition, others do so by enhancing the tradition.

Mixing Pop Genres: SHINee, Shinhwa, TVXQ

"Idol" groups not only cite the R&B music tradition, they enhance it by incorporating R&B elements into multiple genres of pop music, which is a hallmark of Korean music production. The songs of pop group SHINee engage in several genres, yet consistently incorporate R&B vocals. First-generation group Shinhwa has delved into multiple genres including rock-rap and dance over its twenty-year career. "Idol" group TVXQ forays into the R&B ballad despite its solid reputation as a pop group.

SHINee debuted in 2008, the same year as 2PM, but the groups could not be more different. SHINee means "to receive the light," much like an employee receives employment. The five-member group from SM Entertainment originally featured three vocalists, Onew (Lee Jin-ki), Jonghyun (Kim Jong-hyun), Taemin (Lee Tae-min), and two rappers, Minho (Choi Min-ho) and Key (Kim Ki-bum). Introduced as a "contemporary" group with a penchant for bright colors and trendy style, SHINee has drawn on a variety of R&B genres and performance styles since the beginning of its career. This is exemplified by the group's debut hit single from the first album *The SHINee World* (2008), "Noona Neomu Yeppo [Noona Is So Pretty] (Replay)," which Tamar Herman (2018) describes as "a smooth, contemporary R&B pre-break-up track." SHINee released *Lucifer* (2010); its music video featured the complex choreography for which they would also become known. Rino Nakasone, who has worked with Janet Jackson, choreographed routines for "Noona Neomu Yeppo" and "Lucifer," which featured some of the most difficult choreography in K-pop. Tony Testa, who has also choreographed for Janet Jackson, worked with the group on routines for "Sherlock" and "Dream Girl." SHINee went on to become the first Asian artist to perform at Abbey Road Studios in London in 2011 and later became the first Korean group to have an independent concert in London. They continued to release Korean albums, including *The Misconceptions Series* (2013), which included *Dream Girl—The Misconceptions of You* and *Why So Serious?—The Misconceptions of Me*, *Odd* (2015), and *1 of 1* (2016). Like members of other "idol" groups, the members also pursued solo careers. Jong-hyun released two studio albums and one mini-album and earned song credits on SHINee songs as well as tracks for other K-pop artists like Lee Hi and his bandmate Taemin. Taemin has released three albums and several mini-albums. SHINee also officially debuted in Japan in 2011 and later produced an impressive Japanese discography, including *The First* (2011), *Boys Meet U* (2013), *I'm Your Boy* (2014), *DxDxD* (2016), and *Five* (2017). Soon after their Japanese promotions for *Five* in 2017, Jonghyun lost his longtime battle with depression, taking his own life in December of that year. The group performed the rest of the Japanese tour and released the Japanese compilation album, *SHINEE: The Best From Now On* in early 2018. This was followed up by the three-part Korean album series, *The Story of Light*, in 2018.

SHINee is best known for the way the group deploys its vocalists, using R&B within a pop context in unexpected ways. "Symptoms," from the 2013 album *Everybody*, opens with Jonghyun's plaintive solo vocals against the backdrop of a slow-tempo rhythm, followed by Onew's more mellow vocals, providing contrast on this not-quite-ballad. The verses are intermittently interjected with brief phrases of harmony, underscoring the vocal difference. It is the way that their voices follow each other in the song that gives it a classic R&B sound. The verses are peppered with rhythmic breaks and the breakdown has an epic, orchestral feel. Fan reviewers pick up on the unique, quintessentially R&B track. Alice Edogawa (2013) hears an echo of a Broadway song and R&B, while Jakob Dorof (n.d.) describes the track as "an internal discord of portamento synths that lurch woozily toward the chorus catharsis and a huge, key-change bridge."

SHINee's 2015 album *Odd* runs the gamut of styles, yet consistently incorporates R&B elements, giving them new contexts. The promotional track "View" utilizes SHINee's trademark vocals: "On the other hand, like 90% of K-Pop songs today, the real magic is in the melodies, and with SHINee at the helm of 'View,' this mundane disco-lite track tricks the ear to believe it's livelier than it really is" ("An Annotated Listening: 'Odd'" 2015). The song contrasts with the swing-inflected track "Woof Woof," which combines SHINee's vocals and older black popular music instrumentation. Alejandro Abraca (2015) notes that the track "has different genres in it, a mixture of brass, jazz and swing." *Odd* also features "Trigger," which includes R&B with other eclectic elements. An initial series of discordant electronic sounds resolves into a verse with an easy R&B rhythm featuring SHINee's characteristic vocals. The track becomes more electronic on the chorus, but returns to an R&B feel on the verses. Jara (2015b) describes the song as a "neo-soul R&B influenced number" with "a lot happening in the background, from heavy bass and drums, colorful synths, to oriental sound effects and instruments." It also represents a stark shift in the flow of the album: "This is a complete 360 turn from the previous track. 'Romance' was very happy and fun but the album takes a darker turn with 'Trigger.' With R&B beats, trap elements, the infusion of xylophones and big bass drops, the track contains a handful of sounds that are rarely mixed together but seem to work well with the lyrics" (Abraca 2015). With the album *Odd*, SHINee demonstrates its tendency to put familiar R&B elements in new contexts. This combination of multiple genres is a hallmark of SM Entertainment music production, which Yoo Young-jin links to music like Janet Jackson: "Listening to that kind of music and watching those performance [*sic*], I wanted to show a variety of performance elements within in a song. Like setting a certain flow and breaking it, or putting stop-brakes during the music or slowing down the beat rather than just taking one flow from beginning to end of a song. In a way, I guess you could say that it is like putting five remix versions in one song" ("[Interview] Record Producer Yoo Young-jin" 2010a).

While SHINee references multiple genres within a single release, Shinhwa, the longest-running male "idol" group with its original members, has cited R&B with different genres throughout its twenty-one-year career. Shinhwa's sound balances its three singers, Lee Min-woo, Shin Hye-sung, Kim Dong-wan, and three rappers Eric (Eric Moon), Andy Lee, and Jun Jin (Park Choong-jae). This personnel structure made the group different from g.o.d, which featured a single powerhouse R&B vocalist along with other singers and rappers. Shinhwa, which in English means "myth" or "legend," debuted under SM Entertainment in 1998 with "Hae Gyul Sah [The Solver]" from the album of the same name and emulated the visuals and sound of 1990s R&B, a dance track with rapped verses. The music video featured the members in shiny track suits reminiscent of hip-hop performers Sean "P.Diddy" Combs and Missy Elliott, performing choreography on a giant swinging pendulum in a post-apocalyptic landscape ("Shinhwa—Hae Gyul Sah" 2010). Shinhwa continued to distinguish themselves from other male "idol" groups when they embarked on a darker concept for their second album *T.O.P* (1999) as well as the hit song "All Your Dreams" from the 2000 album *Only One*. Shot with a blue-gray color palette, the music video shows the members working menial jobs ("Shinhwa—All Your Dreams" 2013). A love triangle emerges between one of the working-class members of the group and a rich suitor, both vying for the affections of a girl. In their down time, the members hang out with each other, but are also harassed by other youth and end up involved in a fight. Created in the mold of H.O.T., Shinhwa's versatility and sophisticated choreography would distinguish the group throughout its career and influence later K-pop groups. After *Only One* (2000), Shinhwa's album *Hey! Come On* (2001) also produced the video for "Wild Eyes" with choreography that utilized chairs, which has been emulated by later K-pop groups including SHINee and BTS.

By 2002 Shinhwa had earned the distinction of being the longest running K-pop group to date when it released *Perfect Man* (2002) and *Wedding* (2002). That same year, Shinhwa shocked the K-pop world when the members declined to renew their contracts with SM Entertainment. When they joined Good Entertainment, the group became involved in music production and choreography for the albums *Brand New* (2004) and *Volume 9* (2008). Like g.o.d, Shinhwa participated in television appearances by hosting *Let's Coke Play Battle Shinhwa* (2005), a competition show to create a new "idol" group. While continuing promotions as a group, the individual members also pursued solo careers. Hye-sung has the most active solo career with seven studio albums, followed by Min-woo with four and Dong-wan with two. After all the members completed their military service, Shinhwa reunited in 2012 under its own entertainment agency, Shinhwa Company, for group promotions and released *The Return* (2012), followed by *The Classic* (2013), *We* (2015), and *Unchanging: Touch* (2017).

Throughout its career, Shinhwa has delved into multiple genres while continuing to engage with R&B musical elements. Shinhwa's early albums feature more aggressive rapping combined with rock elements that surpass a standard pop track. Of the eleven tracks on the *T.O.P* (1999) album, the followup to the debut album, at least eight are dominated by aggressive rap and heavy sounds created by synthesizers and electric guitars. Shinhwa also incorporates rap with rock and even classical music for "All Your Dreams." That track from *Only One* (2000) opens with a grand orchestral overture in the style of classical music, which transitions into heavy rock guitar complemented by synthesizer sounds. The rap vocals barge their way into the track, loud and in Korean, followed by group harmonies that soften the track on the chorus. Near the end, the guitars transition into a musical sequence dominated by the synthesizers, gesturing toward electronic dance music. This type of rock/rap hybrid gained notoriety in the US mainstream with Run-DMC's collaboration with Aerosmith on the 1994 song "Walk This Way," but this was the culmination of Run-DMC's own fusion of rock and rap nearly a decade before. "Rock Box," from the group's debut 1984 album *Run-DMC*, features original guitar compositions by session musician Eddie Martinez, who also appears on the title track from Run-DMC's 1985 album *King of Rock*. Run-DMC's use of rock also has an aesthetic impact, allowing the sonic landscape of hip-hop to expand: "The pair created a stoopid-fresh sound that fit the noise of rock guitars as easily as ghetto raps..... Even without overtly political lyrics, loud, hard-rocking rap music was threatening to overturn the music industry status quo by bringing new life to rock and roll from an urban black source" (Vincent 2004, 482–83). While Shinhwa emulates the rock-rap hybrid, they also enhance it with the addition of synthesizers in "All Your Dreams."

Building on its reputation for performance, Shinhwa transitions from rock-rap tracks to more dance tracks in subsequent albums. Shinhwa cites disco in "Rain on a Sleepless Night" from the group's 2004 *Winter Story 2004–2005* album, which opens with a swell of strings and harmonized female vocals that contrast with the male vocals. Rather than the standard verse-chorus structure, the song emphasizes the disco rhythm. This disco-inflected version differs greatly from Kim Gun-mo's 1992 version, which foregrounds his mellow rap and deemphasizes the disco elements. The group returns to the disco sound in 2012 for "Be My Love" from the album *The Return*. This track features large-scale disco orchestration with a spoken-word intro straight from the 1970s accompanied with string orchestration accented with flutes and a disco beat. Both tracks, ten years apart, indicate how Shinhwa uses disco instrumentation and the R&B-inflected vocals along with softened raps to complement the dance elements of their songs throughout their career. An album review suggests the song "would fit very well into the Disco genre and one can imagine a music video for this track being full to the brim with sequins and sparkle" ("Album Review—May: Shinhwa" 2012).

Shinhwa expands into other modes of electronic dance music in later releases like *The Return* (2012). Jung Bae (2012) notes that the album "features the old Shinhwa charisma while also adopting modern dance-pop conventions": "The ominous club-tune intro, stuttered chorus, autotuned and dub-step are not like anything we've heard from them before." Even though they engage with multiple styles, the group remains committed to a diversity of vocals that draw on R&B harmonies. Min-woo, one of Shinhwa's three singers, explains how this diversity of vocals works: "Hye Sung took the center spot in vocals while Eric took charge of the rap. The members all have different tones. Hye Sung has ear-catching vocals. Dong Wan has a powerful voice that I personally like. It's the voice that can express various styles in dance songs. Eric likes stylish tones, like me. Jun Jin's voice has confidence and has good techniques" ("[Interview] Shinhwa" 2015). This is the quintessential Shinhwa sound that remains in an even modern dance track like "Venus" (2012): "Give it a few more listens, and the old style will start to surface. The chorus, while split in beat and controlled in melody, still packs a punch with that thumping drum-machine and mass harmony" (Jung Bae 2012). Over the course of twenty years, there is hardly a genre Shinhwa has not tried, yet the group continues to place R&B elements in new contexts.

Another SM Entertainment group, TVXQ, also demonstrates its musical diversity by foraying into R&B territory, even though it has a solid pop reputation. TVXQ is an acronym for Tong Vfang Xien Qi, the Chinese form of the Korean Dong Bang Shin Ki, which means "Rising Gods of the East." TVXQ is also known as Tohoshinki in Japan. This male group debuted in 2004 with five original members: U-know Yunho (Jung Yun-ho), Max Changmin (Shim Chang-min), Kim Jae-joong, Park Yoo-chun, and Xiah (Kim Jun-su). The group filled the void at SM Entertainment left by H.O.T.'s disbandment and Shinhwa's departure, developing into a major "idol" group. The group's debut album, *Tri-angle* (2004), featured three promotional tracks that demonstrated the group's musical and visual versatility: "Hug," a light pop track with a funky dance breakdown in the middle; "The Way U Are," an uptempo dance track driven by rhythm and hip-hop elements; and "Tri-angle," an eclectic track that ranges from a Mozart sample to a rock interlude performed by SM Entertainment's band TRAX. Between 2006 and 2009, TVXQ released *O-Jung.Ban.Hap* (2006) and *Mirotic* (2008), the title track of which produced one of the group's biggest hits, described by *Billboard* as a "simmering electro-pop song" and as "a dark, sultry tune that thrives on its offbeat production" and consisting of "powerful vocals," "a reverse bass beat, fizzy synths and layered harmonies" ("100 Greatest Boy Band Songs of All Time" 2018). TVXQ also released several Japanese albums, including *Heart, Mind and Soul* (2006), *Five in the Black* (2007), *T* (2008), and *The Secret Code* (2009). In 2009 Kim Jae-joong, Park Yoo-chun, and Kim Junsu filed a lawsuit against SM Entertainment, left the agency, and released music as the trio JYJ, including *The Beginning* (2010), a rare English-language K-pop album, *In Heaven* (2011), and *Just Us* (2014). Kim Junsu and Kim Jae-joong also released several solo albums, and Jae-joong and Park Yoo-chun also starred in K-dramas. Remaining members Yunho and Changmin continue as TVXQ at SM Entertainment, returning as a duo in 2011 with the album *Wae: Keep Your Head Down*, three years after the release of *Mirotic*. They have released several Korean albums, including *Catch Me* (2012), *Tense* (2014), *Rise as God* (2015), and *New Chapter #1: The Chance of Love* (2018), as well as several Japanese albums, including *Tone* (2011), *Time* (2013), *Tree* (2014), *With* (2014), and *Tomorrow* (2018).

Well-known for its dynamic choreography, eye-catching videos, and catchy songs, TVXQ also has a reputation for R&B ballads. Whereas there are slow songs by African American singers that would cross over to the pop chart, certain R&B ballads would only chart on R&B charts and be largely heard on urban radio stations. Richard Rischar (2004) explains using Anita Baker as an example: "'Just Because' and several other Baker hits continue to be played on black radio, while on pop radio (including adult contemporary stations), Baker's appearances are much more limited" (408). Richard Ripani (2006) points to the "quiet storm" style originated at WHUR, the radio station at historically black Howard University. This style emulated the slow yet sophisticated R&B ballads exemplified by Smokey Robinson with a song of the same name (132). Such R&B ballads sometimes involve a soliloquy that reflects the vocalist's thoughts or a conversation between vocalists within the song. The sentiment of such songs can be complimentary, such as "Float On" from the 1977 album *Float On* by the Floaters, which opens with a spoken-word intro, which sets up the song to describe the ideal woman, complemented by a subtle combination of bass and strings. The rest of the song alternates between subsequent members describing their ideal woman and a repeated harmonized chorus. Other times, such songs reflect a feeling of regret. "Have You Seen Her" from the Chi-Lites' 1971 album *(For God's Sake) Give More Power to the People* features a protracted spoken-word introduction where the vocalist looks back on happier times before his lady left. "Fire and Desire," a duet by Teena Marie and Rick James from James's 1981 album *Street Songs*, opens with a narrative in the intro where the vocalist meets an old love, and recall their past relationship with regret. "Kiss and Say Goodbye," from the eponymous 1976 album *The Manhattans*, is a breakup song from the point of view of one of the lovers. In all of these examples, the mood is dictated by the different vocals at play. While the Chi-lites' song features male vocals with different vocal ranges, the duet between Marie and James sounds different because of the interplay between male and female vocals.

TVXQ occasionally leaves its usual pop fare to create such R&B ballads. "Hey Girl" (2006) represents a full-fledged R&B ballad. The opening piano is slowly overtaken by a recognizable slow-jam beat. The chorus features the harmonies of the five members, building in intensity throughout the song like a traditional R&B ballad. One fan reviewer described the track as "a nice, smooth and very sexy little rnb number, that really showcases the boys vocal talent; especially JaeJoong and Junsu, who really blew me away with their tones" (kawaiineyo 2008). As a duo, TVXQ relies on R&B ballad instrumentation for "Before You Go," which opens with a sexy 1970s-esque R&B guitar riff and sparse instrumentation that prominently features percussion and progressive vocals. The guitar riff and other instrumentation are reminiscent of The Isley Brothers' "Voyage to Atlantis" from its 1977 album *Go for Your Guns*. A. Scott Galloway (2017) notes that this album represents a shift in the Isley Brothers' sound, when three younger Isley Brothers, who were musicians, joined the group: "Their contributions became so identifiable with the Isley's sound that they were brought in as full-fledged members before they'd even graduated from Long Island University. This shifted the dynamic from a singing group into a band prepared to throw down with that decade's mighty warriors, which included the Commodores, Average White Band, Earth, Wind & Fire, Ohio Players, Rufus, and Parliament-Funkadelic." Andrew Hamilton (2003) describes the iconic track "Voyage to Atlantis" as "a staple of their live concerts, its opening strains acknowledged by deafening, enthusiastic applause" (342). TVXQ's invocation of the R&B ballad relies on a similar interplay of vocal harmony and R&B instrumentation.

Citations of Performance

In addition to musical intertextuality, Korean pop acts also cite the choreography and styling elements of African American popular music culture. Drawing on these images provides alternatives to reductive representations of Asians.

Choreography and Male Idols: Rain (Bi)

African Americans bring a different aesthetic to the music video, one that draws on dance to enhance a musical performance and demands precision to complement the music. K-pop male idols like Rain (Bi) cite the performance aesthetics of 1990s R&B male singers, emulating the smooth and dynamic choreography and disrupting images that declare Asian men unattractive and undesirable.

From their inception, Korean pop groups have depended on visuals, perhaps more so than other genres under the K-pop umbrella. Scholars comment on the "pretty" appearance of members of male pop groups like SHINee, who "reveals an androgynous sexuality of handsome boys stripped of traditional masculinity" (Kim C.-N. 2012, 119). Jung Sun (2011) argues that male "idol" groups reflect a *kkonminam* aesthetic, one that revolves around "men who are pretty looking and who have smooth fair skin, silky hair, and a feminine manner" (58). Media tends to focus on the bodies of female K-pop "idol" groups. In Japan, "the focus of the camera is aimed explicitly at the SNSD members' legs when they perform 'Genie,' objectifying their bodies through its attention to their tight short pants and red high-heeled shoes" (Jung and Hirata 2012). However, other visual aspects are significant, aspects influenced by African American music culture. In K-pop's early stages, Seo Taiji and Boys took advantage of the rise of the music video, emulating the styles of their African American hip-hop counterparts: oversized clothes, tracksuits, and gold chain necklaces. This was a stark departure, for John Lie (2014) recalls how adults recoiled at their first television appearance (77). Michael Fuhr (2016) says such videos represented a "shift to image-centered pop music, which was no longer confined to the standards of the old TV stations, but available also to the new ones brought about by the approaching era of music video television in Korea" (54).

Because "idols" are known for their ability to sing and dance, choreography plays a large role in their performances. As a result of the popularity of Seo Taiji and Boys, music videos featured choreography inspired by breakdancing and synchronized dance: "What is especially of note here is Korean b-boy culture. Started in the mid-1990s, when independent Korean b-boy crews began to be formed, Korean b-boys performing routines with a high level of technical difficulty have swept international competitions in the 2000s, being recognized as an additional *Hallyu* product" (Kim C.-N. 2012, 72–73). Sophisticated choreography supported by performance-based music, derived from black American music, are a defining characteristic of later "idol" acts. Shin and Kim (2013) coded music chart data and described results where hip-hop and dance music specifically linked to K-pop's emergence in the mid- to late 1990s dominated: "The dance music produced before the emergence of the large entertainment house was qualitatively different in style from the music promoted under the entertainment house system. The dance music performances from the early 1990s looked and sounded nothing like today's K-pop." As K-pop developed, its "idol" groups became known for "harmonizing dances" or "'military style dance' (*gun-mu*), which stresses all members to dance perfectly in sync" (Shin and Kim 2013). However, such dance performances also cite the dance style that supported black American popular music.

Black American popular music influenced the choreography of K-pop "idol" music videos, just as it did at the beginning of the popularization of music video by MTV in the 1980s. John Seabrook (2012) notes the impact that MTV had on Lee Soo-man, founder of SM Entertainment: "He became fascinated with the music videos that were a staple of programming on the newly launched MTV. If there is a single video from the eighties that captures many of the elements that later resurfaced in K-pop, it's Bobby Brown's 1988 hit 'My Prerogative.' . . . Brown's dance moves—a swagger in the hips, combined with tight spins that are echoed by backing dancers—also found their way into K-pop's DNA." Music videos for R&B and hip-hop represented a distinct kind of video aesthetic, one that diverged from MTV's initial offerings. MTV's early aesthetic was one that was devoid of African Americans. An interview with Buzz Brindle, an early director of musical programming at MTV, offers an explanation for the lack of black American music videos on MTV prior to Michael Jackson's "Billie Jean" in 1983: "It was difficult for MTV to find African

American artists whose music fit the channel's format that leaned toward rock at the outset" (Christian 2006). Andrew Goodwin (1992) echoes this sentiment, linking MTV's programming choices with genres: "MTV followed the music industry in defining 'rock' in essentially racist terms, as a form of music that excluded blacks. It based its playlist on the 'narrowcasting' principle of American radio that viewed rock and 'urban contemporary' (i.e. dance music, often produced by black artists) as incompatible. Consequently, blacks were largely excluded from its screens" (133). By the time Lee of SM Entertainment encountered MTV, he was more intrigued by the dance-performance aesthetics of black music videos than the other offerings of the channel.

The kind of music video that inspired K-pop revolved around dance music that required complementary choreography. Veteran SM Entertainment producer Yoo Young-jin (2010) links the music he makes to performance: "For me, songwriting is something that makes the stage performance and music become one. People call it 'a song' but I want to make music that fulfills both the eyes and ears, like a musical production" ("[Interview] Record Producer Yoo Young-jin" 2010a). Yoo also sees a strong connection between the music and dance: "There may be some songs that you can't understand if you just listen to the music. Because they were made to be heard and seen on stage at the same time" ("[Interview] Record Producer Yoo Young-jin" 2010a). This is especially the case with "idol" groups. Mariel Martin, a choreographer who has created dance routines for the Korean pop groups 2NE1, notes that her routines must be concerned with vocals: "Different ones sing at different times.... There will be parts where one is singing and the other ones will be doing the dancing, one will break off and be singing" ("ML | Adventures with YG Entertainment" 2011). Moreover, Yoo built his signature style for performance on R&B elements: "There are notes in a rhythm too and basically if you think of connecting those 'rhythm notes' as a chord progression, you can come up with an infinite number of melodies. A rhythm is not a sub-unit of melody, it is the main unit of a song. Lyrics are important to some songwriters while for others, melody is key. In my case, I think about the rhythm first and add other stuff with the arrangement" ("[Interview] Record Producer Yoo Young-jin" 2010a). This influence can be seen in Yoo's signature SM Performance sound. Fuhr (2016) notes that producers like Yoo's "sense of stage performance, visual imagination, and black music had a tremendous impact on the composition of K-pop songs" (83).

The distinct combination of music and performance is a staple of African American popular music performers, hearkening back to routines by Motown's Cholly Atkins. Charles Sykes (2006) notes that Motown songs featured "slick musical arrangements, like the well-coordinated outfits their artists wore when they performed live. Stage routines were choreographed to project an air of 'class' and 'sophistication,' very much within the range of acceptability for mainstream audiences, but with a subtle edge that spoke 'young,' 'cool,' 'Black,' 'urban,' and 'Detroit'" (432). There was a blending of R&B-based vocals, music created for choreography and showmanship. No 1960s group exemplified this more than the Temptations. Many of their performances featured members in coordinating outfits, which were often suits. But even more dynamic were the performances themselves, which incorporated several of Atkins's techniques. The group was made up of five members, who were all vocalists, but often songs featured a lead vocalist. The Temptations featured dynamic choreography for the backup singers, even when they were not being featured. While the lead vocalist held the attention of the audience, the rest of the members engaged in dynamic choreography to punctuate their backup vocals, especially in parts of the song where they were not singing. In a performance of "The Way You Do the Things You Do," the other members provide harmony in the verses and chorus, but it is not continuous ("The Temptations" 2012). In between, their dance moves involve drops to the floor and quick returns to the microphone. During the breakdown, all four backup vocalists form a line and engage in choreography that features complex footwork in unison. The Temptations replicated the unison and precision on performances of slower tracks like "My Girl" ("The Temptations" 2016). Even with the slower tempo, the choreography evokes the Temptations' trademark smooth transitions and dramatic arm movements and unison.

Later black performers would develop such choreography further. In the 1970s, the Jackson 5 took the blend of vocal performance and dance to another level by incorporating the lead vocal into the choreography in addition to synchronized dance movements of the backup dances. In a 1973 appearance on *Soul Train*, during the performance of "Dancing Machine," Michael Jackson performed the robot, a dance where he enacts very precise and robotic movements in synch with the breakdown of the song ("The Jackson 5" 2014). Choreography became more sophisticated and complex as Jackson moved on as a solo performer. Moves such as the moonwalk force audiences to follow the dancing body wherever it goes. The solo performer who executes choreography well and synchronized routines for groups of dancers form the foundation for performance for K-pop "idol" artists. Gil-sung Park (2013) argues that the focus on singing and dancing at SM Entertainment used Michael Jackson as a model because he "regularly showcased his revolutionary combination of singing and dancing skills in various music videos on MTV" (22). Michael Jackson's dance performance introduced the notion of using choreography to highlight individual vocal performance. The metaphor of mechanization, often used to describe Korean pop groups, was also used to describe Jackson's choreography, deemphasizing his dancing prowess and distilling his style to a limited repertoire of dance moves. Judith Hamera (2012) argues that Jackson's virtuosity is grounded in a strong work ethic, both in terms of its creation and the context that surrounds it. His dancing prowess challenges the mechanistic characterization of dancers who can execute such precision moves: "In his testaments to the hard physical labor of performance, he also challenged romantic construction of the virtuoso as perfect human motor by insisting that dance was actually work, not the transcendence of it" (Hamera 2012, 760). His choreographed dances perfectly complement K-pop music made for the performance. Male and female K-pop "idol" groups undergo years of training to learn how to perform similarly intricate and complex routines. Such training represents the same kind of work ethic that Jackson demonstrates. Known for groups with large numbers, Korean pop groups use their members to execute creative movements. Not only central for performers, choreography factors into fan interaction. Groups often release rehearsal or dance practice videos as a gift to fans, allowing viewers to see the entire routine uninterrupted, a must for fans who perform cover dances.

While Korean pop performers utilize choreography, they draw on different performative elements from black American popular music culture in their music videos. Male performers like Rain (Bi) oscillate between smooth and dynamic performances of 1990s male R&B singers. Rain (Jung Ji-hoon) began his music career as a solo artist with the debut album, *Bad Guy* (2002), but gained popularity through the release of his second album *Rain 2* (2003) and the hit single, "Ways to Avoid the Sun." Following the success of this album, Rain embarked on a world tour that took him to destinations around the world, including the United States. Rain later released several albums, including *It's Raining* (2004), *Rain's World* (2006), *Rainism* (2008), and *Rain Effect* (2014). He launched his first independent agency in 2007, J. Tune Entertainment, which managed the popular "idol" group MBLAQ. J. Tune Entertainment eventually merged with JYP Entertainment, but Rain would go on to establish his own agency, R.A.I.N Company in 2015. In ways that make him truly an "idol" pioneer, Rain successfully parlayed his career beyond his music and developed an acting career. He starred in the popular Korean drama *Full House* (2004) as well as the film *I'm a Cyborg, But That's Ok* (2006), directed by Park Chan-wook, who also directed critically acclaimed films like *Joint Security Area* (2000) and his vengeance trilogy, *Sympathy for Mr. Vengeance* (2002), *Oldboy* (2003), and *Lady Vengeance* (2005). In the United States, Rain emerged in the mainstream when he appeared on the comedy television show *The Colbert Report* to answer the host's dance challenge in 2006. Rain went on to appear on *People* magazine's 2007 list of "Most Beautiful People in the World" and star in Hollywood films *Speed Racer* (2008) and *Ninja Assassin* (2009).

Scholars frequently associate Rain with a globalized Asian image. Hyunjoon Shin (2009) notes that "Rain, at least since 2004, was globalized Asian pop.... Rain and JYP [Park Jin-young] try to deny the 'Asian' characteristics of Rain's music in the Asian market and present Rain as a distinctively unique product" (515). Sun Jung (2011) notes that Rain fans in Singapore indicate that "Rain appeals to them because he is an 'Asian artist,' who is able to perfectly recreate American popular culture, and who is as good as American pop idols. This suggests that they recognize that American popular culture is localized in Rain's performances" (107). Focusing on Rain's globalized image obscures the African American elements at play. Singapore fans recognize the influence of R&B singers like Usher, but nevertheless characterize the performance as emanating from American pop culture (Jung S. 2011, 107).

However, Rain exemplifies many performance aesthetics drawn from African American popular music videos. Part of Rain's sound can be attributed to the influence of Park Jin-young, who not only wrote and produced for R&B artists such as Omarion and Tyrese but also exhibited a "personal preference for American black music.... Influences from Soul, Funk, Disco and R&B characterize the label's hybrid sound that Park in the same interview described as 'black music with a K-pop feel'" (Fuhr 2016, 69). Rain employs choreography based on that type of music, creating an image that also mirrors that of black male R&B singers. The music video for "It's Raining" (2004) captures much of Rain's signature style ("RAIN 3rd" 2012). It opens with a shot of a semi truck surrounded by several individuals on motorcycles. These shots are interspersed with shots of Rain in a dressing room lined on both sides with clothing, where he lounges on a lighted white couch with a black tiled background wall with his shirt open. The next shots send the viewer down an exhaust shaft to a club with a DJ on a raised dais and a crowd of people dancing. Back in the dressing room, Rain takes off his shirt to prepare for his entrance. The back door of the truck opens to reveal Rain, dressed in all black: a leather jacket, sleeveless leather vest with silver buttons, black pants, a black hat, and a belt with a huge silver buckle. Security quickly whisks him through the crowd of paparazzi. Back at the club, the music stops, and Rain appears on a stage under a circular ceiling with a chandelier. Surrounded by arched doorways, Rain begins his dance solo, but is soon joined by backup dancers. This choreography is dynamic with sharp arm and leg movements. The sequence is interspersed with shots of appreciative female members of the audience. At least one of Rain's backup dancers is female, but she functions more as just another member of the dance crew. Toward the end of the song, water falls from the ceiling onto the stage, adding visual interest. The performance ends with enthusiastic cheers from the audience. At the end of the video, Rain returns to his dressing room to lounge on the white sofa.

This video cites similar music videos by African American male artists who gained popularity in the 1990s, like Usher (Raymond Usher). The music video for Usher's "Oh Yeah! Ft. L'il Jon and Ludacris" (2004) opens with images of Usher in the midst of laser lights on a stage, intercut with scenes of him walking through a crowd in a dance club ("Usher—Yeah!" 2015). For his stage performance, he wears jeans, athletic shoes, a white blazer over a striped collared shirt, and a white T-shirt accessorized with a necklace and cufflinks. When walking through the club, he wears black pants, black dress shirt open midway, and a cap, acknowledging others with a hat tip as he passes. A woman sits next to Usher briefly, then goes to the dance floor. Usher follows, and they start to dance suggestively with each other. Usher is joined by other male and female backup dancers, who also dance with each other in a suggestive way. This is a classic club video, and Rain cites the performative aspect. As sexy as Rain's performance may be, it is less sexual than Usher's, as Rain does not dance with a female protagonist and his female backup dancers are dressed less provocatively. Rain's music video cites the club atmosphere that centers on the choreographed performance of the singer complemented by backup dancers. Rain's dance performance is tamer, but his wardrobe mirrors Usher's. The response by the women in the audience suggests that Rain comes off just as sexy as Usher in his music videos.

Rain also cites the performance of slower songs by male R&B singers. The music video for "How to Avoid the Sun" (2003) opens with a sunrise behind a group of office buildings, placing the video in an urban setting ("Rain 2nd" 2012). The next scenes show Rain running in slow motion through city streets. Rather than being chased, Rain seems to be trying to avoid the sun. These dramatic and dynamic scenes are juxtaposed with the acoustic guitar and slow tempo of the song. Rain enters an underground garage, where he is joined by backup dancers. Here, he exchanges a leather jacket trimmed in fleece with another leather jacket, allowing the viewer to see his well-toned arms showcased by a tattered tank top. He completes his look with a pair of aviator sunglasses. Unlike the dynamism of "It's Raining," this choreography is fluid, complementing the slower tempo of the song, with more seductive arm and leg movements. The dance sequences are interspersed with scenes in a dimly lit room where Rain dramatically throws objects, pushes items off a desk and smashes a television—all in slow motion. The latter part of the video showcases Rain's rap verse, which features a close-up. The earlier fluid movements are replaced by more hip-hop inspired movements of throwing hands. This performance parallels the music video for Usher's "You Make Me Wanna" (1997). A mid-tempo track with a prominent Latin guitar riff, the music video opens with several versions of Usher in different outfits ("Usher" 2009). One is more casual with a tank top and suspenders, while another wears a silk shirt and dress pants. The choreography includes a modified moonwalk where Usher glides over the floor. Usher's backup dancers are all dressed casually with caps, tracksuits, and athletic shoes. As with Rain, Usher's choreography is sharper and more dynamic, with more defined arm movements and footwork during the breakdown, and more fluid throughout the song.

Both of Rain's music videos utilize distinct performance elements from African American male R&B videos, providing more visual choices beyond those commonly associated with Asian men. Eun-young Jung (2010) identifies a common image of Asian men, "desexualized, maligned Asian male stereotypes (e.g. a kung-fu master who can kick-ass but cannot speak English or a computer geek who could figure out all the rhythms but couldn't figure out how to get a date" (221). Rain adapts the performance style of African American male R&B performers of the 1990s, a style based on sexiness, which is rarely attributed to Asian men. Rain's videos draw from the styling and choreography of black male R&B singers, which is distinct from other modes of masculinity. As a result, black performative aesthetics allow Rain to exercise visual options different from those often open to him as a Korean man.

Glamour and Female "Idols": Wonder Girls

While Rain cites performance aesthetics of African American male singers, Wonder Girls cite the retro styling of 1960s black girl groups for images that counter reductive images of Asian women.

Scholars often focus on the images utilized by K-pop girl groups. Some focus on hyper-feminine images. E.-Y. Jung (2010) assumes a limited range of concepts for Korean girl groups that focus on "their cute, sexy, exotic Asian female images" (229). Others focus on images that rebel against feminine norms. Roald Maliangkay (2015) points to the inclusion of punk elements as a way to disrupt conformity in 2NE1's music video for "I Am the Best": "The very Lady Gaga-like glam-punk fashion and stage sets as well as the recalcitrant and masculine vocal style and performance are interrupted from 2:25 by a scene in which the styling of the girls is street-punk, albeit with lots of makeup and fake eyelashes, polished chrome spikes and perfectly groomed punk hairdos" (99). Stephen Epstein with James Turnbull (2014) point to a continuum of tropes in K-pop girl videos, all of which "focus on the female image as visual spectacle" that promotes a passivity in service to men or renders men without agency or just defines women in terms of men (318). However, none of these scholars recognize the way black American girl groups influence K-pop girl groups.

K-pop girl groups have drawn on visuals and performance of African American girl groups from the beginning. The video for first-generation K-pop girl group S.E.S's debut track "I'm Your Girl" (1997) featured the members performing choreography in oversized jeans in black and white and laughing in the upbeat song ("S.E.S—Im Your Girl" 2010). The music video for Fin.K.L's "Blue Rain" (1998) featured the members performing the slower-tempo single in oversized pants on the stoop of a house, bringing to mind the doo-wop tradition ("[MV] Fin.K.L" 2019). First-generation K-pop groups reflected the visual style and ethos of 1990s girl trio TLC in their debut images. TLC popularized urban-inspired outfits for girls in contrast to body-conscious clothing and having fun among themselves instead of performing for men. The music video for the group's 1992 hit "What About Your Friends" exemplifies this idea. The video opens with a montage of women walking a catwalk in a dimly lit room, wearing an array of shiny catsuits, mini-skirts, and heels ("TLC" n.d.). The text "NOT!" in red is superimposed on these images and a slide transition takes the viewer to a more colorful urban scene with background dancers all dressed in baggy jeans, black suspenders, and white T-shirts. The members of TLC emerge wearing oversized jeans in bright colors and layered tops. Other scenes reveal the members dancing in graffiti-covered white overalls. Goodall (1994) notes, "Realizing the most accepted version of femininity is 'high fashion' (primarily consisting of miniskirts and heels or tight clothing which accentuates the female's body), the group refuses to remain within these confines, sporting baseball caps and baggy pants" (88). When first-generation K-pop girl group music videos emphasize fun times in an urban environment, they hearken back to images introduced by black American girl groups like TLC.

While first-generation K-pop girl groups drew from the bright urban style of 1990s black girl groups, subsequent girl groups like Wonder Girls draw on older visuals of African American girl groups. E.-Y. Jung (2010) reads Wonder Girls' concept for the single "Nobody" as "an image that again brings to mind the stereotypical China doll look, and perhaps even the trope that all Asians 'look alike'" (227). However, the music video for Wonder Girls' "Nobody" also directly emulates the styling options exemplified by black American girl groups of the 1960s. Fan reviewers make the link between the music videos and black girl groups of the 1960s. Askjeevas (2009) describes it as "a sequin-studded retro R&B number that evokes *Dreamgirls* and the days when soulful girl groups reigned supreme." Writing for the K-pop media outlet *soompi*, Motoway065 (2008) describes it as "very upbeat with Motown sounds from the 60s and 70s." The music video for "Nobody" opens with Park Jin-young, founder of JYP Entertainment, performing his own song "Honey" on a 1950s stage with a backup band with Wonder Girls acting as his back-up singers ("Wonder Girls 'Nobody'" 2008). In the next scene, Park relaxes on stage while the Wonder Girls practice their choreography in the background. Park is approached by two men with a new song on sheet music. The pianist reveals that it is "Nobody," and Park agrees to perform it. However, right before the performance, Park humorously gets stuck in a bathroom without toilet paper. While the managers appear flustered backstage, the Wonder Girls move their microphones to center stage and perform the song. They are dressed in shiny, clingy sheath dresses and elbow-length gloves. They perform a choreographed sequence in two staggered lines which makes all of the girls visible. The audience applauds enthusiastically and the mangers backstage are ecstatic. JYP finally arrives on stage in an effort to receive some of the glory. The next scenes of the music video show the success of the Wonder Girls as a result of that performance, including adulation from a DJ, performance on the music charts, and media coverage in newspapers. Wonder Girls perform the song on a 1960s television show against a purple background and dressed in bold print sheath dresses, colored stockings, 1960s-style earrings and heels. The scene morphs into a television screen and a little girl dancing along. The scene transitions to another performance on a stage. Here, they are dressed in sequined dresses with fringe. They descend steps in front of a light-filled center panel with a huge "W" in lights framed by sparkly curtains.

The shifts in fashion during the video hearken back to the styling of 1960s black American girl groups like the Supremes. Jacqueline Warwick (2007) notes that ethnic girl groups of the 1960s intervened in racial discourse: "Accessing the social world [of higher class groups] was an explicit and important goal for all performers at Motown Records, and other girl groups whose members were marked as ethnically different were able to assimilate by virtue of their self-preservation" (80). In particular, African American girl groups became "emblems of girlhood for white, middle-class suburbia during the years of the Southern Civil Rights Movement" (Warwick 2007, 8). They function in the same way for Wonder Girls, representing an alternative visual image. The changes in wardrobe by the Wonder Girls echo the kinds of options reflected in the Supremes' fashion choices. Many are familiar with the elaborate ball gowns worn by the group during their performances, but some may forget how they took on the mod girl look during their British tours from 1964 to 1967. Charlotte Greig (1989) reminds us that "Mary [Wilson] too seemed at home in short plastic dresses and big earrings" and that Diana Ross's "thin figure was the height of fashion and she looked terrific in every outfit she wore" (120). However, the fact that black women donned the trend of the time and made it their own signified something different. They effortlessly transitioned from trendy casual wear to their iconic sequined dresses. Wonder Girls emulate those options, drawing specifically from the 1960s, where black girl groups incorporated a new era of style that showed women of color could be stylish. The backdrop of the 1960s should not be lost on viewers, when segregation and negative stereotypes were still in effect. Wonder Girls emulated the variation of styles of 1960s black girl groups, citing black glamour to avoid being limited solely by stereotypes like the China doll.

Image, Music Quality, and Global Crossover

More than other artists under the K-pop umbrella, promotions that focus on image and music quality drive the intertextuality that Korean pop groups exhibit. The Korean casting and training process mirrors artistic development employed by black American music producers like Berry Gordy, founder of Motown. Both meticulously crafted images that resonated with audiences and music with high production value. In doing so, the K-pop "idol" groups enact a global form of crossover.

Image and Music Quality

Korean entertainment agency CEOs mirror Gordy's use of image and music quality in the casting and training process. Drawing on their own experiences in creating music, they become adept in ensuring quality music production.

As discussed earlier, Korean pop entertainers undergo an intensive casting and training program. As trainees, they practice vocals, choreography, foreign languages, and other skills they will need for extramusical activities, including event hosting, television appearances, product endorsements, and magazine photo shoots. While there are many trainees, relatively few are chosen to debut in an "idol" group, and even fewer groups have successful careers that span years. The Korean training system, pioneered by SM Entertainment and followed by YG Entertainment, JYP Entertainment, and a slew of smaller agencies, utilizes a training process where trainees learn "singing, dancing, and how to act like a star" (Shin and Kim 2013).

Many compare the K-pop casting and training system to the Japanese idol system. The production process used by Johnny's Entertainment represents the epicenter of the idol training system in Japan, where "idols" refers to "those who sing and act simultaneously," as opposed to "artists," who focus on singing (Jung and Hirata 2012). The system has produced many male groups since the 1960s, including such long-running groups as SMAP and Arashi. This model uses the teen members of new groups to target teenage audiences: "The audience for teenage pop music and those who performed teenage pop music were interchangeable. Idols and their audience, though on opposite sides of footlights, occupy the same plane" (Brasor and Masako 1997, 59). Bevan (2012) calls the Korean casting and training system a "tweaked interpretation of the one first put to use by Johnny & Associates." Others assert that Korean CEOs adjusted and improved on this model by introducing more systematic management of talent (Jung and Hirata). However, promotion and production strategies used for Korean "idols" also mirror those undertaken by Berry Gordy at Motown Records in the 1960s. Journalists frequently use the factory metaphor to make the connection between the training and marketing strategies of Korean entertainment agencies and Gordy's Motown. John Seabrook (2012) says that Lee Soo-man, the founder of SM Entertainment, employed "a sophisticated system of artistic development that would make the star factory that Berry Gordy created at Motown look like a mom-and-pop operation." Jon Matsumoto (2012) observes that "the preparation that some go through is reminiscent of the rigorous artist development practices employed by Barry [sic] Gordy's Motown Records in the '60s."

In the 1960s, Berry Gordy adapted the Hollywood casting and training system to a training program with a similar focus on image at Motown. The Hollywood casting and training system, orchestrated by Jewish film heads, revolved around the creation of image. Devoting a whole department to the pursuit, publicity departments pioneered marketing strategies where the studio handled interviews and managed stars' reputation. Publicity also created the aura of glamour through the production of fashion images and artwork in addition to shooting movies (Davis 1993, 154). People like Ann Straus, fashion editor at Metro-Goldwyn-Mayer, were responsible for getting stars ready for magazine covers and layouts: "Straus believed in using real jewelry and beautiful clothes. . . . Her arrangements with the shops and designers was that they would receive credit for any fashions used, and that she would return clothing in the same condition it left the store" (Davis 1993, 155). Gordy tweaked the Hollywood model to address the realities of his African American talent. He achieved this during the training process using people like Maxine Powell, former charm school and modeling business owner, "who taught singers how to walk, talk, hold a microphone, and generally provide the acts with that polished, groomed, and polite presence that made it possible for them to cross over" (Early 2004, 116).

Like Gordy, Korean CEOs utilize artist development focused on the construction of image. They produce a wide variety of images that enable "idols" to promote beyond music. Part of this is due to structural changes that occurred in the Korean entertainment industry in the 2000s: "The major entertainment agencies which had produced the first-generation idol groups evolved into sprawling organizations incorporating the development and training of stars in addition to production and management, thus intensifying their strategy of one-source multi-use" (Kim C.-N. 2012, 101). Entertainment agencies also build on the anticipation by fans of their most successful acts through a Korean mode of promotion involving teaser images (which may be completely different from the actual concept images that accompany the promotion), multiple concept images for different versions of the music release, different concept images for Japanese releases, and additional concepts for the album repackage. For example, for its 2011 album *Mr. Simple*, SM Entertainment released teaser images of each of the ten active members of the "idol" group Super Junior, showing the members in colorful, over-the-top outfits. However, the concept images for the music video featured the members in outfits that were significantly toned down and reflected the chic video with choreography in front of sculpted white walls. *Mr. Simple* was followed up by a completely different concept for *A-CHA*, its repackage. A repackage contains the tracks of the original music release along with additional songs or remixed versions of original tracks. The teaser image for *A-CHA* centered on the theme of photography, with the members featured with camera equipment. The music video for the additional track "A-Cha" featured the members performing choreography against a tunnel-like background with a shaky cam ("Super Junior 'A-Cha'" 2011). In K-pop promotion, more than one image is associated with a musical release. Participation in extramusical activities represent additional opportunities to produce more images.

Korean CEOs and Gordy both coupled carefully crafted images with high music quality. Quality music production through the efforts of producers was the hallmark of Motown. Before he was a music mogul, Gordy was also a songwriter writing for artists like Jackie Wilson and became knowledgeable about not only the elements of music production, but also its promotion (Early 2004, 51). Early (2004) asserts that "Gordy became an intuitive intelligence, something that actually stood him in good stead in the game of trying to anticipate and predict hit records" (45). Such experiences allowed him to understand what people liked about music and fueled his ability to put it into the music Motown produced. Gordy used his musical intuition to create music with undeniable quality. The musical production of Motown was innovative, changing the landscape of pop music.

Like Gordy, many Korean CEOs are able to ensure music quality in part because they possess prior experience in the creation and promotion of music. Lee of SM Entertainment was a former pop star himself, achieving a certain level of popularity in Korea, first as a member of the folk duo April and May, and later as a solo singer. These efforts secured him accolades as one of the top ten singers in the country. He also gained experience in public musical tastes as a DJ and host of the radio show, *Viva Pops*, and later host of his own television talk show, *Together with Lee Soo Man*. According to Mark James Russell (2008), Lee "credits his deejaying job for keeping his musical tastes broad and in step with what audiences liked" (151). Park Jin-young maintains his dual role as CEO and artist at JYP Entertainment. Park debuted as a solo artist in 1994 and scored a number of hit songs in Korea under his stage name the Asiansoul. Park was also responsible for producing Rain, one of the most successful solo Korean pop artists, and has composing credits on many of the early hits of the artists on his label, including g.o.d, 2PM, Rain, and GOT7. Yang Hyun-suk, former member of Seo Taiji and Boys and founder of YG Entertainment, has a reputation of being involved in all of the musical production at the company. In an interview with *Kstar10*, Yang notes, "I'm knowledgeable enough about [music] to have discussions with my artists thanks to my experience. I can coach them about performing on the stage as I have a lot of experience from my days of Seo Taiji and Boys. It is true that I dropped many other things, but I could never give up communicating with artists and creating music itself" (Lennon 2013). These experiences of Korean CEOs make them privy to the musical tastes of the public.

While Korean agencies will use foreign music producers for various elements of the music, the final music production remains in-house like with Motown, and is almost always overseen by Korean producers. Chris Lee explains that at SM Entertainment, Lee is "not happy to just outsource the music to some composers and then record the songs with the artists. For him, producing involves a meticulous step-by-step process of refining, changing, and finishing the song" (G.-S. Park 2013, 24). The result is "modifying the original creative work to make it more viral to the actual listeners, whoever and wherever they may be" (G.-S. Park 2013, 24). Yoo Young-jin of SM Entertainment explains how he transforms songs to make them appeal to Korean audiences: "I don't take a song from a foreign songwriter and just use it. Their songs are incredibly simple in terms of melody, lyrics and arrangement so I add certain parts to the song that I think are necessary to succeed in Korea. Sometimes I take the sub-melody in the original composition and make it the main melody, or even make a new one from scratch. If a song has a great overall flow but a weak climax, I make it stronger" ("[Interview] Record Producer Yoo Young-jin" 2010a). Korean music producers see themselves as active participants. Korean producers do not see themselves as cogs in a wheel, but as individuals who are knowledgeable about music and serious about making unique music. Several Korean music producers, like Yoo Young-jin and Teddy, are former artists themselves. They may make music for mass consumption, but they also see themselves creating music that participates in a musical legacy, and notably, an African American one. Yoo Young-jin contextualizes his ambition in African American musical terms: "Culture is a shock. Look at how the Michael Jackson's moon walk for 'Billy Jean' changed [the trend for] the entire world. I too would like to create such a moment someday" ("[Interview] Record Producer Yoo Young-jin" 2010b). The production of Korean pop also involves a deliberate process. Moreover, the production strategies are quintessentially Korean. G.-S. Park (2013) notes that even the outsourcing and remixing of music at the heart of K-pop "reflects a Korean-style work ethic that involves a tenacious persuasion of global producers for creativity outsourcing despite apparent impossibility" (31).

The talent pool at Korean agencies include singers, songwriters, and producers as well as the singers and dancers, which also contributes to music quality. A quality performance is the goal of the intensive training process. G.-S. Park (2013) observes that the successful training program of SM Entertainment requires "a steady supply of high-quality performers": "K-pop artists must dance and sing exceptionally well, both alone and groups" (25). The casting and training system also introduces potential stars to a musical repertoire, functioning as a mode of instruction, "a specific training and education system, called the 'academy system' [that] is central to this arrangement.... Not only singer-dancer-actor aspirants but also those who want to work for the company can get the relevant education in a classroom located in the entertainment companies' buildings" (H.-J. Shin 2009, 510). Trainees learn the industry and the musical legacy of the music they will perform. They learn the songs created for their groups as well as the popular songs by other groups. In some cases, these songs are from earlier Korean pop groups. Given the popularity of H.O.T.'s "Candy" (1996), it seems like required learning for many subsequent pop groups. INFINITE performed the song and its accompanying choreography in 2010, the same year of its debut. Boyfriend also performed the song and choreography in similar outfits originally worn by the members of H.O.T. on *Music Bank* in the same year of its debut, 2011. First-generation girl group Fin.K.L's "Now" (2000) has been performed by subsequent female idol groups as well. Girls' Generation, who debuted in 2007, performed the song and its choreography on a 2009 episode of *Music Bank*, and Girls' Day, who debuted in 2010, sang the song on a 2014 episode of *Picnic Live*. Fiestar, who debuted in 2012, performed the song and its choreography on the concert program *Concert 7080* in 2015. Pop groups will also learn their contemporaries' songs as well as American pop and R&B songs. In this way, Korean pop entertainers develop a knowledge of musical traditions that they will bring into their own music, thereby ensuring musical quality. This emphasis on musical quality and promotion and production strategies are part of a larger game plan.

Crossover

Gordy's strategy of crossover contained global aspirations, making it perfect for the goals of global distribution by Korean CEOs. While some critique the crossover used by Gordy and Korean CEOs as solely motivated by maximizing profit, the strategy also results in an unprecedented degree of influence on the musical landscape.

Berry Gordy enacted crossover in order to shape the image of African Americans in the public imagination. Reebee Garafalo (1993) describes crossover as "that process whereby an artist or a recording from a 'secondary' marketing category like country and western, Latin or rhythm and blues achieves hit status in the mainstream or 'pop' market" (229). Early (2004) alludes to motives other than profit on Gordy's part: "Gordy had little interest in, or his temperament had little tolerance for, being a petit-bourgeois merchant. He somehow wanted to shape and influence taste and music and not merely supply a product to fulfill a need" (53). Motown emerged during the age of segregation in the United States. Garofalo (1993) notes that the 1950s, the dawn of pop music, saw the emergence of "race records" in the United States: "The race market developed as an undercapitalized subindustry, during a period when the society-at-large was still legally segregated. With some notable exceptions, African-American artists were systematically barred from radio performances and live appearances in established white venues" (235–36). Race records not only described who performed and to which audiences, but also the kind of music performed. Segregation contextualized this division in the music. Early (2004) observes that "The Sound of Young America," Motown's motto, suggested "something subversive and perverse, a cannily contrived insult at mainstream America, cloaked as seemingly innocent diversion" (108–9). The "race records" of the 1950s and the soul and black pop in the 1960s had a distinct musical sound, which made crossover possible. Gordy sought what Philip Brian Harper (1989) calls "crossover appeal," an "appeal across racial boundaries considered to divide the general popular music audience" (102). Gordy used crossover, based on high music quality and image construction, to make African Americans recognized by mainstream audiences during a time when they refused to do so in everyday life.

Gordy's notions of crossover were not limited to the United States. When critics focus solely on what they describe as assimilation tactics at home, they overlook Gordy's global aspirations. Andrew Flory (2014) explains the impact of Tamla Motown: "Between 1963 and 1965, Motown slowly established business relationships within the British entertainment industry, culminating in a large-scale tour of the UK in May and June of 1965. Much of the work of Motown during this period was supported by the activities of the Tamla Motown Appreciation Society, which actively promoted knowledge about African American music and artists through member events and newsletters" (114). Tamla Motown represents an element of Gordy's global strategy, which included European tours for his largest acts.

Similarly, Korean CEOs utilize the combination of image and music quality to cross over globally. This crossover strategy distinguishes the Korean creative and business strategies from the Japanese "idol" system. Global aspirations are central to Korean pop. Its use of social media, including Twitter, YouTube, and Instagram, has propelled Korean pop groups beyond the nation's borders to East Asia and the rest of the world. Increasingly, Korean artists venture to other countries on world tours that include stops in such destinations as Moscow, Helsinki, Warsaw, Istanbul, Chile, and Buenos Aires. In 2018 SM Town held a family concert featuring all of the artists on the label in Dubai, United Arab Emirates. Conversely, the Japanese pop music industry focuses on the local scene. International fans of Japanese groups have limited access to music on major digital music outlets like iTunes. Videos posted of Japanese artists by fans are subject to swift take-down while Korean videos flourish. Global J-pop fans go through extra efforts to even attain physical copies of Japanese releases or see television appearances by their favorite groups. Until the early 2000s, Japanese pop acts rarely toured in East Asia (McClure 2001). Rather than emulating the Japanese pop music industry in this regard, Korean CEOs reflect the global outlook of Gordy.

Some see drawbacks to the kind of crossover enacted by Gordy and the Korean CEOs, citing profit as the only motivating factor for both. Kim Chang-nam (2012) argues that the Korean casting and training system "reaps considerable profits by selecting and molding trainees in their early and mid-teens" (84). Similarly, Gordy has often been criticized for capitalizing on the innovative aesthetic he fostered in order to curry favor with mainstream American audiences. George (1988) sees Motown, as "black-owned, secretive, rigidly hierarchical, totally committed to reaching white audiences" and Berry Gordy, its founder and longtime CEO, as committed to mainstream standards: "His message was, 'Don't worry, I just want to be like you.' That's what his dreams of acceptance in Hollywood and Las Vegas, and the slogan, 'The Sound of Young

America' were meant to communicate" (88). Gordy has also been criticized for blatantly seeking profit at the expense of his artists. George (1988) reduces Gordy's work to an example of sheer capitalism: "Gordy clearly stated that his goal was to buy into mainstream standards. He was amassing wealth and expanding his operation" (88–89). Early (2004) identifies a tension between "the company's own bourgeois-motivated and practically rendered need in a racist society to have an identity of virtue and racial 'commitment'" and its commercial aspirations, driven by Gordy's "equally neurotic need for accommodationist outreach for his white audience" (31, 32). Targeting the mainstream is also seen as part of the profit motive: "Motown's success across racial, social, and cultural boundaries has often generated criticism narrowly focused on the notion that the company's success came with a compromise of Black roots, as evidenced in both music and presentation style" (Sykes 2006, 440). R. W. Stephens (1984) also points to the emphasis on commercial success as one of several factors "that had a deleterious effect on the continued development of soul. What was once a tradition defined by blacks and recorded on many independent labels is now directly affected by the taste of larger audiences, cost benefit analysis, and increasing dominance of the major record companies" (38). The resulting music was largely seen in terms of its function as a product that brings profit.

Others believe music loses its quality with crossover success. George (1988) traces what he describes the death of the rhythm and blues to industry shifts where black artists leave black and black-friendly labels for those controlled by whites and that target mass (read white) audiences. In the process, he asserts that this had a negative effect on the quality of the music itself, despite more widespread popularity, such as the case with disco: "Between 1976 and 1980, two musical forces combined to defunk disco and turn it into a sound of mindless repetition and lyrical idiocy that, with exceptions, overwhelmed R&B" (153). Even though the 1980s produced Michael Jackson and Prince, William Jelani Cobb (2007) opines that "by the 1980s R&B was a wasteland of headlining artists for whom blackness was incidental . . . assimilation and racial neutrality were the order of the day as artists like Michael Jackson, Prince and even former Commodore Lionel Richie cultivated personas that were only vaguely black but wholly marketable" (55).

However, crossover can also diversify the music landscape. Tshepo Mokoena (2017) observes that crossover makes more room for R&B acts in the popular imagination: "Future generations would come to be hemmed in by the same illogically race-based lines that helped facilitate the white-washing of music originally made by African Americans, rather than just widen the scope of what could be marketed as 'pop' on the radio. That legacy, of a separation of 'white mainstream' from soul, funk, jazz, R&B, rap and even country pushed so many genres from both sides of the Atlantic to the margins, even though pop borrowed heavily from them anyway." As David Brackett (2005) notes, "non-African Americans have certainly purchased, consumed, and listened to music classified in this category [R&B]; African Americans have recorded, purchased, consumed, and listened to music that does not belong in this category" (75). The most popular music icons include Michael Jackson, Prince, and Beyoncé, whose music clearly contains R&B elements. Focusing on the race of performers or audiences limits our examination and consideration of their impact on the music and the audience. The music is what resonates with its mass listeners: "But that isn't how music actually *feels* to people. We connect to its rhythms, melodies, harmonies, its beats. The naming of genres, and creation of a hierarchy where 'vapid and commercial' pop sits near 'gritty and real' rock, while the minor players duke it out below, doesn't have much of a place in our society now. Pop's only main rules are meant to centre on how a song is constructed, throwing hooks, verses and choruses into a neat package of about three to four minutes" (Mokoena 2017). Moreover, pop music has always been informed by the aesthetics of black music. Jon Fitzgerald (2007) notes that "the new crossover music is clearly characterized overall by a demonstrable shift in focus toward specific gospel techniques, rhythmic elements, and rhythm-based structures. Few white songwriters of the day used rhythm as a central element or in a structural way" (136). Crossover acts spread the aesthetics of black popular music to a broader audience and shifts the soundscape of pop music.

Cultural Work and Globalized R&B

Crossover, as used by Gordy and Korean entertainment agency CEOs, functions as a strategy of cultural work, using image and music quality to shape perceptions. Gordy tweaked the Hollywood casting model to promote a particular ethnic image that he constructed. Korean CEOs use similar strategies to shape the country's global image. Enacting cultural work makes Korean pop groups part of a global R&B tradition.

Korean CEOs use dynamic images and quality music production to engage in cultural work. Craig Stroupe (n.d.) defines cultural work as "the process by which writing or pictures reinforce current structures of feeling, thinking or acting in a culture, or enable individuals in a culture to rehearse new patterns of feeling/thinking/acting that history has made necessary." When cultural production functions as cultural work, it has an impact on the way individuals perceive something, often altering their perceptions. Often, the cultural production achieves such changes using new strategies or strategies deployed in new ways. The casting and training system utilized by Korean CEOs has always been, in part, about effecting some kind of representational change, which is a part of cultural work.

To suggest that Korean pop music engages in cultural work challenges dominant ideas that view it as merely trendy with little staying power. For many, pop music describes songs that follow a particular formula: "They have a good rhythm, a catchy melody, and are easy to remember and sing along to. They usually have a chorus that's repeated several times and two or more verses. Most pop songs are between two and five minutes long" ("What Is Pop Music?" n.d.). The catchiness contributes to its popularity, a popularity measured by charts based on sales and radio play and more recently by downloads and streaming. Such popularity has also been fueled by technological developments, including records, CDs, and digital music that made pop music accessible to large numbers of people. Garofalo (1993) notes that for *Billboard*, the pre-eminent charting entity, "pop is the most important category; it defines mainstream culture.... A recording is listed on the pop charts only after it is distributed and sold in mainstream outlets" (235). As a result, "pop music" refers not only to a genre but to a mode of music subject to particular marketing strategies that are guided by popular tastes. Roy Shuker (2001) "equates the 'popular' with commercial, cultural forms of entertainment, and regards the markets as an inescapable feature of popular culture" (3). Pop is also considered disposable because it is seen as a commercial venture aimed at youth culture, whose tastes shift frequently. Shuker (2001) points to the differences in preferences based on age: "Younger adolescents, particularly girls, prefer 'commercial pop' (e.g., Britney Spears, S Club 7); older adolescents express greater interests in more 'progressive' forms and artists (U2, Hole). That girls enjoy chart pop music more than boys reflects the segmented nature of the market" (199). Younger listeners are not associated with acts that have longevity and more musical gravitas. Because of its links to popularity and mass production, some see pop music as "the poorest type of 'dumbed down' music that is easy to listen to and enjoyed by people who know little about, or do not appreciate, more complex music" (Wall 2003, 2). The logic goes that simple music appeals to the masses, while more complex music requires more discerning tastes. Pop music is a part of the former.

Korean pop music, using crossover strategies, goes beyond being trendy. It seeks to shape perceptions, much like the original Hollywood model that Gordy tweaked. The Jewish movie moguls in Hollywood used images to show what people aspired to be: "Americans wanted to see enticing images of themselves on the screen, projected in baroque movie palaces with lights twinkling from the ceiling, thick carpets, exotic alcoves, grand staircases, ivory elephants stationed at entrances, and ushers in splendiferous uniforms waiting to escort them to velour seats" (Davis 1993, x). The image had an impact on the culture beyond, for Neal Gabler (1989) notes that Jewish film moguls "could simply create a new country—an empire of their own, so to speak—one where they could not only be admitted, but would govern as well. . . . They would fabricate their empire in the image of America as they would fabricate themselves in the image of prosperous Americans. They would create its values and myths, its traditions and archetypes" (6). However, what Jewish moguls sold back to the American public was stripped of the ethnic and cultural elements that banned their own entry into American life. The image promoted through the Hollywood casting system traded on the power of image to erase ethnic culture.

Gordy tweaked the Hollywood formula to effect crossover as one of the goals of the cultural work of artist development at Motown. Glamorous images and phenomenal performances underscored showmanship that promoted an image of African Americans as artists who challenged stereotypes: "Black acts at Motown and elsewhere had always worn their sharp mohair suits and silk gowns with . . . much pride and joy, seeing them as symbols of how far they had come from humble beginnings. . . . Motown made the earnest bid for mainstream success and respect a matter of black pride" (Ward 1998, 267). Such images can perform work, especially for ethnic groups. Anne Anlin Cheng (2011) argues for "celebrity as a politics of recognition and glamour as a politics of personhood" through which we can "revise some of the deepest assumptions that we have about raced bodies and their presentations" (1023).

Rhythm and blues as practiced by Motown represented cultural work because it effected a cultural change by shifting pop music itself. It was initially positioned opposite pop music. Going back to the 1950s, pop music initially included songs by Frank Sinatra and Tony Bennett, whose style Martha Bayles (1994) describes as "smooth, polished vocal music set to an orchestrated background" (108). On the other hand, rhythm and blues represented "black oriented" music that mixed elements of swing and the blues with vocals derived from gospel (Bayles 1994, 111). This new form of music threatened pop music, as an article in *Variety* from 1955 shows: "The established pop vocalists are finding the current rhythm and blues phase of the music biz to be tough sledding. . . . The major diskers are not finding it easy to crack the r&b [sic] formula. . . . The kids not only are going for the tunes and the beat, but they seem to be going for the original interpretations as well" (Brackett 2005, 77). Rhythm and blues not only represented a different mode of music, it also provided the foundation for rock and roll and changed the pop music scene by introducing soulful vocals and rhythm-driven tracks that promoted dance and choreography in ways that continue today. Fitzgerald (1995) identifies Motown's role as an innovator in the development of pop music itself and points to how the musical team of Holland-Dozier-Holland "elevated rhythm to new structural status," creating "a new style of mainstream popular song . . . where the hidden architecture supporting the melodic/lyric hook is now primarily rhythmic" (8). After this point, it is almost impossible to talk about pop music without recognizing its R&B foundations, an influence that went beyond the black people who initially created it or its initial black American audiences. Rhythm and blues influenced pop music so much that "in late 1963 *Billboard* discontinued its rhythm & blues chart for over one year, apparently because it was similar enough to the more general Hot 100 music chart as to be redundant" (Ripani 2006, 81). Pop may go by a plethora of names, but much of it still retains the elements of R&B within a pop context. Ward (1998) suggests that Motown "forged a flexible house style which appealed across regional, racial and even generational boundaries" (262). That influence in pop music not only represented a measure of mainstream success, but also a recognition of the craft behind the musical production that made African Americans the envy of all.

Similarly, Korean music producers, who have great influence on the sound of K-pop, are known for high-quality music production and, when coupled with images, undertake cultural work. G.-S. Park (2013) observes that the Korean mode of music making relies on a particular kind of production that is local: "Thus far, however, only Spanish and Korean singers have been able to generate such wide success without relying on the global 'track guys' [melody composers who create popular music] indicating that these countries have been able to localize their music in a way that other countries cannot easily emulate" (29). Foreign producers who attend music camps in Korea sponsored by Korean entertainment agencies also recognize the quality of this distinct form of Korean pop music. Rodnae "Chikk" Bell describes the difference between American music production and Korean music production: "The average American song is four melodies, maybe five. The average K-pop song is eight to 10. They are also very heavy in the harmonies" (Leight 2018). Kevin Randolph adds: "The one-loop beat doesn't work over there. . . . You definitely get to stretch. No other style of music has that many parts in their songs" (Leight 2018). This high music quality is inextricably linked to the image of Korean pop artists, who engage in the kind of cultural work we also see in Motown. The casting and training system makes it possible for Korean artists to use quality music as a springboard for parlaying their image. For example, government agencies and non-profits call on such artists to promote causes that produce a positive image of Korea. In 2015 the "idol" group MONSTA X was selected as ambassadors for Girl Scouts Korea because of its image: "We chose MONSTA X as ambassadors due to their diverse talents and charms. Their active and healthy persona fits Girl Scouts' image" (K. Do, 2015). Beyond Korea, the "idol" group BTS delivered a speech at the United Nations as part of UNICEF's *Generations Unlimited* initiative. The focus on image and music quality makes this possible.

Moreover, like Gordy, Korean agency CEOs promote an image of their own making rather than one thrust upon them by others. Given the experience of events like Japanese colonialism, this was sorely needed: "The experience in the Japanese schools engendered ambivalent feelings towards their own language, history and culture" (Eckart et al. 1990, 263). Rob Wilson (1991) details a number of instances of "a grandly orientalist rhetoric of Korean misrepresentation/underrepresentation": "If Asia is a territory of vast misrepresentation subject to recurrent tropes of Western orientalism, Korea remains more simply an enclave of sublime forgetting. . . . North/South 'Korea' still comprises for postmodern Americans a forbidding and forgotten landscape of belligerency" (239). In other words, Koreans face a global context where the image of their country remained distorted by others. Image has thus become a mechanism where Koreans create their own version of themselves. As Seabrook notes, "*Hallyu* has erased South Korea's regional reputation as a brutish emerging industrial nation where everything smelled of garlic and kimchee, and replaced it with images of prosperous, cosmopolitan life" (Seabrook 2012). While this is often described as soft power, it also represents a specific, ethnically informed strategy of cultural work. Korean agencies mirror Gordy's strategy to rehabilitate the image of Koreans globally. Korean CEOs like Lee Soo-man want to represent Korea well: "What I set forth was the idea of 'culture first, economy next.' I believe if the culture of a country becomes known to foreign people first then the economy of that country would thrive through those people. The same dream that shared with the artists, fellow employees and staff members is no longer just a dream. Now our dream has finally become reality" ("Korean Entertainment Agency Takes Its Acts Globally" 2011).

Korean CEOs, and black music producers like Gordy who preceded them, used the casting and training system and the quality of musical production to achieve crossover. Crossover includes the impact of image, combatting reductive ones and replacing them with ones based on work ethic, virtuosity, and quality of performance and music. Korean pop music uses the image of talented and hard-working performers who make and perform high-quality music to dispel the view of the country as weak, unstable, and lacking leadership. Korean entertainment agency CEOs seek to use Korea's culture to project a self-determined image onto the global stage. It ties its creative and commercial cultural production to its national image through cultural work that worked for Motown decades earlier. By making music that simultaneously emulates and enhances the R&B tradition, CEOs and their pop artists become a global branch of R&B.

3

"SOUL BREEZE"
Korean R&B Groups and Soloists

The reunion of first-generation Korean pop group Shinhwa kicked off a series of reunions and comebacks for other older K-pop groups, including the return of Korean R&B duo Fly to the Sky after a four-year hiatus with its ninth album, *Continuum* (2014). Like its first-generation "idol" counterparts, the group came back to enthusiastic fans in Korea, selling out its three-day concert "Continuum: The Return" at Blue Square Samsung Card Hall. Before the reunion, the duo released the first single from the album along with a video, "You You You" in early 2014. By August, Fly to the Sky was performing live as a special guest at SMTown Live World Tour IV in Seoul, alongside some of the most successful pop groups at the agency, including SHINee, Girls' Generation, EXO, and TVXQ. Fly to the Sky's reunion and subsequent interaction with Korean pop groups show how Korean R&B also resides under the larger K-pop umbrella. Korean R&B artists exhibit intertextuality by emulating R&B instrumentation and gospel-inflected vocals and enhancing the R&B tradition by invoking multiple R&B genres and vocal styles. Their music videos cite the dynamic performance and distinctive styling of African American singers. Through this intertextuality, Korean R&B artists participate in a global R&B tradition, expanding its musical legacy beyond the black/white racial binary.

From "Idols" to R&B Artists: Fly to the Sky and 4MEN

While Korean R&B artists are seen as more serious than their Korean pop counterparts, several began in the "idol" model, showing a relationship between the two styles of music that links them within the overarching category of K-pop. Fly to the Sky and 4MEN transitioned from "idol" groups with a focus on appearance that appealed to a teenage audience to R&B artists, with an increase in songs with slower tempos and a focus on vocals.

Korean R&B developed right alongside Korean pop groups. Kim C.-N. (2012) reminds us that Koreans had access to R&B through the popular music that it influenced: "Considering the fact that the progression of Korean popular music unfolded under the profound influence of pop and rock from the United Kingdom and the United States, where African Americans were prominent music pioneers of popular music, it should be noted that their impact indeed permeated the overall history of Korean popular music" (33). The proliferation of K-pop begun by Seo Taiji and Boys prominently featured the sound of rhythm and blues, which continued to underwrite early contemporary Korean pop acts. Lie (2014) points to Kim Gun-mo as a significant figure in Korean R&B in the wake of Seo Taiji who "managed to integrate new influences seamlessly into both an R&B-infused music and pop ballads.... Kim came to be known as The Stevie Wonder of South Korea" (82). Made up of Lee Joon, Kim Jo-han, and Jae Chong (Chong Jae-yoon), the Korean group Solid garnered a reputation for establishing R&B as a force in K-pop: "A few K-pop artists tried out R&B prior to Solid's appearance, but none was as committed to the genre as Solid was. With good voice and considerable (albeit not necessarily overwhelming) talent, Solid managed to popularize R&B as a genre in Korea" ("50 Most Influential K-pop Artists" 2010). Solid paved the way for later pop groups whose sound was influenced by 1990s R&B. These groups frequently featured at least one member who emulated black vocals, which was a new development as "R&B was virtually non-existent before 1992 in South Korea" (Lie 2014, 82). Because both draw from R&B musical aesthetics, the boundaries between Korean "idol" acts and Korean R&B performers have always been fluid. Moreover, large Korean entertainment agencies that house "idols" also house Korean R&B artists. Fly to the Sky began its career at SM Entertainment, home to the first successful male "idol" group, H.O.T., and remained for a time, even after they made the transition to R&B duo. Big Mama, the female Korean R&B vocal group, spent most of its career with YG Entertainment, who managed globally successful "idol" groups 2NE1 and BigBang. Park Hyo-shin, a veteran R&B singer, spent time at Jellyfish Entertainment alongside "idol" groups VIXX and gugudan.

While Korean R&B groups have links with "idols," they also represent a distinct mode of popular music. Other R&B artists reside on smaller labels that cater to Korean R&B artists. Typically, Korean R&B singers do not receive the same level of exposure as their "idol" counterparts. As a result, their music does not generate the same amount of critical response from global fan reviewers. Nevertheless, global K-pop fans recognize these Korean R&B acts. YouTube abounds with playlists dedicated to individual R&B artists as well as Korean R&B in general. Comments show that global fans follow these groups and their music with great enthusiasm.

The development of the "idol" turned R&B duo Fly to the Sky illustrates how Korean R&B differs from Korean pop. Fly to the Sky, made up of Korean singer Hwanhee (Hwang Yoon-seok) and Korean American singer Brian Joo (frequently referred to as Brian), debuted in 1999 at SM Entertainment with the mid-tempo single "Day by Day," from the album of the same name. The group released its second album *The Promise* in 2001, but its third album, *Sea of Love* (2002), marked the group's shift to R&B with the promotional track "Condition of My Heart," written by African American R&B singer Brian McKnight. The group would go on to release two more albums, *Missing You* (2003) and *Gravity* (2004), leaving SM Entertainment for PFull Entertainment in 2004. After the release of *Transition* (2005), *No Limitations* (2007), and *Decennium* (2009), Brian and Hwanhee pursued solo careers, placing Fly to the Sky on hiatus until the 2014 reunion and the release of *Continuum* (2014). Since then, the duo has remained active, releasing several mini-albums, including *Love & Hate* (2015), *Your Season* (2017), and *I* (2018).

Fly to the Sky began as a pop act much like other early "idol" groups. Both Brian and Hwanhee were recruited to SM Entertainment through the audition process and subsequently entered the trainee program. They were part of a "systematized traineeship" that "involved training the artists in subjects ranging from singing, dancing, rapping, composition, and musical instruments to foreign language and manners" (Shin and Kim 2013). They participated in activities meant to popularize their image and target a teenage audience with a sound influenced by R&B dance genres and hip-hop. The title track from their debut album *Day by Day* (1999) bears little resemblance to the R&B ballads that form the foundation of their later career. It is a mid-tempo pop song that sounds like it would fit in well at a 1980s prom with its synthesized effects and the regular beat of a drum machine. The duo alternates vocals in the verses and sings in unison in the chorus. Fly to the Sky's sound emulates much of the pop of the 1990s, such as Whitney Houston and Boys II Men. The group's uptempo tracks allowed them to perform choreography like others "idols." "What You Want" from the 2001 album *The Promise* opens with a funky guitar riff, which leads into gospel-inflected backing vocals, along with syncopated bass and handclaps. When Fly to the Sky performed the song on the music show *Inkigayo* in 2001, they performed a high-energy synchronized dance routine complete with backup dancers and fan chants from the audience

("Fly to the Sky—What U Want" 2019). Both Hwanhee and Brian are dressed in black tracksuits with silver necklaces.

Like other "idols," they leveraged their image through music videos and extramusical activities like appearances on television shows. In addition to the standard interviews to promote new releases, they made the rounds on Korean television. Hwanhee appeared on the first season of *We Got Married*, a Korean variety show that places celebrities into couples and follows their "married life." The duo also hosted the radio show *1010 Club*. The duo also made music videos that appealed to their largely female fanbase. The music video for "Day by Day" lacks a narrative and features a series of images focusing on the duo in their well-furnished urban apartment ("Fly to the Sky—Day by Day" 2009). The video follows the members in routine activities and invokes standard music video tropes, including slow-motion shower scenes. Both are well-dressed, and the video features plenty of close-ups to capitalize on their appearance. The aesthetics of Fly to the Sky's early work conformed to the tastes of youth audiences, relying on the optics of the duo's good looks and revealing the influence of "idol" promotion in the construction of their visuals and style.

However, beginning with the 2002 album *Sea of Love*, Fly to the Sky focused more on vocals and less on appearance. Fly to the Sky's transition to R&B included not only an increase in slower-tempo songs, but also a tendency to use their vocals in the sophisticated and polished production of 1990s R&B. Ripani (2006) describes "urban" or "urban contemporary" as a music category distinct from rap that "includes under its umbrella not only the smooth and soulful ballads formerly associated with the quiet storm style, but also up-tempo dance and funk songs" (134). Many Fly to the Sky songs work on vocal tensions that evoke emotion and highlight the dynamic between Hwanhee's more husky and intense voice and Brian's more mid-tone vocals and rap ability. Brian's "Beginning of the World's End" from the 2008 remake album *Recollection* reflects his tendencies toward R&B pop and rap music styles. The mid-tempo song begins with a pop-friendly guitar lick, later joined by another guitar as well as piano. Brian's voice enters after a twenty-second intro with little tonal variation. Brian is backed by vocals that are barely noticeable, consisting of stock "oohs" and "aahs." In "Wish," from the same album, Hwanhee's more soulful voice is complemented by minimal instrumentation in the form of piano with finger snaps in the intro. This leads to a mild swell of orchestration featuring strings and chimes. Hwanhee breaks up the standard verse-chorus structure with vocal ornamentation that utilizes more of the vocal range. He uses melisma at the end of the verses to build vocal momentum going into the choruses. Hwanhee's greater tendency for emotional intensity and vocal ornamentation is also evident in his version of the duo's track "Sea of Love"

(2002). In the original version, Brian and Hwanhee enact their typical vocal arrangement, alternating vocals in both the versus and choruses. However, in Hwanhee's version, he incorporates more vocal ornamentation. Rischar (2004) asserts such vocal aesthetics are hallmarks of R&B ballad singing: "Common timbral markers indicate its 'blackness'" in R&B ballad singing, and include "a throaty attack to the initial word of a phrase" and "a rise a step up after finishing a cadence on a chord tone" (424–25).

Together, Brian and Hwanhee engage in vocal interplay that contributes to the duo's R&B sound. Korean singer Kim Dong-ryul popularized a version of "Drunken Truth" on his 2008 album *Monologue*. His version has a slow tempo and a soulful guitar intro, and demonstrates his strong vocal talent. However, Fly to the Sky's version for the album *Recollection* (2008) features R&B vocal techniques and the interplay of voices. Dispensing with a musical intro, the track begins with Hwanhee's vocals operating at a lower register with melisma and other vocal ornamentation and complemented by backing vocals in doo-wop style with no instrumentation. The second verse features Brian's sweeter vocals over the same doo-wop backing vocals. As the song continues, Hwanhee employs more melisma in his vocal parts, complemented by the swell of instrumentation that fills out the sound with drums, bass guitar, and keyboards. Brian and Hwanhee continue to alternate in their vocals to the end of the song. In a largely a cappella context, the song uses the differences in the vocal style of Hwanhee and Brian to create dynamism within the song. "Don't Marry," from the 2007 album *No Limitations*, is a slower-tempo track that also demonstrates their distinctive vocal dynamic. The track opens with a melancholy piano and soft string instrumentation that form a sonic backdrop for Hwanhee's melisma, giving way to Brian's more controlled vocals. Just as resonant against the lone piano, Brian's vocals alternate with Hwanhee's, which come in to contribute to the buildup and decrease in intensity over the verse. By the time the percussion enters late in the song, the alternating rise and fall in intensity resolves in a final climax where both singers are singing different lyrics at the same time. The exchange works because their voices are different.

The soulful interplay between two voices against the backdrop of highly polished production by Fly to the Sky recalls other acts like American R&B duo K-Ci & JoJo. K-Ci (Cedric Hailey) and JoJo (Joel Hailey) began as a part of the R&B group Jodeci, but their sound later diverged from Jodeci's gritty and suggestive music. Alex Henderson (2003) points out the influence of older R&B genres for the duo's 1997 album *Love Always*: "It was clear that the great soul music of the 1970s was very much on K-Ci and JoJo's minds when they made this album" (382). Fly to the Sky mirrors the duo's R&B vocal style. In a review of the group's 2000 album *X*, Henderson (2003) notes: "One thing that's never in doubt is the Hailey Brothers' skills as vocalists; while a lot of urban contemporary artists get over on image alone, K-Ci and JoJo really do have impressive vocal ranges" (382). Writing for *Ebony*, Joy Bennett Kinnon (1998) attributes their vocal-centric style to their gospel singer parents: "Their strong gospel roots have tempered what has become known as the Hailey brothers sound. The brothers, in short, can wail. Known for lushly layered, yet powerful vocal harmonies, the brothers bring their all to a song" (178). Fly to the Sky echoes the vocal dynamism of K-Ci & JoJo by making distinct vocal interplay key to their signature style.

Like Fly to the Sky, 4MEN, a Korean R&B group, also began with "idol" tendencies, but later developed a reputation for R&B ballads. 4MEN debuted a year before Fly to the Sky in 1998 with Happyface Entertainment, and has experienced several personnel changes over the years. Original vocalists included Yoon Min-soo, Jeong Se-young, Han Hyeon-hee, and Lee Jeong-ho. Yoon departed the group in 2006, replaced by J1 in 2006. Soon after, all of the remaining members departed, and three new members joined: Shin Yong-jae, Kim Young-jae, and Kim Won-joo. Despite numerous personnel changes, 4MEN has created a substantial discography, with eight albums released between 1998 and 2017: *FOUR MEN* (1998), *Iroke Chonildongan Moumyeon Ibyori Sarajindago Hetda* (2000), *Andante* (2006), *The 3rd Generation* (2010), *Sorry* (2010), *The Artist* (2011), *1998 (The 5th Album)* (2014), and *Remember Me* (2017).

4MEN began with an "idol" concept, but developed a more sophisticated R&B style. The covers of the group's early albums make them virtually indistinguishable from their Korean pop counterparts. Their first two albums featured images of the members, and the cover of *Iroke Chonildongan Moumyeon Ibyori Sarajindago Hetda* (2000) used styling that appealed to teenagers. With a colorful abstract background behind them, the members are dressed casually. Three of the four members wear plaid shirts over white t-shirts. One has on a baseball cap and another sports shades. The group tended to perform pop ballads. For example, "Namanui Neo" from the 1998 album *Four Men First Album* is comprised of electronically generated beats and music that brings to mind a 1980s dance for teenagers. However, albums from 2006 to 2009 do not feature any images of the members, and subsequent albums feature more mature styling. The cover for *The Artist* (2011) features the three members of the group in a black and white photo. All the members are wearing suits, and none of the members make eye contact with the camera. The music from this album reflects a different mood, more informed by R&B vocals. The track "Love Sick" opens with a plaintive piano that gives an organic feel to the song. Soft percussion and fingersnaps complement the more mature vocals. As Arnold Artega's (2011) review notes: "'Love Sick' is reminiscent of the smoothness of

Boyz II Men (with whom they've held a concert with already). It's tame, but in 4MEN lingo, that really means it's only less explosive than other tracks. In this case, that approach is appropriate since the overall feel is soft and colorful." This is different from the mid-tempo track "A Riddle" from the same album, where bright horns bubble up to take center stage in the instrumental intro that leads to the vocals. Unlike the smoothness of "Love Sick," "A Riddle" features 4MEN "serenading their emotions through exhilarating melodies and bright harmonies. The song builds in thin, quick layers, ferociously mounting beautiful coats of singing one after another" (Artega 2011). 4MEN attribute their style specifically to R&B: "We want our fans to know that Korean singers also understand R&B and soul music well and Korean traditional ballad music and K-soul of R&B sentiment have been popular in Korea before the start of the K-pop heat" (Nini 2015).

While 4MEN and Fly to the Sky both had pop origins and transitioned to a more R&B sound, they sound different from each other. Fly to the Sky relies on the interplay between two different voices, while 4MEN relies on the multiple individual vocals and group harmonies. Other Korean R&B groups continue to illustrate Korean R&B's broad intertextuality through emulation.

Emulating Soul Instrumentation and Gospel Vocals: Brown Eyed Soul and Big Mama

While Korean R&B artists cite elements of the R&B tradition, they do not do so in the same way. Some Korean R&B groups combine harmony with soul instrumentation, while others draw on gospel-inflected female vocals.

Soul Aesthetic: Brown Eyed Soul

Korean R&B group Brown Eyed Soul emulates the R&B tradition by combining harmonies with 1960s and 1970s soul instrumentation in complex musical arrangements. The group's use of vocals with instrumentation that features horns recalls R&B bands like Earth, Wind and Fire and Sly and the Family Stone.

Brown Eyed Soul is the brainchild of Na-ul (Yoo Na-ul), a Korean R&B singer and musician who was also a member of the Korean R&B duo Brown Eyes, another Korean R&B act. Just as the style of music of the group draws on black American popular music, so too does the name of the group: "Brown Eyed Soul is derived from 'Blue Eyed Soul,' which describes black music— R&B or soul music—performed by white artists. The group replaced 'Blue Eyed' with 'Brown Eyed,' a term that symbolizes Asians" ("Brown Eyed Soul

Interview" 2007). Such deliberate naming coupled with their consistent R&B sound shows that the group consciously aligns itself with the R&B tradition. Founded in 2003 with vocalists Jungyup (Ahn Jung-yup), Sung Hoon, and Youngjun (Go Young-jun), Brown Eyed Soul has released several albums, including *Soul Free* (2013), *The Wind, the Sea, the Rain* (2007), *Browneyed Soul* (2010), *Thank Your Soul* (2014), *Soul Cooke* (2015), and *Soul 4 Real* (2016). While the members rarely make frequent public appearances like their "idol" counterparts, individual members collaborate with other artists on albums and soundtracks for Korean dramas. Na-ul is the most prolific. In addition to three solo albums and three mini-albums, Na-ul also collaborated with the Korean hip-hop duo Dynamic Duo, singer-songwriter Younha, and Korean pop singer Kim Junsu, member of the "idol" group JYJ and former member of the "idol" group TVXQ.

Brown Eyed Soul's signature style combines vocals and musical elements of soul music. Many associate soul with a cultural moment in black communities in the 1960s and 1970s. Mark Anthony Neal (1999) argues that "1960s soul became primarily linked to evocations of black communal pride. In this regard, soul came to represent an authentic, though obviously essentialized blackness that undergirded the Black Power and Civil Rights movements that soul music had come to be associated with" (94). Some also see soul as an empty marketing category that converted blackness into a product to be bought and sold (Neal 1999, 95). At the same time, soul also represents a rich music tradition in R&B: "Soul presented a remarkable blend of melodic and harmonic fluidity and rhythmic certainty and drive, all built upon the solid rock of repetitive, yet inventive, bass, drum, piano, guitar and horn figures. Above all, however, soul borrowed from gospel a breathtaking expressive freedom for its finest individual and collective vocalists" (Ward 1998, 184). This distinctive style made its way to Korea, bringing "the tough but sensuous singing style unique to soul" into the Korean musical imagination (C.-N. Kim 2012, 33). Soul also captures an inclusive impulse, one that may explain why Brown Eyed Soul finds its home in the musical style. Kelley (1997) sees soul as a flexible concept: "That is why, even at the height of the Black Power movement, African American urban culture could be so fluid, hybrid and multinational" (25).

No matter the song, Brown Eyed Soul's vocals are always on display, showcasing individual members' voices as well as group harmony utilizing various R&B aesthetics. An analysis of his vocals reveals that Na-ul "is a vocalist who knows how to perform and control his voice to truly enhance the musical message of songs in various genres but finds his niche in the R&B, Soul, Ballad, Funk and Gospel music where he excels in terms of musical ideas, compositions and harmonic knowledge" ("Brown Eyed Soul Vocal Analysis" 2015).

Such musical expertise is replicated in the group's signature harmony. Glorious group harmony interrupts the stark sound landscape provided solely by finger snaps in "Love Ballad (Piano Version)" (2010). This version of the song begins with the chorus rather than the verse. With a subtle piano creeping into the background at some point, the track uses a simple verse-chorus form but the momentum and intensity is driven by the vocals. As the song reaches its end, the lead vocal improvises over the backing vocals, using vocal ornamentation and gravelly gospel vocals to achieve even greater intensity. The sparse orchestration of the song puts all of the attention on the vocals, making use of both the vocal harmony of the group in the choruses and the strength of individual vocals of the members on the verses.

These signature vocals are often accompanied by horns to evoke a 1970s soul sound. "Dream," from the 2007 album *The Wind, the Sea, the Rain*, opens with bright horns, accompanied by string orchestration and a funky rhythm. The intro resolves to piano, with horns providing an accent. During the verses, voices harmonize while alternating with the horns. Horns also punctuate the group harmony in the choruses. Horns are also featured in tracks with slower tempos, like "I'll Make Way" from the 2010 album *Browneyed Soul*. This track begins with the verse, with sparse orchestration and a slight echo over chimes and a subtle synthesizer supporting a lone vocal. Horns with chimes brighten the track leading into the verses and the horns up the intensity leading into the chorus, which features soft group harmony and a fuller rhythm provided by more pronounced drums. As the vocals intensify on the chorus, so too do the horns. The song ends with a repeated chorus that features vocal improvisation over group harmony, as well as horns and bass with vocal accents in the outro.

Brown Eyed Soul's horn-inflected songs like "Dream" and "I'll Make a Way" emulate the soulful sound that emerged in the United States in the 1970s with R&B groups like Earth, Wind and Fire, a band that has strong musical roots in jazz. That group's founder, Maurice White, began his career as a studio musician, eventually becoming the drummer for the Ramsey Lewis Trio at Chess Records in the late 1960s. White left the trio in 1970 to form Earth, Wind and Fire, which Ricky Vincent (1996) describes as "a wide-open percussion-filled jazz-pop act, a cross between the visuals of Sly Stone, the melodies of his Memphis roots (growing up with Booker T. Jones of the MGs), and the rhythms of Africa" (186). In addition to its distinctive percussive style, the group is also known for "syncopation over a variety of choppy rhythm breaks" and "surges of spectacular horn breaks that challenged Kool & the Gang" (Vincent 1996, 187). This combination of jazz rhythms and horn interludes help create Earth, Wind and Fire's signature sound: "Rather than incorporate the horns primarily for emphasis or punctuation, as James Brown or the Stax bands had done, EW&F

wove them into the arrangements, playing fluid secondary melodic lines and then unexpectedly leaping into the foreground. Along with the early recordings of such EW&F contemporaries as Kool and the Gang and the Commodores, this sound would spawn an entire school of horn-based R&B pre- and proto-disco groups, including Slave and Brass Construction" (Light 2008). Such arrangements can be heard in the group's uptempo tracks like "In the Stone" (1979), which highlights the group's horns: "With just a handful of horns and overdubs, White was attempting to re-create the full horn sections he had worked with in the Chicago jazz clubs" (Light 2008). The intro opens grandly with prominent horns supported by string orchestration. After the extended intro, the horns drop out, leaving a lively guitar, synthesizer, percussion, and bass guitar. The horns punctuate the vocals on the verses, adding interest. During the choruses, group harmony combines with falsetto, complemented by horns. During the breakdown, the song resolves into a different set of repeated choruses, initially with a sparser instrumentation with subtle horns in the background and later with increasing intensity.

"That's the Way of the World," from the 1975 album of the same name, opens with a simple but effective electric keyboard, drums, and bass, but is quickly elevated by the dawning of the horns on the song's musical horizon. They provide a contrast to the newly introduced syncopated rhythm. The overall easy vibe of the track provides the backdrop for Philip Bailey's signature falsetto as well as the vocal harmony and counterpoint. The song's loose structure allows for much vocal improvisation without discernable regular verses typical of pop songs. Horns have often been used in the group's songs with a slower tempo: "The soft studio ballads were extended with long, sultry saxophone solos; the lead vocals of Philip Bailey and Maurice White soared into the skies; rich percussion draped the arrangements like fine lace" (Vincent 1996, 187). These uses of the horns define the Earth, Wind and Fire sound, a sound that also emerges in Brown Eyed Soul songs.

In addition to Earth, Wind and Fire's signature 1970s soul sound, Brown Eyed Soul also emulates the 1960s sound of Sly and the Family Stone. The group consisted of Sly Stone (Sylvester Stewart), the group's lead singer, and band members Freddie Stone, Rose Stone, Cynthia Robinson, Greg Errico, Jerry Martini, and Larry Graham. Its eclectic lineup made it unique, featuring both male and female musicians as well as black and white members. While the group is well known for its contributions to rock music, Stephen Thomas Erlwine (2003) notes the group's unique sound is important to soul music as well: "The Family Stone's arrangements were ingenious, filled with unexpected group vocals, syncopated rhythms, punchy horns, and pop melodies. The music was joyous" (624). Songs like "Dance to the Music" (1968) capture the group's signature sound: "Prior to this record no one, not even the Family Stone, treated soul as a psychedelic sun-splash, filled with bright melodies, kaleidoscopic arrangements, inextricably intertwined interplay, and deft, fast rhythms" (Erlwine 2003, 624). At the same time, this sound highlighted "audaciously fused soulful vocals, Latinate horns and psychedelic rock flourishes," as opposed to the jazz-inflected harmonies of Earth, Wind and Fire (Ward 1998, 358). Vincent (1996) elaborates on the inclusion of horns and guitars: "Jerry Martini's shouting saxophone fired up the best of the blues vibes, yet the jagged staccato horn rolls he and Cynthia locked into revealed a be-bop sensibility at the same time. Brother Freddie Stone's chopping guitars twanged with a freaky, lighthearted feel of James Brown's band *at the circus*, while the entire soup rode along Larry Graham's pulsing, popping, punching, never-before-heard fuzz bass, and Sly's genius for tension at the organ" (Vincent 1996, 89).

Brown Eyed Soul also emulates Stone's brand of soul. "Brown City," from the 2003 album *Soul Free: #1*, opens with groovy horns that give way to a lone horn and complemented by the rhythm punctuated by bass and an intermittent guitar, with a bit of scat-singing added for good measure. This simple instrumentation on the verses contrasts with the more complex instrumentation on the chorus, which highlights the horns. By alternating relatively simple rhythm on the verses and more complex rhythm on the chorus, the song becomes more varied as the song progresses. The subsequent verses begin to feature more accents of an electric guitar with the horns and contributes to its Sly and the Family Stone sound. Brown Eyed Soul's "Can't Stop Loving You" from the 2010 album *Brown Eyed Soul* opens with bright horns and an uptempo, versatile rhythm that is also reminiscent of Sly and the Family Stone. The song carries the horns throughout the verses, while the guitar provides accent and the bass guitar improvises. The chorus features call-and-response between the group harmony and the lead vocal, punctuated with some falsetto improvisation. After a breakdown, during which the instrumentation and orchestration drop out, the music builds up to include an extended guitar solo and the eventual reintroduction of horns as the song fades out.

While Brown Eyed Soul draws on soul bands, other Korean R&B artists emulate other R&B vocal traditions.

Female Gospel Tradition: Big Mama

Big Mama draws from a distinctive black female vocal tradition informed by gospel, a tradition that includes female soul singers like Aretha Franklin rather than male soul singers like Sam Cooke and Ray Charles.

Big Mama was a female Korean R&B group founded in 2003 with YG Entertainment, the same year that Brown Eyed Soul debuted. A four-member female group made up of Shin Yeon-ah, Lee Young-hyun, Lee Ji-young, and Park Min-hye, the group quickly established a reputation for solid vocals in the R&B tradition. During its nine-year career, the group released several albums, including *Like the Bible* (2003), *It's Unique* (2005), *For the People* (2006), *Blossom* (2007), and *5* (2010). Big Mama's incorporation of vocal ornamentation and vocal etiquette draws on older artists like Aretha Franklin and those who came in her wake, including Whitney Houston, Mariah Carey, Anita Baker, and the 1990s female vocal group En Vogue, who also traverse wide terrain in older black vocal styles. Jon Pareles (1992) notes that En Vogue also features four equally strong singers: "There's not a weak voice in the group, from Ms. Jones's alto, with its carefully applied touches of rasp, up to Ms. Herron's flamboyantly sustained high notes and Ms. Ellis's swooping melisma. In nearly every song, one singer takes the verses while the other three join in with harmonies on the chorus, a euphonious support group." En Vogue's debut album, *Born to Sing* (1990), features doo-wop, gospel-inflected tracks, and urban contemporary.

Big Mama incorporates vocal techniques drawn from gospel. Rischar (2004) describes that the function of the drive section, or "the section at the end of a song in which a chorus or phrase is repeated indefinitely while a soloist improvises above it," is expressivity and joy, and often is accompanied by "a thickening of the musical texture" (433). Gospel uses "drive" to create a sense of emotional dynamism, where "the repeating cycle commonly supports a soloist of some sort . . . and a responsorial element provided by the choir or congregation. The emotional level of the soloist gradually builds, and over time the process moves the entire congregation to a higher level of religious excitement" (Ripani 2006, 45). That musical expression ranges from sorrow to exuberant joy. Ripani (2006) describes gospel vocals that contain an element that "begins at a low emotional level and builds to a high point" (144). In addition to Korea's own emotional music, the country has a musical tradition influenced by gospel. Music from the black church makes its presence known in the sacred music of Korean churches. The Heritage Mass Choir is one such example. Sonya Beard (2010) describes Kim Hyo-sik, the choir's worship leader known as a Korean "Kirk Franklin," and the eighty-member choir as "the R&B-infused, hip-hop–flavored gospel choir." Their experience made them the subject of the documentary *Black Gospel* (2013), which documents their travels to Harlem and the American South in an effort to improve their performances. The choir reveals its desire to understand the aesthetics and context of gospel through their choir school "where they learn about black gospel techniques and the history of gospel music" (Beard 2010). Such convergence does not surprise blogger Gail Song Bantum (2009): "While some may find the adaptation of African-American style gospel unusual, in many ways, this seems to be a natural point of connection between the worship life of Korean and African American Christians despite each group's relative ignorance of the other. Growing up in Pentecostal Korean churches and later worshipping in African American churches, I have always been struck by the deep and almost desperate moments of worship, yearning, and exaltation in both places." Korean R&B groups like Big Mama have directly engaged the gospel tradition, covering such staple spirituals as "His Eye Is on the Sparrow."

Gender also informs the black popular tradition that influences Big Mama. In the African American tradition, men such as Ray Charles and Sam Cooke were instrumental in translating the gospel impulse into pop music for the masses. Through a musical and textual analysis of black pop songs from 1963–66, Fitzgerald (2007) discovered that "the new crossover music is clearly characterized overall by a demonstrable shift in focus toward specific gospel techniques, rhythmic elements, and rhythm-based structures" that white songwriters used (136). Charles is often credited for this transformation: "The gospel vocal style itself, as typified by Ray Charles, consists of a variety of features of the blues system, such as use of blues-scale notes, pitch blends, glissando, melisma, gravelly vocal style, and extreme vocal range (falsetto and full voice) (Ripani 2006, 73). Similarly, Sam Cooke promoted gospel elements in pop music, reflecting "a definite gospel sound, complete with the melismatic turns and emotional delivery he was famous for as a gospel singer prior to his crossover into the secular music world" (Ripani 2006, 74). While writer-producers created songs for black pop performers and used stylistic elements of the black musical tradition, "Motown, the dominant new force in black pop crossover music, supplied its performers with songs written and produced by black writer-producers who had extensive first-hand experience of black musical traditions (gospel in particular)" (Fitzgerald 2007, 129). Male R&B singers with gospel backgrounds used musical and vocal elements from the gospel and blues traditions to create a sound palatable for the American mainstream. Robert Stephens (1984) notes: "[Motown] attracted and maintained a large white following through skillful use of 'pop' music elements, and remained equally popular in the black community by using gospel elements and driving R & B rhythms" (30).

At the same time, female songstresses like Aretha Franklin drew on a distinctly female vocal tradition. Franklin's musical style diverged from Charles and Cooke both in terms of quality and gender: "Aretha employs not only the percussive vocal style of her R&B predecessors and contemporaries, but she also has a keen sense of how to stretch the melodic boundaries that allows her to do some more soaring, seemingly effortlessly" (Davis 1992, 22). Her transformation of those elements produced a different thread of the black music tradition because she was a woman, unique even among the explosion of girl groups in her day. Thulani Davis notes: "For black women, Aretha is the voice that made all the unsaid sayable, powerful and lyrical, before the black women writers stepped in the '70s to tell us the stories. She was more rockin', more earnest, just plain more down front than the divas of jazz, Sarah and Ella, and certainly more than the Supremes and all the coy girls of Motown" (Davis 1992, 21). It was this female perspective and subjectivity that made Franklin's version of "Respect" so different from the original: "She took Otis Redding's 'Respect' and turned it inside out, making it deeper, stronger, loading it with double entendres, refashioning it as a self-styled creation" (Wexler and Ritz 1992, 16). As the lead, she also created a unique style: "If Aretha sings a standard, all the old intentions are there, but she will always up the ante, propelling the song with total commitment. Aretha operates on such a level of dynamic intensity and so personalizes the lyric, that she eclipses everyone who ever sang the song" (Wexler and Ritz 1992, 23). Many praise Aretha's strong voice, but Wexler and Ritz (1992) also credit the interplay between her voice and the Sweet Inspirations, comprised of Cissy Houston, Estelle Brown, Sylvia Shemwell, and Myrna Smith, who often back up Franklin's vocals and "were also instinctively creative about parts and harmonies" (13). Moreover, Franklin blazed a trail for women to use their powerful voices in almost any genre: "In a way, the title Queen of Soul is unfair to Aretha Franklin. It implies that she ruled in only one sector of the musical universe, when she actually reigned over virtually everything she touched and touched every kind of vocal vernacular music of her time" (Marsh 1992, 25).

Big Mama follows Franklin in its incorporation of elements of gospel. "Start," from the 2005 album *It's Unique*, opens with a group gospel shout, followed by handclaps and gospel rhythm on bass. The upbeat chorus uses all the members' vocals, which act as a choir behind improvised vocals of the lead. This track also features other vocal elements from gospel, such as moans. The slower temp track "Follow Inner Light" from the same album showcases how the singers build on each other's voices using vocal technique. Opening with the twinkling of chimes, the song begins with a lone melismatic vocal and sparse instrumentation from a piano. As the song continues, the lead vocal increases in intensity, adding vocal ornamentation and vocal improvisation that travels over several octaves, as well as echoes a kind of call and response. Like Franklin, Big Mama exercises a variety of vocal arrangements that draw on gospel, including the arrangement of their voices to mimic the vocal depth of a choir and the use of vocal adlibs.

Enhancing the R&B Tradition with Multiple Genres: Park Hyo-shin, Lyn, Zion.T

Korean R&B artists also enhance the R&B tradition by invoking multiple styles and genres, a hallmark of Korean music production. Korean R&B artists draw from styles and genres that may depart from the expectation of the R&B ballad or slow jam. Korean R&B singer Park Hyo-shin invokes the styles of such different vocalists as Michael McDonald and Kenneth "Babyface" Edmonds. Korean R&B singer Lyn draws on music genres such as jazz and hip-hop throughout her career. Zion.T oscillates between classic R&B and hip-hop.

Park Hyo-shin

Park Hyo-shin has a reputation as a solid vocalist who frequently draws on the ballad. Park has released several albums, including *Things I Can't Do for You* (1999), *Second Story* (2001), *Time-Honored Voice* (2002), *Soul Tree* (2004), *The Breeze of the Sea* (2007), *Gift: Part 1* (2009), *Gift: Part 2* (2010), and *I Am a Dreamer* (2017). Beginning with *The Breeze of the Sea*, he embarked on a new singing style that caught the attention of listeners: "The man who started the so-called 'cow calling technique,' which is a vibrato singing technique, had decided to retire that singing method. His decision comes seven years after his debut, at a time when the Korean music scene is dominated by Korean rhythm & blues" ("Park Hyo Shin's Interview" 2007). His engagement with the R&B vocal tradition remained consistent. His R&B-inflected songs often feature vocal ornamentation and instrumentation, which is distinct from his non-R&B ballads. "Love . . . That Common Word" from his 2001 album *Second Story*, is a typical Park Hyo-shin ballad. Opening with piano introduction, the orchestral instrumentation swells right before the introduction of his vocals. The verses begin with the piano, underscoring his low register, and later add additional instrumentation in the form of bass and drums. On the chorus, the song builds, as do his vocals, showcasing his vocal strength. Here, his vocals lack ornamentation. In contrast, "It's Gonna Be Rolling" from the 2002 album *Time Honored Voice* features both R&B instrumentation and vocals. In an intro with bright horns, syncopated rhythm, and vocal ad-libbing from Park Hyo-shin, the track establishes its musical links to R&B early. The verses are punctuated by electric guitar, supplemented by the horns. By the time we get to the chorus, gospel-choir-like vocals support his singing. After the guitar solo and a vocal bridge, the song trails off with his continued vocal adlibbing.

However, Park Hyo-shin utilizes a variety of vocal styles reminiscent of different African American R&B vocalists. "Now and Forever" from his album

The Breeze of the Sea (2007) is a 1990s R&B track where Park utilizes vocal ornamentation on the intro against the backdrop of a subtle electric piano and well-placed handclaps. Here, his tone is mid-range, very much like Kenneth "Babyface" Edmonds, who is probably best known for his work with other artists but who also is a singer in his own right. Edmond's "Everytime I Close My Eyes" is the type of vocal performance one hears on "Now and Forever": "In 'Everytime I Close My Eyes,' the earnest, cliched sentiments are rendered listenable via a slick background arrangement.... Edmonds has a light voice that vacillates from sounding sweet to sounding gritty thanks to a slight catch in his throat. He tends to bathe his voice with wispy background vocals, an effect that, when matched with his instrumental backing, gives his songs a slightly ethereal feel" (V. Stephens 2001, 133). Conversely, Park Hyo-shin goes for a lower register and grittier sound on "You and Me" from T*ime Honored Voice* (2002), which blends a subtle Latin guitar riff with vocal ornamentation in the vein of Michael McDonald. Formerly a lead singer for the Doobie Brothers, McDonald later embarked on a solo career that produced hit songs including "I Keep Forgettin'" (1982) and the collaboration with James Ingram, "Yah Mo B There" (1983). McDonald credits R&B for his distinctive low, gravelly, resonant singing style: "Because I'd always wanted to be an R&B screamer, I realized early on that I wouldn't sing for very long if I kept trying to sound like James Brown! So out of necessity my voice just developed into the R&B tenor you hear today" (Lewis 2018). Park Hyo-shin even changes vocal styles within songs. "Wonderland," from the 2017 album *I Am a Dreamer*, creates an ethereal opening with a crooning style backed by female vocals with a rhythm guitar accompanied by electric keyboards that introduce a groovy rhythm. The smooth vocal style is reminiscent of the vocals of jazz crooner Nat King Cole. As the song goes into the chorus, his vocal ornamentation begins to appear. However, by the second chorus the rhythm changes, and he employs more gospel-inflected vocals that lead into a call-and-response bridge with choir-like backing vocals. The latter part of the song continues with more improvised vocals with the same R&B backing vocals. Here, Park Hyo-shin's vocals draw more on contemporary R&B vocals, which sound different from the jazz-inflected crooner style.

Lyn

Probably the most wide-ranging engagement with black popular music styles comes from Korean R&B singer Lyn. Lyn (Lee Se-jin) has released several albums since her debut in 2000: *My First Confession* (2000), *Have You Ever Had Heart Broken?* (2002), *Can U See the Bright?* (2004), *One and Only Feeling*

(2005), *The Pride of the Morning* (2007), *Let Go, Let In, It's a New Day* (2009), *6½ New Celebration* (2009), *6th Part 2 'Candy Train'* (2010), *Le Grand Bleu* (2014), *9X9th* (2015), and *#10* (2018). Throughout these releases she draws from a variety of genres. She utilizes R&B vocals on ballads with more pop-oriented instrumentation. "Love . . . It's All Lies" from the 2009 album *Let Go, Let In, It's a New Day* uses string instrumentation with a bit of guitar. Here, Lyn employs very little vocal embellishment but still produces a black pop sound. One reviewer calls this incarnation of Lyn a "sweet soprano that may not have Mariah Carey's range but can pull off a very similar style" ("Lyn Preaches Love" 2013). Lyn also produces songs that reflect a Korean pop sensibility. "Breakable Heart" (feat. Yong Jun-hyung) from the 2015 album *Le Grand Bleu* includes a rap verse from the member of pop group BEAST (later known as Highlight). Although best known as a ballad singer, Lyn regularly features hip-hop instrumentation and guest rappers on her tracks. Both "Fly High" and "New Day" from *Have You Ever Had Heart Broken* (2002) features the hip-hop group CB Mass, made up of members who will go on to be members of veteran groups Epik High and Dynamic Duo. CB Mass provides a rap intro for "Fly High" and an intro and rap verse for "New Day." The group's contribution provides a counter to Lyn's sultry voice, as the rappers employ a more aggressive flow. The combination is reminiscent of the music of Mary J. Blige, an R&B singer best known as the Queen of Hip-Hop Soul. While Lyn's voice is very different from Blige's "robust, dark voice," which she uses to "move around melodies in a pleasingly unruly way," both exhibit a tendency to work with hip-hop artists: "[Blige] was notable for being one of the first R&B singers to be at ease working with MCs. . . . [On Method Man's 1995 'I'll Be There for You/You're All I Need to Get By'], Blige sings in an uncharacteristically airy and soft way. . . . In the background, though, she throws in subtle ad-libs as if singing along to the radio" (Frere-Jones 2008). Similarly, Lyn contributes to a hip-hop vibe in these two tracks.

In addition to the inclusion of hip-hop artists, Lyn demonstrates her versatility by blending the slick production of urban contemporary with the organic feel that comes from the inclusion of acoustic instruments as a backdrop for her R&B vocals. While Lyn moderates her vocal ornamentation on the track "Time Enough" from *Can You See the Bright?* (2004), the song highlights the acoustic guitar even more. With a more open feel on the verses, the choruses have denser instrumentation that comes with the kind of production that characterizes urban contemporary. Backing vocals provide more sonic interest and a prominent bass raises the profile of the rhythm. The guitar continues to provide flourishes throughout. This instrumentation allows Lyn's vocal ornamentation to shine.

Despite a tendency to draw on a variety of contemporary styles, Lyn does not neglect older styles of vocal-centric black popular music. Her 2015 album *9X9th* represents a radical departure from her usual style in that it has jazz instrumentation on nearly all of the tracks. Jazz guitar and percussion as well as a swing rhythm that changes for the chorus and again for a piano solo drives "A Bitter Love Goodbye" (2015). Lyn's vocals are in a higher register, without the ornamentation found in her more R&B-inflected songs, but she utilizes more jazz vocalization, where her voice follows the rhythm. "Look At Me" (2015) combines a string arrangement, piano, horns, and guitar reminiscent of a slower version of John Barry's jazz arrangement behind the James Bond theme. Here, Lyn employs more jazz-inflected vocals. "Only You" (2015), a mid-tempo cool jazz song, highlights her lilting voice, which has counterpoint with the saxophone. As the song develops, Lyn even throws in some scat singing. Lyn's music career is emblematic of the type of enhancement we find with Korean R&B artists. She effortlessly takes on different genres that fall within the tradition of R&B music. The variety of the genres is characteristic of Korean music production, and it allows the listener to hear R&B genres in a new context. A listener who delves into her catalog is treated to R&B vocals in pop, hip-hop, and jazz environments.

Zion.T

While Lyn is an R&B vocalist who delves into multiple genres, hip-hop vocalist Zion.T occupies a different musical space. He clearly links himself to R&B: "When I first appeared in the music scene and people got interested in me, I was known rather for the rarity of my music than for its quality. At that time, there were not many hip-hop R&B vocalists, so I was the only vocalist in such a position. That was why other musicians sought to work with me" ("[SS Interview] Zion.T" 2017). Glasby (2017) identifies Zion.T as part of a generation of Korean R&B artists that includes Dean, Jay Park, and Crush who "are generally signed to independent or subsidiary labels, meaning they're less constrained than their predecessors and current pop contemporaries, with fewer boundaries on their sound and who they choose to work with." They collaborate with each other and share the tendency to combine the innovative and creative impulse of hip-hop with the staples of R&B music. Dean cites a variety of R&B performers as well as music producers such as Pharrell Williams, the Underdogs, and Timbaland as influences (Barnes 2016). He credits early exposure to R&B as a significant influence on his music: "I can't remember exactly when, but I remember watching a video of a famous R&B singer performing. I watched how he performed and then I felt the genuine reaction from the crowd. The whole energy in the atmosphere was so amazing that I started to feel something different inside me" (Brungardt 2015). Similarly, Crush recounts early fondness for R&B vocalists like Marvin Gaye and Donny Hathaway as well as more recent singers like Maxwell, D'Angelo, and Erykah Badu (HP Cheung 2016). At the same time, these vocalists have been influenced by hip-hop. Dean began his career as a member of a hip-hop crew with Keith Ape and cites Kanye West as one of his biggest hip-hop influences. Crush was the youngest member on Dynamic Duo's Amoeba Culture label and cites the group as a huge inspiration (Sharon 2016). Like dedicated MCs, Dean wants to be recognized for his own style: "I don't wanna be just another generic R&B singer. I want to be my own artist. I've been trying to make my own brand of style and music, so it's important to me to come across as different. I see myself having my own sound and style as an artist, and I see people loving it. I see myself creating my own culture and community off of my music and artistry" (Brungardt 2015). These artists consciously connect hip-hop and R&B with the idea of expanding both. Dean observes: "Due to the fact that Hip-Hop and R&B have the same roots, I was able to explore R&B, Soul, and other similar genres" (Lyon 2015). These vocalists embody the blending and mixing impulse of hip-hop within an R&B context through the use of multiple genres. Dean says he is "more concerned with crafting a sound unique to me as an artist. Blending the elements of 90s R&B, hip hop, EDM, garage, indie rock. I want to construct a future R&B sound" (Brungardt 2015). Crush sees his fellow R&B artists going beyond conventional R&B: "We try a lot of experimental music; we try different genres, we try to mix things up and try to collaborate with other R&B artists from other countries as well . . . we constantly look for new challenges and new things, new genres—that's what I think others should do, and we're doing that already too" (Melendez 2016).

Korean hip-hop R&B acts like Zion.T lean toward alternative R&B. There have been efforts to describe some modes of contemporary R&B as different from previous incarnations. Miles Raymer (2014) points to how alternative R&B differs from more commercially popular R&B: "The style's consistent performance and genre-wide disinclination to court controversy or indulge in hard-to-sell artistic statements made it a safe investment, and majors snapped up developing acts quickly enough to forestall an independent insurgency." Others suggest that the production setup of alternative R&B is more conducive to a different style, as DJ Jazzy Jeff, who heads A Touch of Jazz Production, explains: "Now we're starting to get real instrumentation, with people writing a lot more soulful and meaningful songs. But you still have a touch of modern technology in there, which is cool, because it can't go back to what it was in the '70s. Every time R&B comes back around, it comes back with the old but with some reinventing" (G. Mitchell 2000, 41). In the 1990s, Kedar Massenburg coined the phrase "neo-soul" to describe a marketing strategy for the kind of music that D'Angelo made: "But soul music is soul music. There's nothing really new under the sun. But, in terms of marketing today, there's the need to categorize music for consumers so they know what they're getting" (Mitchell 2002, 30). Others point to the incorporation of other genres as key to alternative R&B. Barry Walters (2012) notes how those under the alternative R&B banner "map out how the new genre is transcending its initial limitations, merging/mutating with other genres, while shaping both the indie in-crowd and the pop mainstream." However, not everyone supports this kind of characterization of alternative R&B. Aimee Cliff (2014) applauds a full-fledged rejection: "It's not a genre, but more like a door to condescension. By adding the prefix, it sidelines R&B itself by implying it's not experimental, boundary-pushing or intellectual. It throws side-eye at the genre, while at the same time claiming to have discovered something worthy within it. To call someone 'alternative R&B' is pretty much the ultimate musical negging: it feels like it's not so far away from saying, 'This is innovative . . . for R&B.' It allows curious outsiders to have their say while still maintaining a spectre of segregation. It keeps R&B perpetually in another room."

Nevertheless, Zion.T comes off as more experimental compared to Korean R&B singers like Park Hyo-shin. Zion.T was featured early on tracks by hip-hop artists like Dok2 and Simon D in 2011 before releasing his first single as lead artist, "Click Me" feat. Dok2 (2011), which also appeared on his first album, *Red Light* (2013). He has gone on to release two mini-albums, *Mirrorball* (2013) and *OO* (2017), as well as several popular non-album singles, including "Yanghwa Bridge" (2014), "Eat" (2015), "No Make-up" (2015), and "Snow" feat. Lee Moon-sae (2017). Zion.T eventually moved from Amoeba Culture to The Black Label, a sub-label of YG Entertainment. Many find his vocal style difficult to describe but agree that it is not the norm: "I sat for a good thirty minutes—maybe more—of lucubration, deeply contemplating which select set of words would best define Zion.T's none-too-typical singing style. It's odd, but odd in a pleasing sort of way. He departs entirely from the norm with his peculiar voice, delivering perfect pitch with light, airy hums and squeaky clean harmonization that is skillfully layered for your listening pleasure" (Joora 2014). Some focus on his unusual pronunciation, while others note the nature of the vocal he produces: "Funktastic singer Zion.T has one of the most distinctive voices in K-pop. His tenor vocals are tight, his rapping is high-pitched, wickedly timed, and he has this amazing nasal quality to his sound that makes him identifiable anywhere he performs" (Raineo211 2016). The unique nature of his voice provides distinct contrast when he collaborates with other vocalists. Against the electric keyboard stylings and finger snaps, "Two Melodies" feat. Crush, from *Red Light* (2013), introduces Zion.T's vocal, which is a bit nasal compared to Crush's. Unlike Zion.T, Crush has a more typical R&B soulful and smooth voice. Together, they play off one another, much like the vocal dynamic of Brian and Hwanhee in Fly to the Sky. Zion.T's collaboration with Crush sounds very different from his collaboration with Lee Moon-sae for "Snow" from the *ZZZ* album (2018). The slow-tempo track begins with Zion.T's distinct vocals, backed with the jazzy instrumentation with soft percussion. His vocals come off as a crooner style, losing some of the edge it usually features. This contrasts with Lee Moon-sae, whose voice is fuller compared to Zion.T's, thereby achieving the contrast that drives the song. Listeners often are drawn to his voice in their reviews.

Zion.T also demonstrates his ability to blend his unique vocals with innovative instrumentation. He deploys his voice in a more insistent way on the funky track "Dolabeolyo [Spin Spin]" from the *Mirrorball* (2013) album. The track opens with Zion.T's repeated vocals that punctuate the funky rhythm and organ work. The use of a prominent bass and electric guitar is very reminiscent of James Brown's distinctive rhythm. "The Song" is probably one of his most pop-oriented tracks, yet it still provides an opportunity for musical experimentation. Nick (2017) notes: "It has a warm, piano-driven instrumental that recalls everything from Motown to the more classically soulful side of Prince. As we might expect, *The Song*'s verses are an ever-evolving hodgepodge of melodic lines and stream-of-consciousness vocal phrasing" ("Song Review: Zion.T"). Kaito Locke (2017) points to the variety that Zion.T's vocals provide: "His rapping is a bit faster than usual, mixed with cute vocal percussion (the "bap-bap-bap" dubbing) and he hits some beautiful (and delightfully nasally) high notes with clarity." Zion.T's hip-hop R&B results from expanding the vocal and rhythmic-centered nature of R&B and using the creative impulse of hip-hop.

Citation of Performance: Big Mama and Wheesung

Even though Korean R&B artists do not engage in nearly the level of exposure and promotion as their Korean pop counterparts, their music videos nevertheless cite the performance and styling of African American music videos, providing alternative modes of representation that challenge stereotypes. Big Mama, drawing on the styling of black female vocalists, challenge stereotypes of women based on size. Wheesung defies the low-profile performative style of Korean singers by drawing on the choreography and styling of 1990s male R&B singers, much like pop singer Rain.

Women, Talent, and Representation: Big Mama

As women in a music industry dominated by female pop groups that depend on image, Big Mama, as a group with average-sized women, have foregrounded their voices over their appearance: "In a world where female musicians are critiqued by their outward appearances, Big Mama came out blazing with their enormous vocal talent. Unfortunately, it was their 'full-figured bodies' that garnered more attention than their music" ("They Will Even Hear Sound of Our Breath" 2007). Big Mama made a statement about visual expectations of women with the video for the group's breakout hit, "Breakaway" ("Big Mama—Break Away" 2006), from their first album, *Like the Bible* (2003). The video begins with a lone breakdancer spinning under a spotlight on a stage, surrounded by musicians. The camera pulls back to reveal a bar, and later, more of the club's interior. The shot transitions into a shot featuring four women on a different stage. These shots are intercut with shots of someone playing a saxophone. Upon closer inspection, it is clear that these women are not the actual members of Big Mama. These women reflect the ideal of a singer, complete with smaller sizes. In several sequences, the video features close ups of the faces of these women interspersed with longer shots that reveal the full length of their bodies. The women are dressed in ways that draw attention to their bodies in a variety of ways. One wears a miniskirt with a silver tank top that exposes her arms. Another member of the group wears a strapless top with a black skirt that goes to her knee, while the other member wears a halter top with a black skirt that goes nearly to the floor. The women sing in front of classic microphones associated with the 1950s and 1960s. The audience, which appears to be largely male, give approving looks in the smoky atmosphere.

Two-thirds of the way through the video, the camera pans backstage, revealing the members of Big Mama, who ostensibly provide the vocals for the cover group's performance in front of the audience. Unlike the cover group, the members of Big Mama are dressed casually. They wear jeans and knit tops in different colors. Their outfits are not color-coordinated. They sing in front of regular microphones in the midst of backstage equipment. Yet, their performance of the song is more animated than the cover group. They face each other while they sing and exude greater emotion on their faces. The video proper ends when the song ends, but there is an additional vignette at the end, which features the members of Big Mama outside of the club following their performance. Bundled up in coats and scarves, they thank the patrons who leave the club. They even thank one of the members of the cover groups, who rudely brushes past them and does not return their greeting.

The video compares superficial performance and authentic performance. Overdetermined by spectacle in the form of jugglers, breakdancer, and even the cover group, the video shows these performers as superficial compared to the authentic vocal performance that emanates from backstage. The cover group's demeanor and dress draw attention to their bodies and provides a stark contrast to that of the members of Big Mama. The cover group is dressed to be seen and admired, while Big Mama remains invisible. The audience is treated to popular images of Asian femininity and the vocal performance of soul singers, and they seem content with it. The approving looks by the majority male audience seems to suggest that they desire the women in ways that they would not desire the members of Big Mama. The vignette at the end reveals negative judgment by the audience members as well as the cover group. The audience's failure to acknowledge the Big Mama members is a critique of their attraction to the ideal of femininity and a denial of talent of the group. The video makes a statement about a lack of variety in the images of women in music, specifically, that the members of Big Mama would not be accepted by the club audience as glamorous singers despite their talent because of their size.

Other music videos by Big Mama show that women who do not fit the music video norm simultaneously can be glamorous and vocally talented. The African American black popular music tradition is replete with talented singers whose experienced weight fluctuations and remained glamorous. Nichelle Gainer (2014) recalls Aretha Franklin's range of looks: "If Aretha's music gave voice to the everyday 'do right' black woman, her style choices showed you what she looked like when she dressed up: Afros, sometimes dyed red, to match flowing, custom-made gowns from black designers like Stephen Burrows. An all-natural look without makeup, worn with a hand-sewn dashiki. Or a sleek press-and-curl to complement glittering, beaded, low-cut stage gowns, like those she wore in a 1970s advertisement for Fashion Fair cosmetics" (163–64). While the music video for "Breakaway" hides the members, the music video for "Nevermind" puts them in a performance mode that reveals their glamour, much like Franklin ("Big Mama—Nevermind" 2009). The video opens with a series of vignettes featuring different women: a woman whose car has broken down and her cell phone is locked inside; a woman who has an argument in a restaurant with her fiancé; a female rock band who loses a member. Within this context, Big Mama performs the upbeat track on a set that resembles an oversized radio. The front of the radio opens, and the members of Big Mama confidently walk forward. They are all dressed for performance, unlike their casual clothes from "Breakaway." Two are wearing black pantsuits with different tops that show off their shoulders. The remaining members have on dresses. One has on a dress with a shiny gold print. Their accessories include large gold earrings, belts, and necklaces that emphasize a glamorous look. The video includes frequent close-ups of the members as they perform the song. Shots of the performance are intercut with scenes from the women in the earlier vignettes. Already known for their vocal talent, the styling of their outfits sends the signal that they are also glamorous entertainers. Rather than suggesting that appearance is not important, the video suggests that glamour should include a wider array of women.

"Real" Performance: Wheesung

Performance of a different kind is cited by singer Wheesung (Choi Wheesung). While he debuted in the same year as Park Hyo-shin, he has a different sound and persona as a male Korean R&B artist. Wheesung began his career in the idol group A4, but quickly moved on to M Boat, the sister company to YG Entertainment, where he embraced the R&B style that would define his career and took on the stage name Real Slow. He has released several albums, including *Like a Movie* (2002), *It's Real* (2003), *For the Moment* (2004), *Love . . . Love? . . . Love!* (2005), *Eternal Essence of Music* (2007), and *Vocolate* (2009). He has also released several mini-albums and single albums, including *With All My Heart* (2008), *They Are Coming* (2011), *The Best Man* (2014), *Transformation* (2016), and *In Space* (2018).

Wheesung draws on two kinds of styling drawn from African American culture in his videos. He reflects the performance of 1990s R&B singers, creating an image much like the one Rain embraces where he seeks to focus on his sexiness. Such performative strategies differ from those associated with Korean singers. Lie (2012) describes traditional Korean music that "stressed melismatic and raspy vocalization, and the performer stood still" (360). Singers like Cho Young-pil "sang without moving, employed melismatic and *pansori* singing techniques, and relied on his vocal skills, rather than on his looks to achieve stardom" (Lie 2012, 345). Conversely, Wheesung draws on the same performative strategies we saw in chapter 2 that include the stylistic choices and choreography of African American singer Usher. However, his decisions resonate differently as a Korean R&B singer, as many Korean R&B singers do not use highly visible promotional strategies like those employed by "idol" artists. Wheesung's performances in music videos place him front and center, involves choreography, and reveals more of his body. It is akin to the kind of representation of American R&B singer D'Angelo that Keith Harris (1999) describes: "This counter image is suggestive of greater awareness to the physical form and is a stabilizing gender image in that these images are resolutely heterosexual, reclaiming straight masculinity within the trend of the sensitive man willing to expose himself" (66). Like D'Angelo, Wheesung blends the vocals of the R&B soul singer with the spectacle that we see with a particular brand of American R&B singers.

The music video for "Incurable Disease" combines choreography and stylistic choices that are cited from African American performance ("MUSIC VIDEO: Wheesung Incurable Diesease" 2007). The music video begins with a rap intro performed by Masta Wu, a rapper with YG Entertainment. He sports black blazer and hat and holds a hammer as he raps. The camera then cuts to Wheesung, who sports several outfits during the video. The music video consists mainly of choreographed dance with his backup dancers as well as solo shots of himself performing the song against the backdrop of a hallway lined with huge graphics of Chinese characters. His wardrobe is key, and changes throughout the video. In one scene he is dressed in wide-legged pants and a red top with half an arm sleeve in the same material as the pants. His shirt is unbuttoned to reveal his well-toned, bare chest. The outfit exudes a kind of intended carelessness, as his shirt is half untucked. In another scene he wears a black fedora, knit turtleneck with one sleeveless arm, and black pants. His backup dancers are dressed the same way as they perform the fluid choreography that matches the tone of the track. Yet another shot shows Wheesung in a more avant-garde outfit: a sleeveless grey leather halter vest that entirely reveals his bare chest. These are fashion choices, but they also echo the kind of styling enacted by Rain for his music videos, styling he emulates from 1990s R&B singers like Usher. These styling choices emphasize the body. Yet, Wheesung is a Korean R&B singer who is expected to focus largely on vocals over appearance.

Whereas his style for the "Uncurable Disease" video is eclectic, Wheesung opts for a more sartorial look for the video for "Night and Day" ("휘성 WheeSung—Night and Day" 2014). The video features two types of sequences. One sequence follows the narrative of a couple, who reunite after a period and dramatically resume their relationship. The other sequence is a performance by Wheesung and male and female backup dancers, all of whom are dressed to the nines. Wheesung sports two outfits in this video: a dark suit accented with a red tie and a pocket square and a light grey suit with no jacket, a vest over a white shirt and the same red tie. The backup dancers also undergo a costume change during the video. Initially the male dancers are dressed in suits; later in the video, they wear pinstripe suits with no jacket, fedora-like hats, white shirts coordinated with white pocket squares, and vests with contrasting white buttons. At the beginning of the video, the female dancers wear sleeveless vests, black shorts, and black thigh-high boots. Later in the video, they are featured in black skirts with a large ruffled hemline and white linings that are revealed when they spin and sleeveless, vestlike tops. The performance itself takes place on a set where Wheesung sits on a chair on a raised dais amid columns, some of which are ruins, against the backdrop of a cloudy sky. Wheesung hardly performs any choreography, thereby drawing the viewers' attention to his stylistic choices. Suits are not only the purview of African Americans, but black men have historically used fashion in particular ways. Monica Miller (2009) traces black dandyism back to the eighteenth century and positions "the black dandy explicitly among other racialized performers and performers of masculinity in order to read the dandy as a complicated figure that can, at once, subvert and fulfill normative categories of identity at different times and places as a gesture of self-articulation" (5). For men of color, placing such detailed attention on style translates into a particular performance of masculinity. In my article "That's My Man!: Overlapping Masculinities in Korean Popular Music" (2014), I note that men in K-pop "rely on a masculinity based on the sartorial, defined by a concern with tailored clothing and meticulous detail to accessories. The sartorial goes beyond contemporary metrosexual masculinity, which focuses more on behavior such as grooming regimens and buying habits" (126). It is this performative mode that Wheesung draws on for this video.

Korean R&B singers are dedicated to the distinct sound of R&B, songs that would could easily be part of rotation on a black radio station. The decision to base a music career on this type of singing is a conscious one that not just anyone can undertake, for Ripani (2006) asserts that "it has remained difficult ... for any person outside of the African-American community to produce an acceptable black vocal style" (190). When Korean R&B singers commit to the musical aesthetics of R&B, they demonstrate a level of authenticity. They do not rely on just on genre, but draw on a wide variety of R&B-inflected styles, all of which are linked by their use of vocals and instrumentation.

Global R&B beyond Black and White

Through an intertextuality that simultaneously emulates and enhances the R&B tradition, Korean R&B artists participate in a global R&B tradition, extending it beyond an often-invoked black/white racial binary. As a genre of African American popular music, R&B has been subject to debates about authenticity and who can perform the music, with critiques frequently made against white performers for cultural appropriation. However, the authentic engagement with R&B by Korean singers complicate this narrative by demonstrating that nonblack, nonwhite performers can also authentically participate in the R&B tradition. As a result, we can recognize the impact of R&B beyond black American culture.

Authenticity and the vocally intensive genres of R&B have always been central to discussions of non–African Americans who delve into the tradition. The interaction between whites and black musical production has often been characterized as one of misappropriation and theft. Speaking of early African American musical traditions of jazz and the blues, Amiri Baraka (1995) has compared white jazz critics to white jazz musicians who "sought not only to understand the phenomenon of Negro music but to appropriate it as a means of expression which they themselves might utilize" (180). Referring to the relationship as one of exploitation and unequal exchange, he questions whether the essence of such cultural production could be truly acquired by non-blacks: "The white musician's commitment to jazz, the ultimate concern, proposed that the sub-cultural attitudes that produced the music as a profound expression of human feelings, could be *learned* and need not be passed on as a secret blood rite. And Negro music is essentially the expression of an attitude, or a collection of attitudes, about the world, and only secondarily an attitude about the way music is made" (Baraka 1963, 181). These critiques extend to R&B as well: "But R&B now, with the same help from white America in its exploitation of energy for profit, the same as if it was a gold mine, strings that music out along a similar weakening line. Beginning with their own vacuous 'understanding' of what Black music is, or how it acts upon you, they believe, from the Beatles on down, that it is about white life" (Baraka 1966, 186–87).

While Baraka focuses on instances where the engagement by whites results in an inferior and inauthentic rendition of the music, Neal (2005) grapples with examples of white performers whose performances are deemed authentic by audiences, preferring the metaphor "white chocolate" to capture the nuances of his approach: "By 'white chocolate' I mean artists—ostensibly R&B and soul performers—who challenge essentialist arguments about who is *allowed* to sing black music . . . and who also provide examples of white performances of black pop that transcend simple appropriations (and in the worst case theft) and legitimately add to the tradition" (372). Such performers would include singer Teena Marie, a white singer who signed with Motown Records in the late 1970s and whose first album *Wild and Peaceful* (1979) was produced by funk singer Rick James. Initially, many did not know Marie's race, as the album cover did not feature her picture and was marketed to black radio stations, but the strength of her voice reflected her authenticity: "With an earthy voice that was pierced with power in its high registers, she was highly credible as an R&B singer, and many listeners learned that she was white only when they saw her portrait on the cover of her second album, *Lady T*, in 1980" (Sisario 2010). As a result, "she was embraced by the R&B audience, and some of her songs have become ingrained in black musical culture" (Sisario 2010).

These discussions about authenticity and race in R&B are contextualized within the United States. Some argue that the blues, R&B, and hip-hop have all gained mainstream acceptance only when white artists performed them in a way that stripped them of their original essence. However, this narrative focuses on white actors in a particular historical context of the United States. For example, Baraka observes that for every black musical innovation, "there was a commercial cooptation of the original music and an attempt to replace it with corporate dilution which mainly featured white players and was mainly intended for a white middle-class audience" (quoted in Rudinow 1994, 130). Baraka zeroes in on white perpetrators as well as a white audience within a culture that has an established socioeconomic structure informed by race. The commercial cooptation is part of a long legacy of labor exploitation that stretches back to the origin of the country and the rise of slavery as well as later manifestations of unequal labor like sharecropping and racial discrimination in employment.

However, Korean R&B performers invite us to consider R&B outside the United States with nonblack, nonwhite performers. Korean R&B artists complicate the black/white racial binary because they historically have suffered discrimination similar to African American experience. Pushed to migrate by the devastating effects of the Korean War, Korean immigrants to the United States benefited from the Immigration and Naturalization Act of 1965, which replaced the previous quota system based on national origins that limited the number of immigrants from East Asia with a new policy based on new categories, one of which was refugees of war. However, Korean immigrants were not white according to the racial dynamics of the United States. Despite the model minority myth, Korean immigrants and their descendants have been subject to anti-Asian racism, which disqualifies them from the privilege associated with whites. Moreover, American imperialism in Korea also factors into the exclusion of Koreans from whiteness. Nadia Y. Kim (2006) found contradictions in the race-based perspectives of whites in Korea: "Idealized whiteness in media looms large in Seoul residents' inferiority complexes and several informants responded by criticizing whites' penchant for, in their words, 'making themselves better in the movies' or 'idolizing themselves.' Yet, the U.S. military figures more centrally in Seoul residents' rejection of white-American superiority, as evidenced by the massive demonstrations against the United States (and Korean government) on the North Korea-USA conflict issue" (391–92). Such responses demonstrate that Koreans do not consider themselves to be white. Koreans in the music business do not have the history of the theft and distortion that Baraka attributes to white jazz performers.

Instead, Korean R&B artists' authentic engagement with the vocal tradition establishes them as nonblack participants in a global R&B tradition, much like British soul singers. Regarding soul in Britain, Annie J. Randall (2008) notes: "It was a sound that could not be peeled away from the culture it represented and the history that produced it; indeed, by virtue of its *vocal* origins in the *improvised* black church tradition, it was a sound that was comparatively difficult to copy and whiten as R&B had been by rock and roll" (43). In authentically emulating and enhancing R&B, Korean R&B artists create another branch of the R&B tradition.

Korean R&B artists, through their vocal abilities, comfortably fit within a R&B tradition recognized for its global reach and impact. While they differ from their Korean pop counterparts in terms of promotional strategies and visibility, they share their intertextuality. Korean R&B singers emulate the instrumentation and distinct vocals of R&B. Vocal groups like Brown Eyed Soul and Big Mama run the gamut of styles from gospel to 1960s soul. Other singers, like Park Hyo-shin, Lyn, and Zion.T, enhance the tradition by incorporating multiple styles. Both Big Mama and Wheesung cite African American performance in music videos that challenge reductive images of Asians. Through music and video, these artists demonstrate a level of authenticity that makes them a branch of the R&B tradition.

4

"REWRITING THE RÉSUMÉ"
Mainstream Korean Hip-hop Artists

As the trajectory of the Korean R&B group Fly to the Sky demonstrates, the boundaries between genres in K-pop are quite permeable. It is this flexibility that allowed Jay Park to reinvent himself. Park, a Korean American rapper, initially came to the public's attention as the leader of the Korean pop group 2PM, which he left in 2009. He subsequently embarked on a solo hip-hop career and founded his own label, AOMG. In 2017, he signed a contract with Roc Nation, the company founded by hip-hop mogul Jay-Z. The news was also hailed as a validation of Korean hip-hop. Despite this achievement for hip-hop, Park's career moves shed light on Korean hip-hop's location under the K-pop umbrella.

While Korea has a vibrant underground hip-hop scene, this chapter focuses on mainstream hip-hop artists, those who are more accessible to global fans due to their use of social media, interaction with the more visible pop groups, and presence on YouTube in the form of music videos. These Korean hip-hop acts emulate the R&B tradition through sampling and the use of R&B vocalists. At the same time, they enhance the tradition by mixing multiple genres with hip-hop elements and using live instrumentation, which are strategies used in Korean music production. They also cite both limiting and liberating hip-hop tropes in music videos. As a result of intertextuality and citation, mainstream Korean hip-hop artists participate in a global R&B tradition by promoting its innovative musical aesthetics.

Pop and Hip-hop

Mainstream Korean hip-hop is intertwined with Korean pop's origins, management, and use of technology. It also mirrors African American hip-hop's concerns with political and social commentary, lyrical prowess, and authenticity.

Mainstream Korean Hip-hop and Korean Pop

Mainstream Korean hip-hop and Korean pop both draw on the same rap and choreography popularized by African American hip-hop and have brought such elements to a wider Korean audience. Some observers draw stark distinctions between Korean hip-hop and pop because of the latter's lack of political or social commentary. Nevertheless, Korean hip-hop acts share promotional strategies and collaborations with "idols," thus revealing the link between the two.

The origins of Korean hip-hop can be traced back to the early 1990s, just like Korean pop. Both Korean pop and mainstream Korean hip-hop emerged in the wake of Hyun Jin-young (Heo Hyeon-seok), credited with introducing hip-hop to Korea with the group Hyun Jin-Young and the WaWa. An article on *allkpop* explains the context for hip-hop's emergence in the Korean mainstream in the 1980s: "The Roger Rabbit dance was very popular at the time and Lee Soo Man saw that the Korean music landscape didn't really have any performers who would actively dance to the music" (GhostWriter 2016). Hyun Jin-young auditioned and was signed to what was then SM Studio. He debuted in 1990 with the song "Sad Mannequin." While radically different from the kind of Korean hip-hop that followed and the African American hip-hop from which it drew, the video and song introduced the distinct musical and performative elements of hip-hop into the Korean popular imagination: "He introduced a bit of swag, rapping, and hip hop to Korea" (GhostWriter 2016). While his initial album was not successful, Hyun Jin-young later achieved a brief measure of fame. His backup dancers would go on to form two of the most influential early Korean hip-hop groups. Lee Hyun-do and Kim Sung-jae came together as the hip-hop duo Deux in 1993, and Kang Wong-rae and DJ Koo (Koo Jun-yup) formed the group Clon in 1996.

Hyun Jin-young also introduced the idea of choreography in pop music, which the "idols" took up wholeheartedly. Hyun's choreography cited breakdancing, one of the four pillars of hip-hop. Dance would continue to be central to global forms of hip-hop and underwrite the kind of performative style that made its way into K-pop: "At the core of hip-hop is the notion of something called the 'cipher.' Partly for competition and partly for community, the cipher is a circle of participants and onlookers that closes around battling rappers or dancers as they improvise for each other. If you have the guts to step into the cipher and tell your story and, above all, demonstrate your uniqueness, you might be accepted into the community" (Chang 2009, 60). For Koreans, hip-hop dance has become a way of stepping into globalized African American culture. Chang (2008) notes that initially, Korean b-boys were criticized because "they were thought to be mechanical, unable to rock with the beat, and lacking in 'foundation skills,' such as the top-rock and footwork moves that form the historical roots of dance." However, "they mastered routines, the choreographed ensemble moves that are essential parts of a showdown. They immersed themselves in the music and the rhythms. They studied the history of b-boying and hip-hop culture" (Chang 2008). As a result, Korean b-boys have had phenomenal success in global competitions.

Hyun Jin-young is often overshadowed in K-pop history by Seo Taiji and Boys in terms of popularizing hip-hop in Korea. However, Korea experienced the emergence of other Korean hip-hop acts, including Deux, Clon, Turbo, and Jinusean. Tiger JK (Seo Jung-kwon) and his group Drunken Tiger have had the most sustained career, one which shows how hip-hop developed into a variety of styles in Korea. Tiger JK coformed the group Drunken Tiger in 1999. The track "Do You Know Hip Hop" from the 1999 album *Year of the Tiger* showcases a knowledge of the basics of American hip-hop. It begins with a woodwind intro, slightly Asian in nature. The beat drops with an operatic vocal that contrasts with a prominent bass rhythm. Dominated by rap on the verses with some electronic accents, the song features rappers who alternate verses, which lends sonic diversity to the track as they have different styles. The clash of sound at the beginning reflects the ways that American hip-hop DJs would put together different sounds, thereby creating a whole new musical composition. Drunken Tiger's more aggressive track "Monster" from *Feel gHood Musik: The 8th Wonder* (2009) begins with a male voice yelling in English and a dramatic swell of sound followed by sparser instrumentation, punctuated with a heavy horn riff. 2013's *The Cure*'s title track is far more mellow, with an acoustic guitar intro, female vocals, a reggae-inspired rhythm, and a more syncopated rap style by Tiger JK. By the time Tiger JK works with Yoon Mi-rae and Bizzy in the group MFBTY, the sound has been described as more mainstream-friendly and pop-oriented. The uptempo "Bang Diggy Bang Bang" (2015) features a sitar mixed with a more complex beat and alternating raps by Yoon, Tiger JK, and Bizzy, all of whom have distinct rapping styles.

Some wish to draw hard distinctions between Korean pop and mainstream Korean hip-hop. Because pop music makes little political or social commentary and appeals to a wider audience, many reject any connection between K-pop and Korean hip-hop. They view Korean hip-hop as more authentic and characterize pop groups as mere puppets of their agencies. Hip-hop artists are often concerned with a gritty reality as opposed to the upbeat songs, videos with bright colors and dancing that characterize Korean pop groups. Others critique K-pop's use of hip-hop aesthetics, like rap and fashion.

However, mainstream Korean hip-hop and Korean pop acts not only share origins but also leverage the same strategies for engagement with fans. Like R&B and "idol" groups, mainstream Korean hip-hop groups are part of Hallyu, taking in Western, particularly African American music styles, combining them with Korean sensibilities, and redeploying them globally using technology, the Internet, and social media. Some of the early Korean hip-hop acts, including Jinusean, Masta Wu, and 1TYM, shared the YG Entertainment label with emerging pop acts like BigBang and 2NE1. Prior to joining YG Entertainment, Epik High were represented by Woolim Entertainment, which also managed idol groups like Infinite and Tasty before it merged with SM Culture and Contents, a subsidiary of SM Entertainment. Members of Dynamic Duo as well as Epik High maintain Twitter accounts. Like many "idol" groups, Epik High named their fans, who are called High Skool. Other mainstream Korean hip-hop groups participate in extramusical activities and appear on Korean television shows as part of promotions. Dynamic Duo appeared on *Ask in a Box*, a segment created by Loen Entertainment, where celebrities answer questions posted by fans. Tablo was a participant in *The Return of Superman*, a Korean show that follows celebrity fathers as they spend time with their children without their wives around. Like "idol" groups, Dynamic Duo and Epik High perform on music shows like *Inkigayo*, *Music Core*, and *Music Bank* as part of promotions. Moreover, many mainstream Korean hip-hop groups have international aspirations like their "idol" counterparts. In an interview, Jinusean, a Korean hip-hop duo, articulated its desire to expand their market during their career: "We were trying to move out of Korea, into China, Hong Kong, Japan.... A lot of times you'll see singers that go out to Hong Kong, China, Japan, just to perform. But we're trying to go international—we're trying to see outside of Korea" (Johnson 2003). The boundaries between independent Korean rap and a more commercial variety in K-pop can be quite porous.

Mainstream Korean hip-hop and Korean pop acts are also linked by the music itself. Tablo of Epik High recognizes how he is influenced by both pop and hip-hop: "Korean music-wise, even K-pop influences us. Even K-pop of this time.... I'm also influenced by underground hip-hop in the States.... The thing is my tastes go from here to there and everything in between" (S. Kim 2011). Song (2014) describes the hip-hop artist Dok2 occupying his own "thunderground," where "he is neither *under*[ground] nor *over* (mainstream) but somewhere in between" (139). Dok2 has collaborated with a number of "idol" artists including Hyuna, Kim Hyung-joon, and Kim Hyun-joong and has also appeared on mainstream hip-hop tracks by Epik High and Primary. Doing so does not seem to have damaged his underground hip-hop credentials. Moreover, Korean television shows referred to as K-dramas expose global audiences to a wide variety of music, which they also tend to describe as K-pop. Official soundtracks (OSTs) bring together artists from different genres and function as another site where one finds Korean hip-hop and pop. The lead ballad for *Descendants of the Sun*, one of the most watched K-dramas of 2016, was performed by Yoon Mi-rae, also known as Tasha, a female hip-hop artist and member of the Korean hip-hop trio MFBTY, which includes veteran Korean hip-hop artist Tiger JK. The soundtrack also featured songs by pop vocalist K. Will, R&B vocalist Lyn, and rock band MC the Max.

In addition, Korean mainstream hip-hop groups do not see themselves as diametrically opposed to Korean pop. In an interview at KCON 2013, a K-pop convention, Gaeko of Dynamic Duo expressed his delight at the popularity of their single, "BAAAM," and credited Korean pop with the group's visibility: "When we first debuted, we didn't have opportunities to perform in the States. We are here today because of all the efforts that K-pop artists have made throughout the years" (Oak 2013). Tiger JK also does not see antagonisms between the two musical styles: "I used to be against the industry. I was a young blood hating everything about it.... But I embrace it now, not in a 'I'm a godfather, I give my blessing to y'all' way, but I'm older now and being in this biz for a long time, I'm able to understand what the up and coming K-Pop kids go through. These kids are dedicated and they really work hard at it to get to where they are now" (Lena 2010). During an interview with Fuse TV, Tablo acknowledged: "If we're being put under the K-pop umbrella we're okay with that. It's not something we're not proud of or not happy about. I think K-pop is pretty cool.... A lot of people come into K-pop through [boy and girl groups] and then discover people like us and other groups. We're very grateful to them" (Sherman 2015). Many fans also are not bothered by categorizing mainstream hip-hop groups as K-pop. One fan expresses the irrelevancy of making distinctions between K-pop and Korean hip-hop: "I don't know why I still get into debates with so-called Hip Hop heads over Pop being 'real' music or not. I mean, didn't DJ Premier produce for Christina Aguilera? Don't Timberland and Justin Timberlake have a classic album together? End of conversation, suckas! But the same argument extends to our K-pop friends overseas" ("Choice 37" n.d.). Finally, the music industry operates under the premise that hip-hop is under the K-pop umbrella: There are also industry connections: "The Korean music industry in collaboration with the state has been promoting hip-hop as part of K-pop globally. The creative output of the underground hip-hop artists is an invaluable source for the industry while for fans and audiences this genre is an important component of their youth culture as a symbolic signifier of the individual and their social identity" (Um 2013, 61).

Like their "idol" counterparts, mainstream Korean rappers have also made use of technology to cultivate and maintain fan bases within and outside of Korea. Mainstream Korean hip-hop acts interact with their fans like Korean pop acts. They have a relationship with their fans, fostered by the use of social media. Song (2014) argues that Korean hip-hop artists choose to "establish themselves through other channels of media and communication, such as YouTube, Twitter, and Facebook" as well as through "club performances and tours around major cities in Korea" (137–38). In addition, Um notes that even underground rappers use the Internet to marshal fandoms through Korean portals such as Naver and Daum (Um 2013, 59). Korea hip-hop shares links not only with Korean pop but also with African American hip-hop.

Mainstream Korean Hip-hop and African American Hip-hop

In addition to links to Korean pop, Korean hip-hop draws from African American hip-hop's concern with authenticity and political and social commentary.

Authenticity figures prominently in the perception of mainstream Korean hip-hop's relationship to African American hip-hop. Korean hip-hop artists demonstrate authenticity through the rapper's lyrical prowess and rapping skill, especially in English. Jeff Greenwald (2002) argues that "lyrics stand out to many scholars and fans as *the* defining characteristic of hip-hop" (260). *XXL* magazine describes Deepflow as "decked with chopped samples and brusque commandments[,] immediately caught the attention of hardcore hip-hop heads," recognizes Beenzino for his "humorous storytelling abilities," and praises Swings for his focus on punch lines and credits him with making "the art into a sport, outshining his peers with pure wit and mad skills" ("15 Korean Rappers You Should Know That Aren't Psy" 2013). Because English is the language used by black Americans, the developers of the genre, lyrics that utilize it are deemed particularly authentic. J.-S. Lee (2004) notes that "the most striking feature of English in K-pop is the presence of AAVE [African American Vernacular English] features in song texts," which range "from a simple attention-getter for stylistic purposes to assertion of liberated self and exercise of freedom of speech" (434, 446). Sometimes English functions as an allusion to common social and political themes of traditional hip-hop. Several of the English titles of musical interludes on Epik High's *Remapping the Human Soul* (2007) refer to elements of the African American historical experience, including "Runaway," "Slave Song," and "Underground Railroad."

Epik High has produced several all-English tracks, where the lyrical skill can be evaluated using standards most English-speaking listeners could apply. "Follow the Flow" feat. MYK and D-Tox, from the 2007 album *Swan Songs*, presents a critique of those who bring a weak game to MC-ing. "Maze" feat. Dumbfoundead and MYK, from 2009's *[e]motion* (2009), is a slower tempo track with a personal meditation on life choices. Rappers also use English to invoke tropes of the urban environment that spawned hip-hop, which appeal to Korean rappers who have an urban experience in a shifting society. On the album *Map of the Human Soul* (2003), Epik High uses English to describe a relationship to the city characterized by being born there and possibly dying there in "Street Lovin' (feat. Joosuc)" (2003). English is also used to refer to common tropes in hip-hop. "Sunrise" (2004) from *High Society* (2004) riffs on social change with the phrase "the revolution will be televised," popularized by the African American spoken word artist Gil Scott-Heron's poem, "The Revolution Will Not Be Televised." Epik High uses English to dramatize its critique of the state of hip-hop in "Free Music (Tablo and Myk)" from *Map the Soul* (2009), another English-language song that criticizes rappers who take short-cuts to achieve commercial success.

Hip-hop musical arrangements also allow rappers to demonstrate their skill. In lieu of musical orchestration, Epik High's "Supreme 100" from the 2009 album *[e]nergy* features almost no music at all, save for a repeated beat that sounds like it comes from a drum machine. Against the background of ambient sounds of cars passing in the distance, Tablo performs a solo rap with an insistent flow that makes references to civil rights icons Malcolm X and Martin Luther King Jr. The ambient sounds of the street draw a sonic connection to the urban environment that produced African American hip-hop. Similarly, Dynamic Duo's "Pride (feat. Verbal Jint, Double K, The Name)" from *Taxi Driver* (2004) features an intro with no music at all, just a single rapper spitting the rhyme before the beat drops and the music begins. Even without knowing the meaning of the lyrics, the rapping dexterity is clear, and central to the identity of underground rappers and their link to black American hip-hop music: "The complex rhymes and flows . . . are essential technical and aesthetic criteria for 'serious' underground hip-hop artists. The intricate rhythmic articulation of the Korean language is highly regarded" (Um 2013, 58). Korean groups also make use of musical loops and repetition of parts of songs to draw attention to the vocal performance.

Korean hip-hop artists also demonstrate the authenticity of African American hip-hop by adopting its bold expressive form. The aesthetics of delivery reflect the harsh urban realities described by these rappers from a distinctly masculine point of view. Alastair Pennycook (2007) observes that such delivery reflects "a particular story about violence, drugs, and life in the hood, or with a belief that there is something essentially authentic in the description of brutal lifestyles." (103). Part of this aesthetic can be characterized by what Elizabeth Wheeler (1991) calls a "bad attitude," which "refuses to play by the rules of white culture, middle-class decorum, and the law. This stance often gets confused with actual violence" (198). Gangster rap comes to exemplify this delivery style, with "brutal verbal raging [that] borders on anarchy" (Perkins 1996, 19). Dynamic Duo uses this technique on "Ohae [Misunderstood] (feat. Simon D)" from *Dynamic Duo 6th Digilog 2/2* (2012), where various rappers featured on the track employ a tough rap style and rapid-fire delivery that adds edge to the track. Similarly, Dynamic Duo's "Dokjaeja (feat. Sixpoint)" from 2006's *Enlightened* contrasts a synthesizer-tinged intro with no vocals with the strong rap style of the rest of the song. When the beat drops, the instrumentation is relatively simple: a basic beat, with a second rhythm that provides interest. However, the vocal performance takes center stage, along with lots of shoutouts on the chorus. Andrew Bartlett (1994) notes: "Repetition supplies a groove within which the rap can be executed and to which the audience can dance. Balanced against deep bass repetitions are the variations which other sampled material (and the rap) supplies" (645). This occurs on Epik High's "Baegya [White Night]" from the 2007 album *Remapping the Human Soul*, which repeats the same beat and provides only minimal sonic interest with the changing strings on top of it. This focuses attention on the rap performance. Korean hip-hop artists gain a measure of authenticity when they conform to these conventions.

They also share the critical commentary of African American hip-hop. Sarah Morelli (2001) attributes a political and critical impulse to early hip-hop-influenced K-pop groups: "With their fourth album (1995), Seo Taiji and the Boys' music became even more socially and politically charged, targeting problems such as teen runaways and political corruption" (251). Tablo, leader of the respected hip-hop group Epik High, formed in 2001, recalls: "Most songs aren't censored because of language. There are no cuss words or bad words. But if we talk about a social issue, we get censored" ("Censors Attempted to Silence Hip Hop Group" 2007).

Interestingly, the very connection to African American hip-hop and authenticity leads to some tension within the world of Korean hip-hop. Some Korean underground hip-hop artists see the quest for widespread appeal as antithetical to the pursuit of authenticity. Song (2014) adds that underground rappers see their position outside of mainstream music as a "sphere of artistic creativity and freedom whereas the mainstream symbolizes a contested space of conformity and commercialism" (137). The lack of commercial success may suggest greater authenticity to some. Others see certain musical aesthetics, such as the presence of rapid-fire raps, or political and social commentary as the only characteristics of true hip-hop music. However, some of the more eclectic mainstream Korean hip-hop artists engage in more variety. "Hip-hop has a lot of styles. Especially now, there's no genre involved at all. Everything is free-flowing. There are no barriers. Everything is inter-changeable. I just prefer to label ourselves as just, you know, a bunch of guys that do music" (S. Kim 2011). Tablo ascribes to a perception of hip-hop music defined by the notion of fusion and transformation. It is that transformative impulse that Tablo affirms, which may conflict with more sociohistorical modes of hip-hop.

Given their ties to African American hip-hop, mainstream Korean hip-hop artists also engage in other aspects of the black popular music tradition.

Intertextuality and the R&B Tradition: Dynamic Duo, Epik High, Primary

Korean hip-hop acts emulate the R&B tradition through vocals and sampling, and enhance it by incorporating eclectic music strategies, a hallmark of Korean music production.

Citing the "Old School": Dynamic Duo

Dynamic Duo cites the "old school" through samples of distinctive R&B instrumentation and the use of Korean R&B vocalists.

Dynamic Duo consists of Gaeko (Kim Yoon-sung) and Choiza (Choi Jae-ho). Before forming the group, both were members of the hip-hop group CBMASS, which released three albums between 2000 and 2003: *MassMediah* (2000), *Massmatics* (2001), and *Massappeal* (2003). Gaeko and Choiza formed Dynamic Duo in 2004 and released their debut album, *Taxi Driver* (2004), followed by *Double Dynamite* in 2005. The duo went on to release *Enlightened* (2007), *Heartbreaker* (2007), and *Last Days* (2008). After completing their military service in 2009, they released *Band of Dynamic Brothers* (2009), *Dynamicduo 6th Digilog1/2* (2011), *Dynamicduo 6th Digilog 2/2* (2012), *Lucky Numbers* (2013), *Grand Carnival* (2015). Along with their partners, the duo established the Amoeba Culture label in 2006. Dynamic Duo captures the creative impulse of hip-hop in the mission of their label through the symbol of the amoeba: "The single-celled amoeba. It began reinventing modes of convention through its own creativity and imagination. Positive energy fueled this innovation to create a new kind of culture. Amoeba Culture strives to continue our efforts in always creating new ideas and positive energy for the further growth and spread of good music and culture" (*Amoeba Culture* n.d.). With such a long career, the duo are considered veterans of Korean hip-hop.

Dynamic Duo cites black American popular music by drawing on R&B's "old school." Joanna Demers (2006) defines "old school" as a "soul repertoire" consisting of "an elite collection of soul, funk and R&B for their samples, from artists such as James Brown, Curtis Mayfield, Isaac Hayes and George Clinton" (41). "Old school" can also refer to the notion of "back in the day," "a somewhat romantic reference to a time before hip-hop music became popular. The old school refers to a more close-knit community of breakdancers, DJs, MCs and graffiti artists who helped nurture and develop hip-hop as a culture, and who were not necessarily concerned with making money" (McLeod 1999, 143–44). Hip-hop music often engages in "old school" sonic references through the use of samples. Sampling emerged at the dawn of hip-hop music, when DJs isolated the best portions of music and played them on a loop, thereby creating new sonic experiences and dance opportunities for partygoers. Bartlett (1994) notes: "The art of digital sampling in (primarily) African American hip hop is intricately connected to an African American/African diasporic aesthetic which carefully selects available media, texts, and contexts for performative use" (639). Using technology, DJs could then "exploit an infinite number of samples from vinyl, advertising, jingles, television sitcom themes, and movie soundtracks. It is sampling and mixing that gives rap music its self-renewing character" (Perkins 1996, 8). This practice also gave hip-hop practitioners access to older R&B genres: "Samples, especially those taken from records released in the 1970s, often have distinct timbral qualities that distinguish them from more recent digital recordings. These include the compression and distortion common to analog recording, which is often favorably contrasted with the 'crispness' of digital" (Schloss 2004, 70–71).

By sampling music that embodies a particular meaning or references a particular sound, Korean hip-hop artists participate in both archiving and intertextuality, making the practice an aesthetic one: "*Working* the turntables . . . is not far removed from the lofty plateau of *musicianship*, from which sampling is often looked down upon as unoriginal" (Bartlett 1994, 647). Korean hip-hop, like its African American counterpart, engages various genres of R&B in this way. Jae Chong, producer for Korean group Aziatix, "feels that the classic '80s and '90s formula of rhythm, melody, and lyrics is what U.S. hip-hop lacks today" ("Korean Hip-Hop: K-Hop Goes Global" 2012).

Dynamic Duo cites the "old school" through samples of R&B instrumentation. The music for Anita Ward's disco hit "Ring My Bell" (1979) provides the backdrop for Dynamic Duo's raucous rapping on its track with the same name from the 2004 album *Taxi Driver*. Ward's original track from her 1979 album *Songs of Love* features a complex bass line that contrasts with the electric guitar and bell embellishments. Dynamic Duo enhances the rhythm in their version. Rather than just lifting the fundamental elements of the song, the duo makes the rhythm even more prominent. The addition of their raps as well as vocals sung by Na-ul of the Korean R&B group Brown Eyed Soul changes how the song sounds. The inclusion of a male vocal that engages in vocal ornamentation provides a contrast to Ward's sweet voice in the original. The song also samples Ward's lilting voice from the original chorus. While Dynamic Duo's "Ring My Bell" benefits from the uptempo dance rhythm, their sample from Player's hit song "Baby Come Back" from the 1977 album *Player* for "Rewriting the Résumé" from *Enlightened* (2007) depends on a slower tempo. Player's original song has a slower tempo and begins with sparser instrumentation dependent on off-beat phrasing of the rhythm. The mellow verse contrasts to the prominence of the electric guitar on the chorus, which Dynamic Duo samples. Dynamic Duo takes the iconic guitar riff from the song's chorus and repeats it through the song. This looped musical phrase with a simple rhythm gives more focus to the rap.

In addition to instrumentation, Dynamic Duo cites "old school" R&B vocals using Korean R&B singers. The choruses of their songs are often sung, providing an aural contrast to the rapping that occurs during the verses. Vocals are also used as accents during the verses as well. This strategy is also used in R&B rap, which Dawn M. Norfleet (2006) notes "was characterized by sung refrains, often with female voices, high melismatic nasal vocal riffs (as opposed to the full-throated gospel-styled singing of 1970s R&B), harmonized choruses, and street-influenced 'attitude'" (364). The choice of R&B vocals can affect the overall feeling of the song. Sometimes, Gaeko of Dynamic Duo will supply R&B vocals for songs. Both "Guilty" from *Band of Dynamic Brothers* (2009) and "Without You" from *Dynamic Duo 6th Digilog 2/2* (2012) are mid-tempo mellow tracks that features Gaeko's soulful vocals that contrast with Choiza's rapping. "Guilty" features vocal ornamentation during the intro against the backdrop of acoustic guitar and other natural instruments and returns for the chorus, which is entirely sung. "Without You" also begins with vocal ornamentation which transitions into the chorus where Gaeko's vocals are complemented by backing vocal. Other times, Dynamic Duo makes use of Korean R&B vocalists with distinctive voices in songs that range from ballads to dance tracks. The slower tempo track "Let's Not Despair" from *Enlightened* (2007) features more aggressive rap on the verses, contrasting the strong female vocal provided by Ah-rom of the Bubble Sisters, backed by fuller vocal harmony with an R&B quality. Dynamic Duo also makes use of a group of vocalists, as with "Happy Day" from *Enlightened* (2007), which features Heritage, the Korean mass choir discussed in Chapter 3 with the inclusion of a musical phrase from the gospel song "Oh Happy Day." Sung by the Edwin Hawkins Singers and Mahalia Jackson, the gospel standard features a call-and-response structure. In addition to Heritage's predominantly female voices, the song also features a lone female vocal and smaller group harmonization on the verses, thus providing variety in the use of R&B vocals. It also incorporates gospel instrumentation, such as gospel-inflected organ and guitar, and culminates in the use of the mass choir singing the chorus. The harmony of the group female voices provides a contrasting fuller sound compared to the solo rapping by the male voices on the verses.

While Dynamic Duo cites familiar R&B genres through sampling and the use of R&B vocals, other mainstream Korean hip-hop acts utilize R&B and hip-hop musical elements in ways that seem far removed from hip-hop.

Musical Eclecticism: Epik High and Primary

While Dynamic Duo draws on familiar sources of hip-hop, other mainstream Korean hip-hop artists utilize musical strategies that may seem strange within the context of hip-hop. Epik High's penchant for remixes and tendency to use non-R&B vocalists in hip-hop tracks make for an interesting career. Similarly, hip-hop producer Primary uses a variety of R&B instrumentation to create his signature sound.

One of the most visible mainstream Korean hip-hop groups, Epik High began its career as an underground group and worked with CBMASS, which included members of Dynamic Duo. Made up of Tablo (Lee Seon-woong), Mithra Jin (Choi Jin), and DJ Tukutz (Kim Jeong-sik), Epik High performed with underground hip-hop artists in Korea before joining Woollim Entertainment and releasing its first album *Map of the Human Soul* in 2003, followed by *High Society* in 2004. Epik High's reputation for being a successful hip-hop group emerged in the wake of 2005's *Swan Songs*, which produced hits for the group, including the tracks "Fly" and "Paris." 2007's *Remapping the Human Soul* contained more serious subject matter, drawing the attention of Korean censors. Epik High's next few releases, *Pieces, Part One* (2008) and *Lovescream* (2008), continued to bolster their popularity. Upon the expiration of the group's contract in 2009, Epik High left Woollim Entertainment to establish Map the Soul, an independent record label, mirroring Dynamic Duo's quest to make music in an artist-controlled environment. Under this label, Epik High released *Map the Soul* (2009), a project rather than an Epik High album; *[e]* (2009), consisting of 2CDs, *[e]motion* and *[e]nergy*; and *Epilogue* (2010). During the hiatus of the group where various members completed their military service, Tablo signed with YG Entertainment for solo work in 2011, followed by the other members of the group in 2012. Since that time, the group has released 99 (2012), *Shoebox* (2014), *We've Done Something Wonderful* (2017), and *Sleepless In* ____ (2019). In 2015, Tablo founded the independent label HIGHGRND under YG Entertainment. The sub-label features an eclectic roster that extends hip-hop's innovative impulse: "While [K-pop] remains the predominant genre, you'll also find rapper[s], R&B crooners, electronic experimentalists and Soulful singers among the mix. From the retrofantastic Karaoke-perfect Black Skirts, to the mellow indie-band Kyukoh [*sic*], to impressive flow of rappers Code Kunst and Incredivle, HIGHGRND is a base for all things Korean—music wise—that in our opinion, is redefining the genres synonymous with the country they come from" (Lendrum 2017). In 2017 Tablo stepped down as CEO to focus on Epik High activities.

Epik High enhances the black popular music tradition through an eclecticism that includes sampling, use of female vocals, mixes and the use of different genres that are not the norm in hip-hop. The group offers a wide range of sounds, sometimes making their tracks hard to categorize within hip-hop music, especially hip-hop solely defined by socially relevant lyrics and samples. Some have criticized certain groups who deviate from "the message" and practice a similar eclecticism. Groups like Digable Planets, The Roots, and the hip-hop collective Native Tongues, which included the Jungle Brothers, De La Soul, A Tribe Called Quest, and others, often fail to make it into histories of hip-hop. They share a tendency toward experimentation, expanding the borders of hip-hop through the incorporation of different genres, production techniques, and aesthetic strategies. Shawn Taylor (2007) explains that the Native Tongues' approach was exemplified in De La Soul's album *3 Feet High and Rising* (1989), which provided "a kaleidoscopic, dayglow era" for hip-hop: "Instead of adhering to the fat gold chains, rampant misogyny, gunplay and virulent bandwagonism of the late 1980s hip-hop scene, De La urged their listeners to operate from a position of radical individuality, self-confidence and self-respect, regardless of how out-there people may consider you" (8). Similarly, A Tribe Called Quest focused on the sound, becoming known for their obscure samples: "They steered away from the ubiquitous funk and old-school soul samples of their fellow Tongue members and embraced rock and roll and jazz . . . They were socially relevant, proudly black and whimsical, quirky and confident" (S. Taylor 2007, 9). Such aesthetic choices opened up new vistas for hip-hop. It was this quirkiness that made these acts stand out.

Consequently, such eclecticism is also part of the hip-hop aesthetic. While American hip-hop groups favored sampling from 1970s funk and soul as part of an archiving project of black experience, such actions were always motivated by the quest for a new sound. According to Schloss (2004), sampling's significance is in the wide range of musical traditions it mined: "The authenticity they seek has less to do with ethnic and political identity than with professional and artistic pride.... Certain musical gestures are valued for aesthetic reasons, and one's adherence to this aesthetic confers authenticity.... The significance tends to lie more in the ingenuity of the way the elements are fused together than in calling attention to the diversity of their origins" (64, 66). Schloss (2004) reminds us that hip-hop music practitioners frequently sampled breaks from rock songs, "in spite of their origins in the putatively white rock world" (64). Hip-hop has also sampled from as far afield as classical music. Afrika Bambaataa's use of a fragment of Stravinsky's "Firebird" in "Planet Rock" as captured within the Fairlight Computer Musical Instrument (ORCH5) represents the first sample of classical and "played perfectly into an Afro-futurist cultural project" that "provides a key imaginative linkage to the house and techno music that the Zulu Nation pioneer claimed as the logical consequence of his 'electrifying' hip-hop" (Fink 2005, 350). Sampling is a key element of hip-hop, and the more eclectic the sample the better. Sampling obscure musical snippets or invoking other musical genres results from "digging the crates" or "digging," "the process of acquiring rare, usually out-of-print, vinyl records for sampling purposes" (Schloss 2004, 79). When mainstream Korean hip-hop groups like Epik High invoke eclectic music strategies, such musical experimentation functions "to educate producers about styles of music with which they may not be familiar.... This benefit can accrue with regard to not only genres, but also more specific strategies and approaches to music making" (Schloss 2004, 95). To this end, Epik High expands its parameters by invoking different musical styles and being equally eclectic.

Since nothing is off-limits, Epik High feels free to venture into other genres of music through experimentation with other genres in remixes. The group uses live instrumentation in its remix of "Paris (feat. Jisun of Loveholic)" from *Swan Songs* (2005) to drastically change the nature of the song. The original track opens with Jisun's distorted vocal and simple guitar instrumentation. When the beat drops, the rap starts against the backdrop of an upbeat, poppy rhythm. However, the beginning of the remix, which appears on the repackage *Black Swan Songs* (2006), opens with a dramatic instrumentation that builds suspense with the rapped chorus coming first, followed by a raucous burst of rhythm from a live drum set. The use of live instruments creates more space, making the sounds echo and highlighting the staccato rap. Here, Jisun's vocal is an oasis within the chaos created by the instrumentation and rap. Similarly, the original version of "One" feat. Jisun of Loveholic from *Pieces, Part One*

(2008) has a 1980s pop sound, with a cheerful synthesizer and a steady beat that encourages the crowd to dance. The instrumentation complements the quick flow of both Tablo and Mithra. Jisun's rock vocals also underscore the pop nature of the song, where the beat drops out then floats back up with whispers of the rappers. When reviewing the album, fan reviewer Yeeun (2008) notes that "Jisun's voice always sounds great with the rough texture of the guys' voices." However, "One (Planet Shiver Mix)" from the same album takes the song into electronic dance music territory with a four-on-the-floor beat, electronic effects, and far fewer vocals. Tablo repeats words in a monotone until the introduction of the melody of the original song bubbles up to the forefront, finally resolving in the same dance beat with just a portion of Jisun's vocals. Planet Shiver, an electronic dance music duo on Amoeba Culture, has not only provided mixes for Amoeba Culture artists, but has frequently provided an eclectic array of remixes of Epik High songs, creating a nexus between electronic dance music and hip-hop. Epik High is conscious of its musical eclecticism, for the subtitle for the album states: "No genres. Just music."

In addition to remixes, Epik High also demonstrates eclecticism through its use of vocals that go beyond the R&B genre. Epik High's frequent use of female vocals, unique in a genre where women artists are not plentiful, represents yet another manifestation of the group's innovation. Epik High uses non-R&B vocalists on a variety of tracks that sometimes push the boundaries of traditional hip-hop. "Umbrella" from *Pieces, Part One* (2008) features Younha, a well-known singer who does not sing R&B. Her vocals open the track, complementing the sound of rain and the lone plaintive piano. The structure delays the entrance of the rap and makes the track seem more like a traditional pop song in structure. This mid-tempo song uses natural instruments, and the vocals take most of the space on the chorus. The rap style is more mellow, complementing the lilting quality of Younha's voice. Conversely, Park Ji-yoon, another non-R&B singer, lends her vocal in a higher register to Epik High's song "Gift" from the 2009 album *[e]motion*. This track features a faster tempo and jazz-like percussion complemented by syncopated bass and high-hat cymbals. The rapid but soft rap style echoes the constant rhythm played out on cymbals. "My Ghetto" from *High Society* (2009) hearkens more toward older hip-hop in its use of a hard-hitting rap style and a sample that sounds like the guitar riff from Daryl Hall and John Oates' "Sara Smile" from the duo's 1975 self-titled album. The track features Kim Yeon-woo, a male artist who does not delve into the R&B genre, on the chorus. A versatile vocalist, he has worked with the South Korean group Toy, a group that also included You Hee-yeol, perhaps best known as the host of *You Hee-yeol's Sketchbook* and who has produced music in a wide array of music genres. Kim is a strong singer who tends not to employ ornamentation commonly found with R&B vocals. His inclusion is unique in that hip-hop tracks rarely feature male non-R&B singers. "My Ghetto" shows that Epik High maintains its links to older forms of hip-hop while enhancing it with different vocal choices.

While Epik High reflects the eclecticism of hip-hop, Primary (Choi Donghoon), a music producer on Dynamic Duo's label Amoeba Culture, brings us full circle in the way he deploys a more traditional R&B instrumentation in a variety of contexts. After attending the Seoul Jazz Academy and collaborating with Dynamic Duo, Primary participated in the *Primary Skool* project in 2006, introducing the iconic box that he wears on his head during performances and in videos. In 2011, Primary produced Supreme Team's contribution to an album dedicated to legendary African American producer Quincy Jones. The track was also performed during Jones's visit to Korea. Afterward, he released a series as Primary and the Messengers, which included collaborations with Dynamic Duo, Zion.T, Garion, Jinsil of Mad Soul Child, E-Sens, and Dok2: *Primary and the Messengers Part 1* (2011), *Part 2* (2012), *Part 3* (2012), *Part 4* (2012), and culminating with *Primary and the Messengers LP* (2012). After releasing *Lucky You* in 2015, Primary began a second series which included *2–1* (2015), *2–2* (2015), and *2–3* (2015), culminating in the album *2* (2015). This project was followed by several mini-albums, including *Shininryu* (2017), *Pop* (2017), and *Do Worry Be Happy* (2018).

It is perhaps his jazz background that drives Primary's tendency to invoke R&B genres through live instrumentation, which to some appears to be antithetical to hip-hop. Some see sampling as so central to hip-hop that live instrumentation is sometimes viewed as inauthentic, equating sampling to hip-hop's "firstborn child" (Marshall 2006, 868). This tension drives critiques of hip-hop groups like The Roots, calling the group's authenticity into question for its use of live instrumentation: "The Roots' basic configuration as a live band, often without the audible presence of a DJ or samples, still compromises—according to commonplace, if purist, notions of authenticity—their ability to produce 'real' hip-hop. Whereas a group such as Gang Starr automatically gains credibility by virtue of being a DJ/MC duo (i.e., a classic hip-hop combo), the Roots' lack of a DJ, and the sounds associated with DJ practice and vinyl sources, represents an inherent obstacle to their authenticity" (Marshall 2006, 871). However, hip-hop has a legacy of live instrumentation. While many focused on the explosive emergence of gangster rap, the West Coast hip-hop artists also distinguished themselves from their East Coast counterparts through the use of live instrumentation. Artists like Dr. Dre used few samples and recorded live musicians for his game-changing album *The Chronic* (1992). Marshall (2006) notes that a group like The Roots embodies "many of hip-hop's distinctive sonic features," including "two-to-four-bar funk riffs and jazz progressions that hip-hop producers were sampling at the time" (871). Moreover, ?uestlove reveals a tradition of live instrumentation in hip-hop, citing hip-hop veterans like Afrika Bambaataa, whose groundbreaking track "Planet Rock" does not technically sample Kraftwerk's "Trans-Europe Express": "The Kraftwerk melody was replayed rather than sampled—*interpolated*, to use the current legalese—by studio hand and producer Arthur Baker, though other elements in the song, particularly some percussion loops, are samples" (Marshall 2006, 874). Moreover, Jeff Greenwald (2002) argues for the centrality of live instrumentation in light of the reliance on rhythm: "The drums in hip-hop serve an important role; they not only establish the groove and emphasize vocal style, but they also act as a cultural signifier. The incorporation of various drumming sounds and styles (including scratching) into hip-hop adds breadth and variety to the music beyond lyrical content. The drums in hip-hop define the music as much as any other element, musical or extramusical" (270).

Primary's work invokes this reliance on live instrumentation even as he works with a variety of artists. He has worked with hip-hop groups such as Dynamic Duo and Epik High as well as members from pop groups like Mamamoo and AOA and indie groups like Hyukoh. To all of his projects, he brings a forward-thinking R&B sensibility. Primary frequently makes use of synthesizers and keyboards to produce a funky sound, such as for "High End Girl" from *Primary and the Messengers* (2012), a mid-tempo track that opens with nineties-era synthesizer complemented by bass and highlighted with electronic accents. There are no vocals for sixteen bars, making the listener think it could be an instrumental. It functions like an extended musical dance break that earlier hip-hop practitioners created using two turntables. As the track continues, the rhythm changes by the pre-chorus, increasing in off-beat phrasing. While this track utilize keyboards to provide the driving rhythm, other songs utilize horns for sonic interest, illustrating Primary's "old school organic band sound" (Rhythm.Connection 2013). "2 Weeks" from the same 2012 album bursts forth in a flurry of sound and a rhythm from the 1960s. The verses feature this rhythm, accented by organ keyboards, but the chorus surprises with the inclusion of James Brown-esque horns.

While his R&B instrumentation is consistent, Primary changes it up by using a variety of vocalists. Fan reviewers note how Primary uses uncommon vocalists for his tracks, pairing non-R&B singers with an R&B instrumentation: "What I really appreciate about Primary's music is how well he is able to showcase the talents of singers and rappers he works with and yet each song maintains an essence and quality that is easily identifiable with him as an artist" ("First Listen—Primary" 2015). Saivickna (2015) notes that Primary features singer Kim Bum-soo for the R&B track "See You": "It has a soul-funk which compliments Kim Bum Soo's vocals tremendously. Kim Bum Soo has traditionally been a ballad singer but his voice works so well with this track I honestly think he should stick [to] this genre."

Primary and Epik High demonstrate the sonic diversity within mainstream Korean hip-hop music, thereby enhancing the R&B tradition. In addition to exhibiting musical intertextuality, mainstream Korean hip-hop artists also cite the visuals of African American hip-hop music videos.

Limiting and Liberating Performance: Jay Park and Yoon Mi-rae

Like their "idol" counterparts, male and female mainstream Korean hip-hop artists cite different performative elements from African American popular music in their music videos. Korean American hip-hop artist Jay Park invokes both a playful male swagger as well as reductive images of women drawn from African American hip-hop videos. Conversely, veteran hip-hop artist Yoon Mi-rae cites tropes drawn from black female rappers that promote female agency.

For all of hip-hop's musical creativity, innovation, and influence, its music videos have also received their fair share of criticism. While early hip-hop videos attempted to visualize the wide realities of urban black American life, they also became known for aggressive images of black men and sexualized images of black women. Harris (1999) points to hip-hop fashion as, in part, a strategy of aggression: "The multilayered, oversized clothing, the bandanas, and the baggy pants revealing boxers are fashionably aggressive in their appropriation of 'street' and *couture*, celebrating the accoutrement of prison and gang culture with the sophistication and timeliness of *pret-a-porter*" (66). In her study, Marquita Marie Gammage (2015) finds that "Black female characters in popular rap music videos are reduced to hyper-sexual commodities.... Black women's bodies are used to sell sex, promote a wealthy lifestyle, and illustrate how a man with money can buy anything including human beings" (49). This is something that Railton and Watson (2011) say happens differently for black women in music videos: "White women are defined by sexual sublimity in direct contrast to the presumed hypersexuality of black women. On the other hand, black women's 'hypersexuality' is seen to derive from a series of apparently natural traits that link them to the anima, the primitive and the 'dirty'" (94).

The music videos of Jay Park embody at least two ways that mainstream Korean hip-hop artists cite African American performance. On one hand, Park adds hip-hop swagger to the "boy next door" in the 2013 music video for "Joah"

("박재범 Jay Park '좋아 Joah'" 2013). This is possible because Park also enjoys a reputation as an R&B singer. Taylor Glasby (2018) says that "Park combines restless creativity with a remarkable ear for a hook and a propensity to swerve lanes, traversing dark beats to smooth R&B to tongue-in-cheek pop." The video opens with a wide shot of an urban skyline by a large body of water on a nice day. Scenes of people in a bustling city are intercut with close-ups of Park, who wears a casual yet hip-hop-inspired outfit: red wool hat, red backpack, denim jacket, and red and white plaid shirt. This is just one of several casual outfits he sports that also have hip-hop fashion touches, like gold necklaces, bracelets, and athletic shoes. Park's numerous tattoos are virtually unseen. The video is filled with scenarios where Park flirts with a girl as they walk down the street and sit by the water. She is also wearing casual clothes, just a white T-shirt and jeans in one shot. Park's visual choices hearken to black pop R&B of the 1980s like New Edition's 1984 video for "Cool It Now" ("New Edition—Cool It Now" 2009). New Edition's music video is also set in an urban setting, taking place largely around a basketball court. It also involves pursing a girl in a cute, flirtatious way. While the styling is dated, Park's video is identifiably African American, down to the gold chains and streetwear, which he sports in an updated way. Rap is prominently featured in the song and video. Both Park and New Edition's videos have a pop sensibility.

On the other hand, Park's 2015 video "Mommae" ("박재범 Jay Park—몸매 (MOMMAE)" 2015) features many of the oversexualized images of women that have emerged in hip-hop video. The video opens with a tight shot on a speaker and quickly transitions to a close-up of Park in a red cap and a sleeveless plaid shirt, one of several styling changes that include a fur coat and athletic outfits. A group of Asian women wear white chunky heels, camouflage shirts over crop tops, and what appears to be denim thongs over pink panties that barely cover their bottoms as they lounge provocatively on the floor. These scenes are intercut with other scenes where scantily clad women surround a shirtless Park. In this video, Park showcases his plentiful tattoos. Women hang on Park while he lounges in bed. At other points of the video, Park and his male friends, who are all clothed, lounge around in a game room while Park eats sushi off the lower back of a woman. This is the kind of hypersexualization in black American music videos that the respondents in Gammage's (2015) study note: "This costuming of Black females as sexually revealing, explicit, and provocative is thus the demeaning and devaluing costuming of women, while men remain fully clothed" (45–46). The women in the Park video exist solely for the pleasure of the men. Because there is no primary protagonist among them, all of the women function as supporting actors, sometimes called "video vixens" in hip-hop videos, women who are presented "as affirmations of a male rapper's hypersexualized manhood" and "have never been defined by nonsexual traits nor represented as anything other than sexual objects and property in this genre of visual fantasy" (Balaji 2010, 9). The Asian women in Park's music video have very little agency and conform to stereotypes of black womanhood frequently found in hip-hop videos. Park consistently cites from both black pop and hip-hop performance in his music videos.

Conversely, Yoon Mi-rae draws from black female rappers in her videos, which often include more liberating tropes. She is a biracial, American-born Korean female rapper (with an African American father and a Korean mother) and R&B singer who has been active in Korea since her debut in 1997. While she has had a long career in Korean hip-hop, she remains one of only handful of successful women rappers, much like the early days of African American hip-hop. Even as early African American hip-hop was dominated by black men, these female rappers used the form to tell their own stories or show that they had just as much skill as the men. Most of the early innovators of hip-hop in the United States were men until the appearance of Roxanne. Some crews featured a female MC, like MC Sha Rock with the Funky Four Plus One. In 1984 Roxanne Shante burst on to the scene with "Roxanne's Revenge" (1988), a diss track that entered into the male-dominated genre. In 1988 MC Lyte became the first solo female rapper to release a full album, *Lyte as a Rock*. Queen Latifah became one of the most popular female rappers as a result of hits like 1993's "U.N.I.T.Y." While they rapped about similar themes, these female rappers also took up issues that uniquely affected women. In addition, female vocalists emerged in hip-hop to sing the hook on rap songs. One popular example is Method Man's "You're All I Need" featuring Mary J. Blige (1994). However, they also introduced a different aesthetic due to the nature of their voices.

Yoon Mi-rae presents a different kind of performance citation compared to the women in Park's "Mommae" video, drawing on the legacy of black American female rappers. Her "Black Happiness" is a visual celebration of her biraciality ("[MV] Yoonmirae (윤미래)—Black Happiness" 2015). The music video opens with black-and-white footage of a birthday party framed by a camera lens, followed by a montage of pictures of Yoon Mi-rae as a little girl. She wears a variety of outfits during the video, including a black, off-the-shoulder pantsuit, a chain necklace with a medallion so common in 1990s hip-hop, dangling earrings, and a striped sleeveless turtleneck sweater with baggy jeans and athletic shoes. For the sung chorus, the video shifts to a black background with overlapping images of her under moving black and white lighting that creates soft shadows, wind effects, and slow motion. Many of these images centralize her identity, drawing connections with her past and emphasizing everyday life.

They are reminiscent of videos by Queen Latifah (Dana Owens), known for her empowering videos of African American women. Latifah was distinguished in the 1990s hip-hop scene by her empowering lyrics and music videos that complemented that message, such as "U.N.I.T.Y" (1993) and "Ladies First" (1989). However, Latifah's music videos also reflected a love for community and black culture. The music video for the 1993 song "Just Another Day" ("Queen Latifah—Just Another Day" 2010), also shot in black and white, shows images of everyday black urban life with people enjoying themselves in a celebration of black life despite the incursions of violence, much like Yoon Mi-rae's video.

Even when Yoon Mi-rae's style turns more pointed, as in the 2018 music video for "Kawibawibo" ("[MV] Yoonmirae (윤미래)—KawiBawiBo" 2018), it still reflects strategies drawn from African American female rappers. The video opens with images of riots and violence projected on an abandoned apartment building. The silhouetted figure of Yoon Mi-rae sits in front, wearing urban wear that includes a pair of Adidas, a gold chain, black hat, black tracksuit, and red lipstick. Other scenes feature her with bright purple braids and a blue and white tracksuit. The backup dancers wear a variety of outfits, all of which conform to an urban hip-hop aesthetic. Most have on leggings, crop tops, or T-shirts with jackets or sweatshirts. Others have on shorts that do not reveal much and athletic shoes. All of them have on loose-fitting clothes. Other scenes show the dancers standing behind Yoon Mi-rae with upraised fists. Her video shows the kind of female agency missing from Park's "Mommae," and drawn from black female rappers, for Rana Emerson (2002) notes that a sample of videos by black women performers "demonstrates the significance of verbal assertiveness. Speaking out and speaking one's mind are a constant theme. Through the songs and videos, Black women are able to achieve voice and a space for spoken expression of social interpersonal commentary" (126). Even without knowing the lyrics, the video makes visual allusions to protest through the projected videos on the buildings and Yoon Mi-rae's use of the raised fist. She accomplishes this without objectifying her backup dancers, but bringing them into the critique as they raise their fists too.

Korean mainstream hip-hop artists cite African American popular music and performance. In doing so, they participate in a globalized R&B tradition.

Global R&B and Musical Innovation

Many associate hip-hop exclusively with political and social commentary. Because acts under the K-pop umbrella are typically not associated with social movements, their connection to hip-hop is questioned. However, because they carry on hip-hop's innovative musical legacy, mainstream Korean hip-hop artists can be seen as heirs to a global R&B tradition.

Some associate hip-hop aesthetics solely with social or political commentary. Using a sociological lens, they point to early practitioners of the form in the United States who used rap to articulate the plight of American blacks in urban areas in the late 1970s. During that time, boroughs like the Bronx in New York City were high crime areas with few economic opportunities, poor relations with law enforcement, and rampant drug use and distribution. Grandmaster Flash and the Furious Five's 1982 single "The Message" represents an important example of commentary-based hip-hop that provided a window into the rough conditions experienced by urban blacks from their point of view. This track created a major trajectory in hip-hop music that would be expanded by later groups. Michael Eric Dyson (2004) notes that with the political impulse of hip-hop, "rap began to describe and analyze the social, economic, and political factors that led to its emergence and development: drug addiction, police brutality, teen pregnancy, and various forms of material deprivation." On the East Coast, Public Enemy emerged, whom Jeff Chang (2005) notes produced an art that "would always belie easy sociology." The track "You're Gonna Get Yours" pays homage to a 1998 Oldsmobile and "was also about facing down racial profiling with Black posse power, an act of defiance set within the historical context of Robert Moses' expressway-fueled segregation and Levittown's racial covenants" (231–32). On the West Coast, N.W.A drew attention to the political ramifications of the 1980s: "It wasn't hard for them to notice that the streets were changing. The effects of Reagan's southern hemisphere foreign policy were coming home, making millionaires of Contra entrepreneurs, illegal arms dealers and Freeway Rick" (Chang 2005, 302). These political and economic circumstances spurred a more aggressive style of hip-hop aimed at reportage and critique: "It was as if NWA overturned transnational pop culture like a police car, gleefully set the offending thing on fire, then popped open some forties, and danced to their own murder rap" (Chang 2005, 321). As a result, politically inflected hip-hop becomes the standard, even when hip-hop began to travel globally. Tony Mitchell (2001) notes that rap and hip-hop "are also used in different local contexts to espouse the causes of ethnic minorities . . . and to make political statements about local racial, sexual, employment, and class issues" (10). Hip-hop's critical function appeals globally, drawing those in other countries to articulate their opinions about their own societies. Political engagement becomes a primary element for authenticity in hip-hop.

As a result, failure to exhibit political and social commentary or present an aggressive persona causes some to question a Korean hip-hop artist's authenticity. For example, responses to Epik High's signing with YG Entertainment in 2012 were mixed. Despite YG Entertainment's role in developing early hip-hop acts like Masta Wu, 1TYM, and Jinusean, fans were skeptical because of the agency's development of "idols." K-pop media outlet *seoulbeats* described the use of Park Bom, member of YG's female "idol" group 2NE1, on the title track of 99 (2012), Epik High's first album under YG Entertainment, as a "pointless contribution": "I'm not against Park Bom singing *per se*, but I'm all against YG throwing her into songs by her labelmates for a random (screeched) sentence" ("How Epik Is Epik High's Comeback?" 2012). Another fan sensed a change from earlier Epik High material: "In the past the rest of their album was always packed with deep, passionate and meaningful songs. In '99' however, 90% of the album's songs are exactly the same as the title tracks: poppy and absolutely meaningless" ("R.I.P Epik High 2003–2012 [RANT]" 2012). Both fans describe Epik High's music as meaningless when it does not conform to the expectations of hip-hop grounded in political or social commentary.

Moreover, political commentary also fuels a particular kind of delivery and hip-hop persona. Deviating from it could also bring charges of inauthenticity. Despite being a major figure in Korean hip-hop for decades, Drunken Tiger's 2013 album *The Cure*, the group's ninth, was negatively critiqued for being too emotional, reflecting Tiger JK's personal experiences with illness and the loss of this father: "The dominant theme in *The Cure* is holding onto optimism in the face of hardship and misery. We've seen this message so many times, especially in school, very special episodes of (insert sitcom name here), greeting cards, and on motivational posters, that it loses its ability to compel us, especially in songs without a solid musical backbone. Of the nine tracks on the album, the best are the ones about going H.A.M., not taking heart" ("Drunken Tiger Loses Some bite with 'The Cure'" 2013). This reviewer uses aggression as a defining criterion of authenticity.

The same critique may be leveled if artists find popularity with mainstream audiences. When acts become popular, they run the risk of being perceived as "selling out": "Because the hip-hop community is very protective of its artists, it quickly rejects those considered to be inauthentic, as determined by a number of factors: overexposure by the mainstream media, smiling in photographs, or appearances in certain types of commercials. All of these actions could be perceived as 'selling out,' or abandoning one's street alliances" (Norfleet 2006, 364). "Selling out" is not just about monetary success, but also about relinquishing the role of critique embodied in hip-hop's oppositional stance to the mainstream. Kembrew McLeod (1999) notes that "selling out" results in "the distancing of an artist's music and persona from an independently owned network of distribution (the underground) and repositioning oneself within a music business culture dominated by the big five multinational corporations that control the U.S. music industry" (141, 142).

However, defining hip-hop solely by particular political commentary or expression reduces its complexity, resulting in a limited mode of authenticity. John L. Jackson (2005) writes that restrictive modes of authenticity "can be both 'too tightly scripted' and corrosively mobilized to make social differences appear absolute and natural.... These scripts provide guidelines for proper and improper behavior, for legitimate and illegitimate group membership, for social inclusion or ostracism" (13). When some listeners insist that the only legitimate form of hip-hop music is politically inflected and aggressive, they subscribe to a reductive kind of script. Emery Petchauer (2009) adds that "most commercial media representations of hip-hop portray it as a narrow musical genre synonymous with rap music," a tendency that tends to "eclipse the variety of hip-hop musical and thematic genres past and present" (946–47). Perry (2004) warns, "It is quite dangerous for the critic or listener to interpret [hip-hop] purely as a reflection of social and political conditions, without thought to the presence of artistic choice in every narrative and composition. Purely social scientific interpretations limit analyses and tend toward reductionism" (39).

Such characterizations distort perceptions of the musical aesthetics of hip-hop music. From its early days, its aesthetic credentials were questioned, with many insisting that hip-hop did not even qualify as music, let alone art. Nelson George (1999) points to a critique of hip-hop's frequent use of sampling as a disqualification from considering it as music: "What [the songwriter Mtume] was objecting to was the use of sampling as a substitute for musical composition. It upset him that so many hip-hop producers had no understanding of theory, could play no instruments, and viewed a large record collection as the only essential tool of record making" (90). Critiques of hip-hop come from outside of R&B as well. Keith Richards of the Rolling Stones has lambasted hip-hop and its audience: "'What rap did that was impressive was to show there are so many tone-deaf people out there,' he says. 'All they need is a drum beat and somebody yelling over it and they're happy. There's an enormous market for people who can't tell one note from another'" (Farber 2015). Both Mtume and Richards suggest that hip-hop lacks musical aesthetics because of the way it sounds and the way it is produced. They believe the use and rearrangement of prerecorded musical snippets cannot count as original music production. Such thinking follows the logic of courts that have equated sampling with stealing (Schumacher 2004, 447).

However, recognizing hip-hop's musical aesthetics reveals hip-hop's value, which goes beyond its political message. Hip-hop has a variety of styles and forms which are on display in Korean hip-hop. Elizabeth Wheeler (1991) reminds us of the other major branch of early hip-hop music, "the 'rock-the-house' subgenre, which invites the crowd to dance" (195). Before the appearance of "The Message," hip-hop music was dominated by DJs who developed techniques to keep the music going at parties and MCs who provided an additional layer of appeal, skill, and entertainment. DJ Kool Herc began to focus on the break at dance parties: "The moment when the dancers really got wild was in a song's short instrumental break, when the band would drop out and the rhythm section would get elemental. Forget melody, chorus, songs—it was all about the groove, building it, keeping it going. Like a string theorist, Herc zeroed in on the fundamental vibrating loop at the heart of the record, the break" (Chang 2005, 79). Herc is also credited with developing the "Merry-Go-Round" technique: "Herc began to work two copies of the same record, back-cueing a record to the beginning of the break as the other reached the end, extending a five-second breakdown into a five-minute loop of fury, a makeshift version excursion" (Chang 2005, 79). This technique changed the way people made and heard music. It represents musical innovation. Andrew Bartlett (1994) notes that DJs engage in musicianship: "The turntable places the record at the center of the hip-hop performance, turning the notion of musical virtuosity on its head by using pre-recorded material not only as rhythm but also as melody and harmony" (647). Not only does hip-hop have musical aesthetics, it has participated in groundbreaking developments in music. Sampling represents yet another form of musical innovation. Bartlett (1994) reminds us that sampling provides a link between hip-hop and pop through "the appropriative use of recognizable pop fragments which 'hooked' listeners" (645). Felicia Miyakawa (2007) describes the turntable as "a two-handed instrument" that enabled scratching, "the act of rapidly moving the record under the stylus to produce the rhythmic and/or melodic sounds" (82). More than one scholar has noted an aesthetic link between hip-hop and bebop. Bartlett (1994) notes the aesthetics of sampling mirror bebop's use of contrafact, which "is an expropriated piece of another tune, brought in as the basis for the composition/performance at hand" (648). Sinker (1992) describes hip-hop sampling as something "in the grand syncretic tradition of bebop, not ashamed to acknowledge that technological means and initial building material are always simply what falls to hand" (31). Hip-hop also provides innovative vocals. In referencing the four fundamental elements of hip-hop, H. Samy Alim and Alistair Pennycook (2007) describe rapping as "the aesthetic placement of verbal rhymes over musical beats" (90). Bartlett (1994) refers to another innovation brought to hip-hop by DJ Kool Herc, the "techniques of 'dub' and 'talk over' as "formative aesthetic techniques" (646). Mtume ya Salaam (1995) points to rap vocal style, which can range from a "monotone" to "very dynamic and emotional"; flow, which is a sense of rhythm and timing that "can be delivered in a rhythm cadence"; and sound, which distinguishes one rapper from another (305–6).

The creative impulse exemplified by hip-hop is also aimed at archive creation, which passes the music and creativity on to others. While DJs like to show off their prowess by taking samples from obscure records, they also act as curators for an existing archive of black music that "serves as a miniaturized repository or vast interactive historical material—interactive because all archival material is handled by the archivist, who listens carefully . . . for the beats and snippets which will accompany and be accompanied by vocalized narrative" (Bartlett 2004, 647). DJs are familiar with the context of the archive, but when producing music with samples for an audience, they also engage in a didactic function because they reintroduce other elements of a black music tradition in a new and local context, what Perry (2004) describes as musical intertextuality: "Hip hop's great dependence on the music of an earlier generation, the music artists often recall from their youth, combined with the reconfigurations of that music and its offering back to the general public, constitutes a kind of conversation with the black musical tradition" (34). Those musical snippets mean something. When Korean hip-hop artists engage in the same action, they are involved in a creative act, using techniques pioneered by African Americans, within the context of a contemporary Korean culture.

The use of technology is key in hip-hop's musical innovation. Grandmaster Flash recounts how his curiosity about the way machines work factored into his use of discarded turntable and speaker parts and development of his turntablism. Because there were no systems designed to do what he wanted to do, he had to invent them: "I was going to the technical school for electronics. . . . I had to go to the raw parts shop downtown to find me a single pole double throw switch [in order to hear the second turntable when mixing music], some crazy glue to glue this part to my mixer, an external amplifier and a headphone" (Toop 2004, 237). By creating what he needed, he sparked an entirely new mode of music production. Sampling, vocal styles, and other musical techniques are also based on a principle of inclusion. Hip-hop, as black cultural production, reflects openness to other like-minded individuals to participate in its creative impulse. Marcyliena Morgan and Dionne Bennett (2011) notes that hip-hop "transcends conventional constructions of identity, race, nation, community, aesthetics, and knowledge," and creates the possibility of a "hip hop nation" which is "international, transnational, multiracial, multiethnic, [and] multilingual" (140).

Focusing on the aesthetic allows us to see its innovation. Korean hip-hop artists like Epik High exhibit the same tendency to engage in musical exploration beyond deft rapping skill. Hip-hop represents a departure from certain genres of R&B like disco. Rather than the anemic mode of disco that had developed in the 1970s, early pioneers embraced the lush instrumentation and complex rhythms introduced by groups like the Love Orchestra and The Sound of Philadelphia as well as rhythm and blues and soul records that provided the beats and samples for the new musical form. At the same time, hip-hop encouraged experimentation, as seen with Afrika Bambaataa's incorporation of Kraftwerk in songs like "Planet Rock," the introduction of live instrumentation by West Coast rappers, and the use of jazz by A Tribe Called Quest. Moreover, R&B and hip-hop have been joined together in common usage. *Billboard* maintains an R&B/Hip-Hop chart. So, while hip-hop is its own genre, it maintains a close relationship with R&B, depending on how wide one would extend that umbrella, and links Korean pop music to Korean hip-hop music. Because mainstream Korean hip-hop partakes of the same musical innovation, it can be seen as part of a global R&B tradition.

It is this inclusivity, based on music aesthetics, that invites Korean hip-hop artists to participate. They participate by carrying on the musical innovation of African American hip-hop. They are knowledgeable about the tradition because, as this chapter demonstrates, they draw from the same source material as their African American hip-hop counterparts. At the same time, in the spirit of musical innovation at the heart of hip-hop, they enhance the tradition by utilizing Korean musical strategies that bring in multiple genres. In the case of mainstream Korean hip-hop, this results in relying on unrelated genres, going beyond the "old school" and utilizing live instrumentation in a variety of contexts. Just like their African American counterparts, Korean hip-hop artists push for musical innovation, making them a branch of a global R&B tradition.

CONCLUSION

2016 was a banner year for the Korean group Hyukoh. The four members of the band, Im Dong-geon, Lim Hyun-jae, Lee In-woo, and frontman Oh Hyuk, garnered mainstream media attention. Tamar Herman (2015), writing for *Noisey*, describes the group as an indie wonder: "This summer, the most popular band in South Korea hasn't been a carefully marketed new K-pop phenomenon or a supergroup making a long-awaited return." Writing for *Vogue*, Monica Kim (2017) credits the group with helping "pave the way for the emerging indie scene" in South Korea and contrasts their sound with the more popular modes of Korean popular music: "Their sound is a refreshing counter to the high-octane pop and hip hop that has dominated the industry until now." Because of their indie status, media also characterize the group as divorced from the commercialism they attribute to Korean pop groups. Tamar Herman (2015) described the group as "a soft rock indie quartet" whose music "blends familiar shoegaze and surf rock sounds . . . explicitly positioned as an alternative to the mainstream." Similarly, Urban Zakapa, a Korean group that began as a nine-member group but by 2012 had coalesced into a trio made up of Park Yong-in, Oh Hyun-ah, and Kwon Soon-il, were also hailed as indie artists in contrast with more commercialized K-pop. A reviewer for *seoulbeats* responds to the track "One Who Leaves, One Who Is Left" this way: "I really liked the lyrics and how the song is pretty addicting in a way that doesn't involve auto tune and repetition of same 'hook' words that currently saturate the idol market" ("K-pop's Indie Gem" 2011). Alex (2017) places the group in the indie category in opposition to K-pop: "It's been a long time coming but Korean underground music finally seems to be getting the place it deserves. This isn't a blatant refute to k-pop, but rather, a complement to the mass genre that's commonly characterised by highly synthesised audiovisual effects, key dance moves, exaggerated styling and overstated camera movement to name some. Oh, and of course, the artists and personalities themselves garner true fanatics worldwide." Urban Zakapa frequently appears on K-indie lists. In doing so, they are divorced from K-pop that many feel only describes "idol" groups. A guest writer for *seoulbeats* positions the group completely outside of K-pop: "Urban Zakapa reminded me of artist Sweet Sorrow because they both shared similar musical harmonies and techniques, which is pretty refreshing in the over-autotuned and over-produced world of K-Pop. Aside from the harmonies, their songs have very mellow rhythms, addicting melodies, and sweet lyrics that make you want to sing along" ("K-pop Indie Gem: Urban Zakapa" 2011). Such descriptions suggest that K-indie is unrelated to K-pop. However, *Soul in Seoul* demonstrates that the K-pop umbrella covers a wide array of artists when we view K-pop as a mode of popular music that emerged in South Korea in the 1990s, has global aspirations, and interrogates a kind of hybridity that combines Korean and foreign, particularly African American, cultural elements. Considering K-pop as part of a global R&B tradition has ramifications for music aesthetics, authenticity, and globalization.

The K-pop Umbrella

Placing K-pop within a global R&B tradition highlights K-pop as a diverse style of music largely informed by African American popular music. The indie category obscures the African American influence on K-pop, but the metaphor of the K-pop umbrella captures the diversity of K-pop's musical aesthetics. By focusing on the way a broad array of Korean popular music artists exhibit intertextuality, we see the extent to which black American popular music has informed K-pop. Collaborations further illustrate the porous nature of the boundaries between K-pop artists.

Viewing K-pop as an umbrella recognizes a variety of genres even as it draws attention to the characteristics that the artists share. This book views K-pop comprehensively, including artists who emerged in the 1990s with global aspirations and who also produce hybridized Korean popular music that blends Korean and foreign music cultures. Broadening K-pop beyond "idols" allows a consideration of the diverse artists under the umbrella, much in the way K-pop audiences label artists even though they do not perform pop music. At the same time, many of these artists draw on African American popular music. Korean hip-hop is considered the polar opposite of Korean pop, but they both emulate and enhance the R&B tradition. Dynamic Duo draws attention to R&B instrumentation and vocals through sampling, while Epik High expands the boundaries of hip-hop by engaging in an eclectic array of music genres. They are also legitimately under the K-pop umbrella, discovered and consumed like "idol" groups by global fans.

The dynamics surrounding genre are brought to the fore when critics contrast K-pop with indie music. Indie is deployed like a genre, but the designation originally represented independent music. It initially signified a group or solo artist's relationship to production and more autonomous labels rather than large, corporate ones, i.e., whether or not they are produced by large record labels or more autonomous outfits. However, indie's position outside of the mainstream is not so clear, as Owen Adams (2007) of the *Guardian* observes: "The confusion now is that almost every emerging band since the Strokes [indie band] has been filed under indie, whether or not they're on a major label, independently minded, or creatively self-controlling. They might have lifted their musical approach and image from the Fall, Joy Division, and Smiths indie textbooks, but the unpopular music of yore is the mainstream pop of today." Such shifts make the designation seem somewhat subjective. A group like Hyukoh is not as marginalized as the indie label suggests. In 2016 Hyukoh won the Performance Culture Award at the Seoul Music Awards, the Best Rock Band Award at the Golden Disc Awards, the Discovery of the Year (Indie) at the Gaon Chart K-pop Awards, and Newcomer of the Year and Best Modern Rock Song at the Korean Music Awards. These awards show mainstream recognition. The group also has contributed to an original soundtrack for Korean television dramas (K-dramas) (notably for *Entourage*), as have many "idol" singers. Millions in South Korea, China, and the United States view such dramas. In 2015 Hyukoh signed with HIGHGRND, a sub-label of YG Entertainment, one of the three largest Korean entertainment agencies that produces pop and hip-hop acts. Korean indie groups also develop active, global fan bases like their pop counterparts. In an interview, Urban Zakapa recognizes that they have international fans as a result of promotional strategies used by Korean pop groups: "Since our international fans give it up for our music, we decided to simultaneously release our new album to be available all over the world through the brand new music application called 'Bainil' (www.bainil.com). We believe this will make our fans more easily enjoy our music" (Konser 2014). Being "indie" does not exclude an artist from being a K-pop act.

The indie designation also obscures the influence of black American popular music for groups like Hyukoh and Urban Zakapa. While Kim (2017) describes Oh Hyuk's voice as "slightly husky, yet warm and full of feelings," she overlooks his connections to the distinctive vocals of popular African American singers. Oh Hyuk's voice has complemented his jazzy and R&B-inflected collaborations with hip-hop producer Primary. Oh Hyuk lends his soulful vocals to "Rubber" on Primary's 2 (2015), with the offbeat phrasing so characteristic of the rhythms of soul and R&B and the distinctive rhythm guitar that provides a counterpoint for the bass and the slower tempo. These same soulful vocals come through on the band's cover of Stevie Wonder's "Isn't She Lovely" ("피키라이브 혁오—Isn't She Lovely" 2015). While his performance lacks the vocal ornamentation of the original, it clearly is in the same vocal tradition. The group also cites elements of R&B music aesthetics. The track "Comes and Goes" from the 2015 album 22 opens with an acoustic guitar and the lead singer's voice. However, the beat drops, introducing a funky guitar riff, a faster, more syncopated rhythm and a bass line that provides an unexpected groove. Acoustic music is not the sole purview of indie music. Artists like Erykah Badu represent a mode of R&B that draws heavily on acoustic arrangements and natural instruments. Writing for *Rolling Stone*, Jenny Eliscu (2010) puts Badu in the same company as hip-hop band The Roots and soul singer D'Angelo: "Badu helped build a new soul groove around impeccable live musicianship—bass (often upright), drums and Rhodes keyboard."

Designations like indie show the limitations of using labels that do not focus on the music aesthetics for K-pop artists. While genre designations were originally designed to help the music-buying public, David Brackett (2005) notes that they developed characteristics that created artificial barriers: "Because of the fleeting quality of genre arrangements and levels at any particular point in time, a given musical text may belong to more than one genre simultaneously, either due to shifting perceptions of the context under consideration or because the text presents a synthesis that exceeds contemporary comprehension of generic boundaries" (76). Many designate K-pop as a genre using "idol" groups as exemplars, making it a monolithic genre and suggesting that all the groups are the same. Roald Maliangkay (2015) points to "a significant homogeneity in the sound and performance across all K-pop acts" and a degree of uniformity in appearance, especially for girl groups (19). However, a consideration of a group's sound over the course of its career or the variety of groups that emerge during the same generation clearly shows that groups exhibit a distinctive sound because they draw on different musical elements in different ways.

The SM Station project defies the expectations of those who define K-pop only using "idols" by bringing together "idols," Korean R&B, and Korean hip-hop acts in collaboration. Launched in 2017, SM Station is a digital music project from SM Entertainment, which produced H.O.T., the first successful "idol" group, and some of the most successful "idol" groups, including SNSD, TVXQ, SHINee, EXO, and NCT. Releasing one new digital single a week, the project represented SM Entertainment's continuing efforts to innovate K-pop: "The goal is to bring together, not only, collaborations with SM artists but also artists, producers, composers and company brands outside of the SM label to create a multitude of new music" ("SM Entertainment Is Branching Out" 2016). Initially, SM Station's roster was filled with well-known "idols". The first single, "Rain," was by Taeyeon, member of the veteran K-pop girl group Girls' Generation. Yuri and Seohyun, also members of Girls' Generation, collaborated on the song "Secret." However, later songs featured collaborations with Korean R&B and hip-hop artists, showing the fluid nature of the boundaries between artists. The track "L'il Something" from *SM Station Season 1* (2017) featured the Korean R&B duo Vibe, Chen (Kim Jong-dae), a member of the "idol" group EXO, and hip-hop artist Heize (Jang Da-hye). The upbeat track features a lively guitar as well as funky synthesizer. Blending Chen's vocals in a higher register with Heize's rap contributes to the groovy feel of the song. Some would consider Heize to be out of place in this collaboration, given that she began her career on the second season of the rap competition show *Unpretty Rapstar* in 2014. However, SM Station brings together these seemingly very different artists in one K-pop enterprise.

SM Station also reveals the influence of African American popular music in these collaborations. SM Station uses its platform to showcase less-known Korean R&B artists. MeloMance is a Korean duo made up of Kim Min-seok and Jeong Dong-hwan. Their vocals and instrumentation draw heavily from black popular music. The duo collaborated with Girls' Generation's Taeyeon for "Page 0" from *SM Station X 0* (2018), which opens with a light gospel-inspired piano and some vocal ornamentation from Kim, who sings at a higher register than one might expect. The rhythm picks up on the verses, and Taeyeon and Kim engage in some brief call and response on the second verse. The combination of their voices on the chorus sounds like a choir. SM Station also features collaborations between "idols" and American R&B singers like John Legend. Legend first found success in the United States in 2004 with his debut album *Get Lifted*, which produced the hit single "Ordinary People." Writing for the *Guardian*, Caroline Sullivan (2004) says the album delivers a "soulful elegance": "Nine years as a choir director for his local church make themselves felt in the richness of the piano-based arrangements, which sit beautifully with pared-down, otherworldly vocals." Legend brings this sensibility to the SM Station collaboration with Wendy, a member of the K-pop girl group Red Velvet. Their song "Written in the Stars" from *SM Station X 0* (2018) is an acoustic number with prominent guitar that opens with Wendy's high, lilting vocals. On the pre-chorus, she is joined by Legend, echoing his voice, even in vocal runs. Legend's voice fills out their sound with its lower register. They sing together, even in the brief ad lib before the second verse, where Legend's vocals take over. SM Station collaborations reflect the ways that K-pop is actually consumed. Most listeners are not constrained by genres, which at best operate as broad and slippery categories. Instead, they are drawn to this mode of Korean popular music that is hybrid, globally directed, and informed by African American popular music.

The ease with which such collaboration occurs points to the synergy within K-pop as a branch of a global R&B tradition. Engagement with R&B links many of the artists under the K-pop umbrella. As the book has demonstrated, R&B vocals derived from the gospel tradition links first-generation "idol" group g.o.d with Korean R&B group Brown Eyed Soul. Both are capable of emulating R&B's distinctive vocals. Both also draw from the instrumentation from R&B genres, ranging from funk to classic 1960s soul. An R&B hip-hop vocalist like Zion.T easily works with hip-hop producer Primary, even as some posit hip-hop as a destructive influence on R&B. While "idol" artists like Rain are known for spectacular performances with choreography tailored to the music, R&B singer Wheesung taps into the same choreography. Only by acknowledging K-pop as an umbrella that embraces a wide array of music can we see the way K-pop emulates and embraces the R&B tradition.

Authenticity and Fan Critical Production

In addition to intertextuality, K-pop's place in a global R&B tradition represents a mode of fan-driven authentication. Technology enables fans to access a wide array of K-pop, foster fan communities, and act as critics and arbiters of taste. Their critical production reveals a consistent recognition of the influence of African American popular music on K-pop.

The critical response to the music of "idol" groups and the influence of African American popular music shows the significance of fans in general and fan critics in particular. More so than other types of music under the K-pop umbrella, Korean pop groups generate the most critical response from fans. Consistently, these fans highlight the relationship between "idol" acts and R&B artists and styles. As *Soul in Seoul* has shown, "idols" draw from different R&B styles and genres. g.o.d's (Groove Overdose) reliance on funk instrumentation differs greatly from Wonder Girls' citation of urban R&B expressed by 1990s black girl groups. SHINee experiments with various genres within songs, which Shinhwa has done over the course of its twenty-year-plus career.

The rise of digital music, streaming, YouTube, and Internet sharing sites have had an impact on the circulation of K-pop and its audiences. Oh and G.-S. Park point to the significance of YouTube as a new medium that distributes K-pop, supplanting the model that focused on the fans (369). While this sheds light on the economics, it overlooks how new media functions to expose both Korean musicians and producers to African American music as well as global fans to K-pop informed by black popular music. Through these digital sites, fans influence other fans as well as the popular discourse about K-pop. They are responsible for changes in measure of popularity. In recent years, a greater emphasis has been placed on YouTube views and streaming counts in Korea and in the United States. Informal contact between fans can increase awareness about K-pop. Distinctions between "idol" groups and other kinds of artists under K-pop's umbrella mean little for fans looking for new artists. The K-pop subreddit is a great example of how fans exchange information, enabling others to expand their knowledge and appreciation. Fans post queries looking for groups that sound like other groups and share deeper cuts that never make it to the level of attention to gain traction on YouTube. In my article "Into the New World: Research Suggests Multi-Fandom the Norm for Veteran K-pop Fans" (2018), I find that fans of "idol" groups engage in branching, the tendency to seek out additional K-pop groups after discovering their first K-pop group (2018). This quest is not limited to "idol" performers. This is how fans who initially encounter "idols" come to know about less mainstream Korean artists. Collaborations with more popular artists also expand what fans consider in the K-pop realm. For example, a fan of Beenzino, a Korean rapper, may come across his collaborations with Urban Zakapa. The track "Get" from Urban Zakapa's 2015 album *UZ* features a gospel-like piano complemented by a wailing guitar that contrasts with Beenzino's rap.

As a result, authentication of K-pop's intertextuality rests, in part, in the hands of K-pop fan reviewers. Fans are often belittled for their enthusiastic response to K-pop. However, many fans are drawn to K-pop because they are fed up with the popular music in their country and like the way that K-pop draws on genres of African American popular music. Since many global fans of K-pop are not Korean, this represents the kind of affective transcultural fandom that Bertha Chin and Lori Morimoto (2013) describe, which "frees fandom from the constraints of national belonging, reinforcing our contention that fans become fans of border-crossing texts or objects not necessarily because of *where* they are produced, but because they may recognize a subjective moment of affinity regardless of origin. . . . Nation-based differences or similarities may well appeal to people across borders; but so, too, might affective investments in characters, stories, and even fan subjectivities that exceed any national orientation" (99). K-pop fans who write reviews of the music represent an important subset of K-pop fandom, going beyond the stereotype of the hysterical fan and showing how they articulate what is important to them in the music. Contrary to the negative stereotype of fans, G.-S. Park

(2013) notes their significance to K-pop: "The external community or the agents of interpretation, integration, and institutionalization are numerous, diverse, and exceptionally diligent, evaluating songs on an almost weekly basis through sales charts, fan blogs, fan activities, and concert participation" (19). An examination of their reviews reveals how they identify the influence of African American popular music on K-pop. Such fans are also important in that they are involved in knowledge preservation. They know more about their favorite groups than the average music journalist. This fan knowledge has value. Matt Hills (2002) notes that fan blogs, which house many of the reviews, differ from their fanzine forerunners in that "they are also more public, more globally accessible, more subject to potential surveillance, more able to carry different forms of information and more easily archived" (186). Through reviews, fans pass on information, including information about the influence of African American popular music in this common fan practice. Fan critical behavior also serves to authenticate K-pop's intertextuality and place in a global R&B tradition because it recognizes the ways African American popular music informs K-pop.

The plethora of "KR&B" playlists on YouTube attest to fans' recognition of Korean R&B's intertextuality. It also points to the knowledge of fans. Fans also function as points of cultural exchange, as David Oh (2017) explains in his study on black K-pop fan reaction videos: "Black K-pop fans interest in Korean artists is subversive as it points to a joining of Black and Korean in a polycultural union that imagines racial identities outside the gaze of Whiteness" (5). As a result, they recognize K-pop as a site where Korean and African American musical cultures fuse, but in a way where the African American musical influences remain identifiable. K-pop becomes its own entity and, at the same time, participates in the tradition of African American popular music. Such participation is authentic. The depth to which African American popular music has influenced K-pop through both newer and older genres shows that such engagement is not superficial or accidental. Korean creative professionals are students of the tradition of African American popular music. In other words, fan and audience actions contribute to the spread of K-pop but also to the links between K-pop and African American popular culture, making African American culture more global, one that informs beyond the United States.

The critical reception by fans recognizes that K-pop artists' authentic engagement with R&B genres depends the most on the ability to perform aesthetics that are difficult without watering them down. The pervasiveness of R&B vocals can be found in "idol" groups when they take on the R&B ballad, like 2PM's "Good Man" from *No. 5* (2015). Like many of the R&B ballads done by "idol" acts, the track begins with natural instrumentation, an organ accented by electric guitar flicks and a high vocal, which contrasts with the lower vocals on the verses and harmony in the following pre-chorus. This slow jam mixes harmony with solo vocals and the song features the kind of development of intensity that defines R&B ballads. By the end of the song, the chorus features powerhouse vocals with a great deal of vocal ornamentation. One fan reviewer connects the vocals and instrumentation to older black American popular music genres: "This track certainly grabs you into a world of smoky lounges with its jazz/big band playing. The track is impressive and shows that they can do any genre, with the sultry rap by Taecyeon and rich soulful vocals" (Alona 2013). To achieve this level of authenticity is not just a mimetic performance. Korean performers express the same feelings as their African American counterparts who engage in the same kind of performance. In this way, participation in black popular culture can be based not solely on race but also on ethnicity. Paul Rudinow (1994) offers the use of ethnicity rather than race as the means of entrance to the tradition: "Ethnicity is a matter of acknowledged common culture, based on shared items of cultural significance such as experience, language, religion, history, habitat, and the like. Ethnicity is essentially a socially conferred status—a matter of communal acceptance, recognition, and respect" (128). This mode of ethnicity "leaves open the possibility of the proper initiation of white people and other non-blacks . . . at least in the use of the blues as an expressive idiom and so into the blues community. . . . initiation into the blues community presumably carries with it legitimate access to the blues as a means of artistic expression" (Rudinow 1994, 134). Given that R&B traces its roots to the blues, it makes sense that it affords this kind of access to nonblacks as well. Just as some white R&B performers are seen as legitimate participants in R&B, Korean artists become part of the tradition. Their fluency with a range of vocally based R&B genres, consistent engagement with the instrumentation throughout their careers, and their incorporation of Korean musical strategies make them an active branch of the R&B musical tree.

Diversification of K-pop's Influences

K-pop's place in a global R&B tradition reveals the diversity of global influences on K-pop. Scholars tend to talk about the globalizing focus from the West or the United States that impacts K-pop. African American popular culture fuels K-pop's intertextuality, and in doing so, creates a different dynamic, as it is simultaneously a part yet critical of a larger American culture. Moreover, K-pop draws attention to black American popular music as an influence beyond the United States.

The fascination over the "K" in K-pop has led to a focus on the distinct Korean contribution to the music and its culture. It has also, inadvertently, juxtaposed K-pop with a largely undifferentiated West or America. John Lie (2014) invokes the discourse of globalization to describe influences on K-pop: "Increasingly affluent Asians had also been schooled in the musical competence and cultural sensibilities associated with Americanized popular music, an education that entailed familiarity with the Western soundscape and the domain of recent American popular music as well as with its cultural assumptions, ranging from its rhetoric and poetics to its valorization of romantic love. The inevitable companion of financial globalization was global consumerism, or the globalization of consumption" (169). Lie positions generalizations of the West and American culture vis-à-vis Korean culture. Both are seen as interlopers, for Hyun-key Kim Hogarth (2013) states: "Globalization, which began in the aftermath of colonialism at the turn of the nineteenth century, was largely Western-oriented, non-Europeans trying to emulate their colonial masters" (148). Hogarth figures the West as monolithic and generalized, and sees the United States as merely a Western power.

However, the United States has its own history of internal and external strife. Not all inhabitants agree or can enact imperialistic behavior. Yet, K-pop engages in an intertextuality informed by African American culture, an American ethnic culture. This complicates how we talk about the influences on it. Sangjoon Lee (2015) notes that Hallyu can be seen as "a vehicle for dismantling scholarship on critical globalization studies, in collaboration with the reverse cultural imperialism school, reorienting/recentering globalization practitioners and cultural pluralism theoreticians who are arguing that the predominant center-periphery perspective cannot explain global media relations today and that a new epoch of cultural pluralism has now arrived" (12). By recognizing its cultural pluralism, K-pop, as a product of Hallyu, allows us to parse its multiple influences. K-pop's intertextuality brings to the fore the emulation of African American popular music, which may have originated in the West, but its history shows that it has often been critical of and runs counter to Western culture. The introduction of rhythm-based songs to American popular music by African American artists radically changed its sound, producing a distinctive musical aesthetic that makes up a large part of K-pop's hybridity. Seeing K-pop as a branch of a global R&B tradition invites us to examine the multiple forces at play rather than part of a homogenized Western or American cultural designation.

K-pop's intertextuality also brings to the fore the influence of black American popular music beyond the United States, adding a new dimension to sociohistorical approaches to the study of R&B music. The rise of R&B-based

K-pop mirrors other global manifestations of R&B vocals, like the development of British soul. While the blues had an impact on the rhythm and blues scene in Britain with groups that would go on to be rock legends, like the Rolling Stones and the Animals, black vocals also influenced singers like Dusty Springfield, best known for her pop hits "I Only Want to Be with You" (1963) and "Son of a Preacher Man" (1968), which was also recorded by Aretha Franklin. Randall (2008) says that Springfield's vocals defied expectations in Britain "by quoting other singers and referencing a variety of styles, sometimes subtly, sometimes quite explicitly, often within the course of a single song" while remaining authentic, "a perception that derived largely from the unique timbre of her voice—something that could not be borrowed" (6). Ripani (2006) describes such vocal aesthetics as an essential element of the "cyclic" form that informs rhythm and blues, which includes an element that "begins at a low emotional level and builds to a high point" (44). The African American sacred tradition in the form of gospel used "drive" to create a sense of emotional dynamism, where "the repeating cycle commonly supports a soloist of some sort . . . and a responsorial element provided by the choir or congregation. The emotional level of the soloist gradually builds, and over time the process moves the entire congregation to a higher level of religious excitement" (Ripani 2006, 45). Randall places Springfield within a context of soul in Britain, created by an influx of gospel through records, as well as the career of Madeline Bell, an African American singer who moved to Britain following her run in the gospel show *Black Nativity* in 1962 with the Bradford Singers. Springfield becomes a British extension of American soul vocalists because she maintains the core of the R&B vocal tradition: "Regardless of who was making the music . . . The African American cultural presence as represented by the gospel aesthetic was the ineradicable sonic centerpiece of soul" (Randall 2008, 43). This version of soul travels back to the United States in the 1980s through what some describe as a Brit pop-soul invasion led by Junior, Sade, and Billy Ocean. Rashad Ollison (2015) observes: "In the '80s, mainstream radio had segregated itself and a few black acts from anywhere regularly crossed over into *Billboard*'s top 10. But soul music certainly didn't suffer during that time. The British version of it brought a polished urbanity and keen attention to the songcraft, something we hear to a certain degree in the pop-soul sounds of Adele and Sam Smith." Korean R&B mirrors British soul in that it too expands the R&B tradition beyond the United States. Unlike British soul, Korean artists are invested in the global spread of K-pop as part of South Korea's globalizing project.

Like their British counterparts, Korean R&B artists emulate the distinctive R&B vocal traditions. While Brown Eyed Soul and Big Mama are both vocal groups who excel at harmony, they draw from different aspects of the black popular music tradition. Brown Eyed Soul draws on 1960s soul instrumentation, while Big Mama invokes the black female gospel tradition. Because many of their tracks feature less dense instrumentation, their vocals take center stage in spectacular fashion, which they replicate even in live performances. Korea has produced a fair number of R&B artists, yet they all exude a different style.

Even more than Britain, South Korea represents a far-flung destination where R&B takes root. Unlike the United States, Korea is not a former colony of Britain. It does not share the same language and cultural links. Placing R&B in a Korean context provides even more opportunity for enhancement. Korean artists come from a musical tradition strongly linked to Korean singing culture. Noh Dong-eun (2003) characterizes Korean society as a "singing culture": "Koreans sang their entire lives and lived their songs. They made up new songs according to the circumstances of the moment, and whenever they sang, they danced and played music. And in fact, even today, Koreans feel that life cannot be enjoyed to the fullest unless there is singing" (75). Moreover, Korea's singing culture can be seen in popular television shows that focus on vocal talent. *King of Mask Singer* pits singers against each other in competition, wearing masks to conceal their identity until the end of the program. You Hee-yeol's *Sketchbook* features a live music format and appearances by individuals with strong vocal talent. While Korea's singing culture is different, it is so central that it may contribute to the way that Korean artists interact with R&B's vocal-centric tradition.

The musical production of the band Hyukoh and subsequent collaborations featuring the band's front man Oh Hyuk nicely illustrate how recognizing K-pop's engagement with a global R&B musical tradition has ramifications for music aesthetics, authenticity, and globalization. While the band Hyukoh emerged into the mainstream while labeled indie, its subsequent forays into hip-hop and pop reflect K-pop's musical flexibility as well as a mode of intertextuality that reveals the influence of African American popular music. Hyukoh encourages us to view K-pop, not as a genre, but as an umbrella that covers a wide array of genres. Moreover, reviews of Oh Hyuk's collaborations reveal how fans recognize K-pop's authentic engagement with the R&B tradition, solidifying its place in that tradition. Fan reviewer SJP (2015) describes "Bawling," the title track from Oh Hyuk's 2015 album *Lucky You* produced by Korean hip-hop producer Primary, as "a fun song with groovy, R&B/jazz elements that shows off the strength of Oh Hyuk's voice." The fan reviewer notes the influence of R&B, a move replicated by other fan reviewers of K-pop with such frequency and consistency that it serves to authenticate K-pop's engagement with the R&B tradition. Placing K-pop artists like Hyukoh within a global R&B tradition invites us to look beyond generalizations of the West or the United States. R&B is simultaneously a product of the West and a cultural production poised against it, and K-pop's relationship with R&B invites us to think of African American popular culture as global, both significant within the United States' specific history as well as beyond it. At the same time, K-pop's ties to R&B helps us understand its appeal and impact within a more complex notion of globalization.

DISCOGRAPHY

1TYM. 1998. *One Time for Your Mind*. YG Entertainment. Mp3.
2PM. 2015. *No. 5*. JYP Entertainment. Mp3.
2PM. 2009. *01:59PM*. JYP Entertainment. Mp3.
4MEN. 2011. *The Artist*. Happy Face Entertainment. Mp3.
4MEN. 2000. *Iroke Chonildongan Moumyeon Ibyori Sarajindago Hetda*. MAJOR9. Mp3.
4MEN. 1998. *Four Men First Album*. MAJOR9. Mp3.
Big Mama. 2005. *It's Unique*. YG Entertainment. Mp3.
Brown Eyed Soul. 2010a. *Browneyed Soul*. SANTAMUSIC. Mp3.
Brown Eyed Soul. 2010b. "Love Ballad (Piano Version)." *Love Ballad/Never Forget*. In Next Trend. Mp3.
Brown Eyed Soul. 2007. *The Wind, the Sea, the Rain*. GAB Entertainment. Mp3.
Brown Eyed Soul. 2003. *Soul Free: #1*. EMI. Mp3.
Chi-Lites, The. 1971. *(For God's Sake) Give More Power to the People*. Brunswick Records. Mp3.
Drunken Tiger. 2013. *The Cure*. Feel Ghood Music. Mp3.
Drunken Tiger. 2009. *Feel gHood Muzik: The 8th Wonder*. Jungle Entertainment. Mp3.
Drunken Tiger. 1999. *Year of the Tiger*. Doremi Media. Mp3.
Dynamic Duo. 2012. *Dynamic Duo 6th Digilog 2/2*. Amoeba Culture. Mp3.
Dynamic Duo. 2009. *Band of Dynamic Brothers*. Amoeba Culture. Mp3.
Dynamic Duo. 2007. *Enlightened*. Amoeba Culture. Mp3.
Dynamic Duo. 2004. *Taxi Driver*. Gap Entertainment. Mp3.
EXO. 2014. *Overdose*. SM Entertainment. Mp3.
Earth, Wind and Fire. 1992. *The Eternal Dance*. Columbia Records. CD.
Epik High. 2009. *[e]motion*. Map the Soul Inc. mp3.
Epik High. 2009. *Map the Soul*. Map the Soul Inc. mp3.
Epik High. 2007. *Remapping the Human Soul*. Woollim Entertainment. Mp3.
Epik High. 2006 *Black Swan Songs*. Woollim Entertainment. Mp3.
Epik High. 2005. *Swan Songs*. Woollim Entertainment. Mp3.
Epik High. 2004. *High Society*. Woollim Entertainment. Mp3.
Epik High. 2003. *Map of the Human Soul*. Woolim Entertainment. Mp3.
Floaters, The. 1977. *Float On*. ABC Records. Mp3.
Fly to the Sky. 2008. *Recollection*. PFull Entertainment. Mp3.
Fly to the Sky. 2007. *No Limitations*. PFull Entertainment. Mp3.

Fly to the Sky. 2001. *The Promise*. SM Entertainment. Mp3
Fly to the Sky. 1999. *Day by Day*. SM Entertainment. Mp3.
g.o.d. 2014. *Chapter 8*. SidusHQ, CJE&M. mp3.
g.o.d. 2000. *Chapter 3*. Synnara Records. Mp3.
g.o.d. 1999. *Chapter 1*. JYP Entertainment. Mp3.
Gap Band. 1982. *The Gap Band IV*. Total Experience. Mp3.
H.O.T. 2000. *Outside Castle*. SM Entertainment. Mp3.
Hyukoh. 2015. 22. DRDR AC. Mp3.
Isley Brothers. 1977. *Go for Your Guns*. T-Neck Records. Mp3.
James, Rick. 1981. *Street Songs*. Gordy Records. Mp3.
Jinusean. 2001. *The Reign*. YG Entertainment. Mp3.
Kim Dong-ryul. 2008. *Monologue*. Antenna. Mp3.
Lyn. 2015. *9X9th*. Music&New. Mp3.
Lyn. 2014. *Le Grand Bleu*. Music&New. Mp3.
Lyn. 2009. *Let Go, Let In, It's a New Day*. CJ E&M. mp3.
Lyn. 2004. *Can U See the Bright?* CJ E&M. mp3.
Lyn. 2002. *Have You Ever Had Heart Broken?* KM Culture. Mp3.
MFBTY. 2015. *WondaLand*. Feel Ghood Music. Mp3.
Manhattans, The. 1976. *The Manhattans*. Columbia Records. Mp3.
Ohio Players. 1975. *Honey*. Mercury Records. Mp3.
Park Hyo-shin. 2016. *I Am a Dreamer*. Glove Entertainment. Mp3.
Park Hyo-shin. 2007. *The Breeze of the Sea*. Nawon Entertainment. Mp3.
Park Hyo-shin. 2002. *Time Honored Voice*. Sinchon Music. Mp3.
Park Hyo-shin. 2001. *Second Story*. Sinchon Music. Mp3.
Player. 1977. *Player*. RSO. Mp3.
Primary. 2015. 2. Amoeba Culture. Mp3.
Primary. 2012. *Primary and the Messengers LP*. Amoeba Culture. Mp3.
Run-DMC. 1984. *Run-DMC*. Profile Records. Mp3.
SHINee. 2015. *Odd*. SM Entertainment. Mp3.
SHINee. 2013. *Everybody*. SM Entertainment. Mp3.
Shinhwa. 2012. *The Return*. Shinhwa Co. mp3.
Shinhwa. 2004. *Winter Story 2004–2005*. Good Entertainment. Mp3.
Shinhwa. 1998. *Resolver*. SM Entertainment. Mp3.
SM Station Season 1. 2017. SM Entertainment. Mp3.
SM Station Station X 0. 2018. SM Entertainment. Mp3.
TVXQ. 2006. *"O"-Jung.Ban.Hap*. SM Entertainment. Mp3.
TVXQ. 2004. *Tri-angle*. SM Entertainment. Mp3.
Urban Zakapa. 2015. "Get." Fluxus Music. Mp3.
Ward, Anita. 1979. *Songs of Love*. Juana Records. Mp3.
Wonder Girls. 2012. *Wonder Party*. JYP Entertainment. Mp3.
Wonder Girls. 2008. *The Wonder Years: Trilogy*. JYP Entertainment. Mp3.
Wonder Girls. 2007. *The Wonder Years*. JYP Entertainment. Mp3.
Yaz. 1982. *Upstairs at Eric's*. Mute Records. Mp3.
Zion.T. 2018. *ZZZ*. The Black Label. Mp3.
Zion.T. 2013a. *Mirrorball*. Amoeba Culture. Mp3.
Zion.T. 2013b. *Red Light*. Stone Music Entertainment. Mp3.

REFERENCES

"[피키라이브] 혁오 - Isn't She Lovely (Stevie Wonder)." 2015. YouTube. 2:22. Posted by Pikicast, July 12, 2015. https://youtu.be/bEq_HIQF3XY.
"박재범 Jay Park '좋아 Joah' [Official Music Video]." 2013. YouTube. 4:05. Posted by JAY PARK, April 9, 2013. https://youtu.be/rMtCJC39SqU.
"박재범 Jay Park - 몸매 (MOMMAE) Feat. Ugly Duck Official Music Video." 2015. YouTube. 3:27. Posted by JAY PARK, May 21, 2015. https://youtu.be/gx_mg-1WhWw.
"휘성 WheeSung - Night And Day Official MV." 2014. YouTube. 3:42. Posted by GENIE MUSIC, May 11, 2014. https://youtu.be/napCk8ZVlpw.
"1TYM – 1TYM M/V." 2008. YouTube. 3:48. Posted by YG Entertainment, October 2, 2008. https://www.youtube.com/watch?v=3eHi8VHKym0.
15 Korean Rappers You Should Know That Aren't Psy." 2013. *XXL*. February 12. http://www.xxlmag.com/rap-music/2013/02/15-korean-rappers-you-should-know-thats-not-psy/5/.
"50 Most Influential K-pop Artists: 47. Solid." 2010. *Ask a Korean*. September 12. http://askakorean.blogspot.com/2010/09/50-most-influential-k-pop-artists-47.html.
"The 100 Greatest Boy Band Songs of All Time: Critics' Pick." 2018. *Billboard*. April 23. https://www.billboard.com/articles/news/list/8362499/greatest-boy-band-songs-of-all-time-top-100.
Abraca, Alejandro. 2015. "Album Review: SHINee's 'Odd.'" *KultScene*. May 26. http://kultscene.com/album-review-shinees-odd/.
Adams, Owen. 2007. "What Makes Music Indie These Days?" *Guardian*. August 24, https://www.theguardian.com/music/musicblog/2007/aug/24/whatmakesmusicindiethesedays.
Adorno, Theodor W., with the assistance of George Simpson. 2000. "On Popular Music." *Soundscapes: Journal on Media Culture* 2. http://www.icce.rug.nl/~soundscapes/DATABASES/SWA/Some_writings_of_Adorno.shtml.
Ahn, Ji-hyun. 2014. "Rearticulating Black Mixed-Race in the Era of Globalization." *Cultural Studies* 28 (3): 391–417. doi: 10.1080/09502386.2013.840665.
"Album Review—May: Shinhwa—The Return." 2012. *United Kpop*. June 1. http://www.unitedkpop.com/2012/06/01/album-review-may-shinhwa-the-return/.
Alex. 2017. "Unpacking Korean Indie with Urban Zakapa." *PopWire*. February 8. http://popwire.com.sg/unpacking-k-indie/.
Alim, H. Samy, and Alastair Pennycook. 2007. "Glocal Linguistic Flows: Hip-Hop Culture(s), Identities, and the Politics of Language Education." *Journal of Language, Identity, and Education* 6 (2): 89–100. doi: 10.1080/15348450701341238.

All About Cassiopeia. N.d. "About Us." Accessed September 19, 2019. https://aacassiopeia.com/about/.

Alona. 2013. "Kmusic Review: 2PM's 'Grown' Album." *Officially KMusic.* May 15. http://officiallykmusic.com/kmusic-review-2pms-grown-album/.

Amoeba Culture. N.d. "About AC." Accessed May 1, 2015. http://www.amoebaculture.com/business/front/aboutAC/company.do.

"An Annotated Listening: 'Odd,' By SHINee." 2015. *Is This How You K-pop.* May 25. https://isthishowyoukpop.com/2015/05/25/an-annotated-listening-odd-by-shinee/.

Anderson, Crystal S. 2018. "Into the New World: Research Suggests Multi-Fandom the Norm for Veteran K-pop Fans." *KPK: Kpop Kollective.* June 7. https://kpopkollective.com/2018/06/07/multi-fandom-the-norm-for-veteran-k-pop-fans/.

Anderson, Crystal S. 2014. "That's My Man!: Overlapping Masculinities in Korean Popular Music." In *The Korean Wave: Korean Popular Culture in Global Context,* edited by Yasue Kuwahara, 117–31.

Anderson, Crystal S. 2013. *Beyond the Chinese Connection: Contemporary Afro-Asian Cultural Production.* Jackson: University Press of Mississippi.

Anderson, Crystal S. 2012. "The 'K' in K-pop: Research Finds Korean Language, Culture Appeals to Global Fans." *Kpop Kollective.* December 12. https://kpopkollective.com/2012/12/11/the-k-in-k-pop-research-finds-korean-language-culture-appeals-to-global-fans/.

Annett, Sandra. 2011. "Imagining Transcultural Fandom: Animation and Global Media Communities." *Transcultural Studies* 2: 164–88. doi: 10.11588/ts.2011.2.9060.

Arteaga, Arnold. 2011. "[Review] 'The Artist' by 4MEN." *allkpop.* June 22. https://www.allkpop.com/article/2011/06/review-the-artist-by-4men.

Asakawa, Gil. 2012. "Psy Performs on the American Music Awards, and Racist Haters Come Out on Twitter." *Huffington Post.* November 21. http://www.huffingtonpost.com/gil-asakawa/psy-american-music-awards_b_2171451.html.

askjeevas. 2009. "Single Review: Wonder Girls—'The Wonder Years Trilogy.'" *A Song for XX.* December 13. https://askjeevas.wordpress.com/2009/12/13/single-review-wonder-girls-the-wonder-years-trilogy/.

Balaji, Murali. 2010. "Vixen Resistin': Redefining Black Womanhood in Hip-Hop Music Videos." *Journal of Black Studies* 41 (1): 5–20. doi: 10.1177/0021934708325377.

Bantum, Gail Song. 2009. "The Heritage Mass Choir—Authentic or Assimilated?" *GailSongBantum,* May 15. https://gailsongbantum.wordpress.com/2009/05/19/the-heritage-mass-choir-authentic-or-assimilated/.

Baraka, Amiri. 1966. "The Changing Same (R&B and New Black Music)." 1966. In *The LeRoi Jones/Amiri Baraka Reader,* edited by William J. Harris, 186–209. New York: Thunder's Mouth Press.

Baraka, Amiri. 1963. "Jazz and the White Critic." In *The LeRoi Jones/Amiri Baraka Reader,* edited by William J. Harris, 179–86. New York: Thunder's Mouth Press.

Barnes, Ariel. 2016. "Korean Singer Dean is the New R&B Heartthrob." *Milkxyz.* May 5. https://milk.xyz/articles/korean-singer-dean-is-the-new-rb-heartthrob/.

Barry, Robert. 2012. "Gangnam Style & How the World Woke Up to the Genius of K-pop." *The Quietus.* December 18. http://thequietus.com/articles/11001-psy-gangnam-style-k-pop.

Bartlett, Andrew. 1994. "Airshafts, Loudspeakers, and the Hip Hop Sample: Contexts and African American Musical Aesthetics." *African American Review* 28 (4): 639–52. doi: 10.2307/3042229.

Bayles, Martha. 1994. *Hole in Our Soul: The Loss of Beauty and Meaning in American Popular Music*. Chicago: University of Chicago Press.

Beard, Sonya. 2010. "Gospel Choir Gives Expat Christians a Taste of Home." *Korea Herald*. December 14. http://www.koreaherald.com/view.php?ud=20101214000863.

Benjamin, Jeff. 2015. "2PM Are Subtle, Seductive Gentleman on 'No. 5': Track-by-Track Album Review." *Billboard*. June 18. http://www.billboard.com/articles/review/6598345/2pm-no5-track-by-track-album-review.

Benjamin, Jeff. 2014. "Girls' Generation—TTS on Why New 'Holler' EP Represents Their 'Mind, Body and Soul.'" *Billboard*. September 16. http://www.billboard.com/articles/columns/k-town/6251587/girls-generation-tts-holler-interview-video.

Benjamin, Jeff. 2013. "SHINee Unveil 'Symptoms,' Produced by the Underdogs: Listen." *Billboard*. September 7. https://www.billboard.com/articles/columns/k-town/5748129/shinee-unveil-symptoms-produced-by-the-underdogs-listen.

Beta, Andy. 2015. "Electronic Warfare: The Political Legacy of Detroit Techno." *Pitchfork*. January 30. http://pitchfork.com/features/electric-fling/9588-electronic-warfare-the-political-legacy-of-detroit-techno/.

Bevan, David. 2013. "A Year after 'Gangnam Style,' K-pop Continues to Make Its Mark in America." *Washington Post*. November 8. http://www.washingtonpost.com/entertainment/music/a-year-after-gangnam-style-k-pop-continues-to-make-its-mark-in-america/2013/11/07/cb161c56-431f-11e3-a751-f032898f2dbc_story.html.

Bevan, David. 2012. "Seoul Trained: Inside Korea's Pop Factory." *SPIN*. March 26. http://www.spin.com/articles/seoul-trained-inside-koreas-pop-factory/.

"Big Mama—Break Away." 2006. YouTube. 4:40. Posted by insatiable, April 10. https://youtu.be/8otPjC1-nuQ.

"Big Mama—Nevermind." 2009. YouTube. 4:06. Posted by HeavenlyHeart87, July 11. https://youtu.be/2SymmvQREnQ.

Bogdanov, Vladimir. 2003. *All Music Guide to Soul: The Definitive Guide to R&B and Soul*. San Francisco: Backbeat Books.

Brackett, David. 2005. "Questions of Genre in Black Popular Music." *Black Music Research Journal* 25 (1–2): 73–92. http://www.jstor.org/stable/30039286.

Brackett, David. 2000. *Interpreting Popular Music*. Berkeley: University of California Press.

Brasor, Philip, and Tsubuku Masako. 1997. "Idol Chatter: The Evolution of J-pop." *Japan Quarterly* 44 (2): 55–65.

"Brown Eyed Soul Interview." 2007. *Reika no Rakuen*. December 20. http://reikanorakuen.wordpress.com/2007/12/20/brown-eyed-soul-interview/.

"Brown Eyed Soul's Vocal Analysis." 2015. *K-pop Vocal Analysis*. December 25. https://kpopvocalanalysis.net/2015/12/25/brown-eyed-souls-vocal-analysis-naul-newly-updated/.

Brungardt, Leah. 2015. "An Interview with South Korean Singer, DEAN on Breaking into the American Market, Working with Songwriter Eric Bellinger and Much More!" *All Access Music*. September 22. https://music.allaccess.com/an-interview-with-south-korean-singer-dean-on-breaking-into-the-american-market-working-with-songwriter-eric-bellinger-and-much-more/.

Butler, Mark J. 2006. *Unlocking the Groove: Rhythm, Meter, and Musical Design in Electronic Dance Music*. Bloomington: Indiana University Press.

Cateforis, Theo. 2004. "Performing the Avant-Garde Groove: Devo and the Whiteness of the New Wave." *American Music* 22 (4): 564–88. doi: 10.2307/3592993.

"Censors Attempted to Silence Hip Hop Group." 2007. *Freemuse*. March 1. http://freemuse.org/archives/874.

Cha, Victor D. 1996. "Bridging the Gap: The Strategic Context of the 1965 Korea-Japan Normalization Treaty." *Korean Studies* 20 (1996): 123–60. Doi: 10.1353/ks.1996.0009.

Chace, Zoe. 2012. "Gangnam Style: Three Reasons K-pop is Taking Over the World." *NPR*. October 12. http://www.npr.org/sections/money/2012/10/12/162740623/gangnam-style-three-reasons-K-pop-is-taking-over-the-world.

Chang, Jeff. 2009. "It's a Hip-Hop World." *Foreign Policy* 163. October 12. https://foreignpolicy.com/2009/10/12/its-a-hip-hop-world/.

Chang, Jeff. 2008. "So You Think They Can Breakdance?" *Salon*. June 26. http://www.salon.com/2008/06/26/korean_hiphop/singleton/.

Chang, Jeff. 2005. *Can't Stop Won't Stop: A History of the Hip-Hop Generation*. New York: St. Martin's Press.

Cheng, Anne Anlin. 2011. "Shine: On Race, Glamour, and the Modern." *PMLA* 126 (4): 1022–40. Doi: 10.1632/pmla.2011.126.4.1022.

Cheung, HP. 2016. "Crush's Experimental Journey Beyond K-Pop & Rap." *Hypebeast*. May 18. https://hypebeast.com/2016/5/crush-interview.

Chin, Bertha, and Lori Hitchcock Morimoto. 2013. "Towards a Theory of Transcultural Fandom." *Participations: Journal of Audience and Reception Studies* 10 (1): 92–108.

Choi, JungBong. 2015. "Hallyu versus Hallyu-hwa: Cultural Phenomenon versus Institutional Campaign." In *Hallyu 2.0: The Korean Wave in the Age of Social Media*, edited by Sangjoon Lee and Abé Mark Nornes, 31–52. Ann Arbor: University of Michigan Press.

Choi, JungBong, and Roald Maliangkay. 2015. "Introduction: Why Fandom Matters to the International Rise of K-pop." In *K-pop: The International Rise of the Korean Music Industry*, edited by JungBong Choi and Roald Maliangkay, 1–18. New York: Routledge.

"Choice 37 Talks about G-Dragon & Big Bang on Gumship Interview!!" n.d. *BB*: *bigbangkpop*. http://www.bigbangkpop.com/2012/09/choice-37-talks-about-g-dragon-big-bang.html.

Christian, Margena A. 2006. "Why It Took MTV So Long to Play Black Music Videos." *Jet* 110 (14): 16.

Chua, Beng Huat and Koichi Iwabuchi. 2008. "Introduction: East Asian TV Dramas: Identifications, Sentiments and Effects." In *East Asian Pop Culture: Analysing the Korean Wave*, edited by Chua Beng Huat and Koichi Iwabuchi, 1–12. Hong Kong: Hong Kong University Press.

Cliff, Aimee. 2014. "FKA Twigs Is Right, 'Alternative R&B Must Die.'" *Fader*. September 12. https://www.thefader.com/2014/09/12/popping-off-fka-twigs-beyonce-alt-r-and-b.

Cloonan, Martin. 2005. "What Is Popular Music Studies? Some Observations." *British Journal of Music Education* 22 (1): 77–93. doi:10.1017/S026505170400600X.

Cobb, Jelani. 2007. *To the Break of Dawn: A Freestyle on the Hip Hop Aesthetic*. New York: New York University Press.

Condry, Ian. 2006. *Hip-Hop Japan: Rap and the Paths of Cultural Globalization*. Durham: Duke University Press.

Cooper, Brittney. 2014. "Do Only 'Haters' Think Miley Is Racist?" *HuffPostLive*. February 11. http://live.huffingtonpost.com/r/segment/miley-cyrus-w-magazine-ronan-farrow/52f0161702a7601cee000768.

Cosgrove, Ben. 2014. "K-Pop Pioneers: The Kim Sisters Take America." *Time*. November 8. http://time.com/3490883/k-pop-pioneers-the-kim-sisters-take-america/.

Davis, Ronald L. 1993. *The Glamour Factory: Inside Hollywood's Big Studio System.* Dallas: Southern Methodist University Press.

Davis, Thulani. 1992. "Aretha Franklin, Do Right Diva." Liner notes to *Aretha Franklin Queen of Soul: The Atlantic Recordings*, 19–23. New York: Atlantic Records.

Demers, Joanna. 2006. "Dancing Machines: 'Dance Dance Revolution,' Cybernetic Dance, and Musical Taste." *Popular Music* 25 (3): 401–14. https://www.jstor.org/stable/3877663.

Do, K. 2017. "Bang Shi Hyuk Talks about Why BTS Hasn't Created English Songs." *Soompi*. December 11. https://www.soompi.com/2017/12/11/bang-shi-hyuk-talks-bts-sings-korean/.

Do, K. 2015. "MONSTA X Named as Girl Scouts' New Ambassadors." *Soompi*. December 11. https://www.soompi.com/article/798011wpp/monsta-x-named-as-girl-scouts-new-ambassadors.

Dorof, Jakob. N.d. "Music Review: SHINee—Everybody." *Tiny Mix Tapes*. http://www.tinymixtapes.com/music-review/shinee-everybody.

Duffett, Mark. 2013. *Understanding Fandom: An Introduction to the Study of Media Fan Culture.* New York: Bloomsbury.

Dyson, Michael Eric. 2004. "The Culture of Hip-Hop." In *That's the Joint: The Hip-Hop Studies Reader*, edited by Murray Forman and Mark Anthony Neal, 61–68. New York: Routledge.

Early, Gerald. 2004. *One Nation under a Grove: Motown and American Culture.* Ann Arbor: University of Michigan Press.

Eckart, Carter J., et al. 1990. *Korea: Old and New: A History.* Seoul: Ilchokak.

Edogawa, Alice. 2013. "Gotcha!: [Review] SHINee 'Everybody' Album." *Aliceedogawa*. November 9. http://aliceedogawa.blogspot.com/2013/11/review-shinee-everybody-album.html.

Eliscu, Jenny. 2010. "The Soul and Science of Erykah Badu." *Rolling Stone*. April 15. https://www.rollingstone.com/music/music-news/the-soul-and-science-of-erykah-badu-186821/.

Elliott, Emory. 2007. "Diversity in the United States and Abroad: What Does It Mean When American Studies Is Transnational?" *American Quarterly* 59 (1) (March): 1–22. https://www.jstor.org/stable/40068421.

Emerson, Rana. 2002. "'Where My Girls At?': Negotiating Black Womanhood in Music Videos." *Gender and Society* 16 (1): 115–35. https://www.jstor.org/stable/3081879.

Emmison, Michael. 2003. "Social Class and Cultural Mobility: Reconfiguring the Cultural Omnivore Thesis," *Journal of Sociology* 39 (3): 211–30. doi: 10.1177/00048690030393001.

Epstein, Stephen, with James Turnball. 2014. "Girls' Generation? Gender, (Dis) Empowerment and K-pop." In *The Korean Popular Culture Reader*, edited by Kyung Hyun Kim and Youngmin Choe, 314–36. Durham, NC: Duke University Press.

Eric_r_wirsing. 2016. "[Album & MV Review] Se7en—'I Am Se7en.'" *allkpop*. October 21. https://www.allkpop.com/article/2016/10/album-mv-review-se7en-i-am-se7en.

Eric_r_wirsing. 2015. "[Album Review] 2PM." *allkpop*. June 15. http://www.allkpop.com/review/2015/06/album-review-2pm-no-5.

Eric_r_wirsing. 2014. "[Album Review] EXO-K—'Overdose.'" *allkpop*. May 10. https://www.allkpop.com/article/2014/05/album-review-exo-k-overdose.

Erlewine, Stephen Thomas. 2003. "Sly & the Family Stone." In *All Music Guide to Soul*, edited by Vladimir Bogdanov, John Bush, Chris Woodstra, and Stephen Thomas Erlewine, 624–26. San Francisco: Backbeat Books.

Farber, Jim. 2015. "Keith Richards Blasts Heavy Metal, Rap in Interview." *New York Daily News*. September 3. http://www.nydailynews.com/entertainment/music/keith-richards-plenty-plenty-article-1.2346653.

Fifield, Anna. 2016. "Young South Koreans Call Their Country 'Hell' and Look for Ways Out." *Washington Post*. January 31. https://www.washingtonpost.com/world/asia_pacific/young-south-koreans-call-their-country-hell-and-look-for-ways-out/2016/01/30/34737c06-b967-11e5-85cd-5ad59bc19432_story.html.

Fikentscher, Kai. 2006. "Disco and House." In *African American Music: An Introduction*, edited by Mellonee V. Burnim and Portia K. Maultsby, 315–29. New York: Routledge.

Fink, Robert. 2005. "The Story of ORCH5, Or, the Classical Ghost in the Hip-Hop Machine." *Popular Music* 24 (3): 339–56. doi: https://doi.org/10.1017/S0261143005000553.

"First Listen—Primary '2–1' Mini-Album." 2015. *seoulrebels*. April 9. https://seoulrebels.com/2015/04/09/first-listen-primary-2-1-mini-album/.

Fishkin, Shelley Fisher. 2005. "Crossroads of Cultures: The Transnational Turn in American Studies: Presidential Address to the American Studies Association, November 12, 2004." *American Quarterly* 57 (1): 17–57. http://www.jstor.org/stable/40068248.

Fitzgerald, Jon. 2007. "Black Pop Songwriting 1963–1966: An Analysis of U.S. Top Forty Hits by Cooke, Mayfield, Stevenson, Robinson, and Holland-Dozier-Holland." *Black Music Research Journal* 27 (2) (2007): 97–140. http://www.jstor.org/stable/25433786.

Fitzgerald, Jon. 1995. "Motown Crossover Hits 1963–1966 and the Creative Process." *Popular Music* 14 (1): 1–11. https://www.jstor.org/stable/853340.

Flatley, Joseph L. 2012. "K-pop Takes America: How South Korea's Music Machine Is Conquering the World." *The Verge*. October 18. http://www.theverge.com/2012/10/18/3516562/k-pop-invades-america-south-korea-pop-music-factory.

Flory, Andrew. 2014. "Tamla Motown in the UK: Transatlantic Reception of American Rhythm and Blues." In *Sounds of the City*, edited by Brett Lashua, Karl Spracklen, and Stephen Wagg, 113–27. Basingstoke, UK: Palgrave.

"Fly to the Sky— 약속 + What U Want." 2019. YouTube. Posted by 황황황, July 6. https://youtu.be/dTfxBdtuodo.

"Fly to the Sky—Day by Day." 2009. YouTube. Posted by doolielove, January 6. https://youtu.be/uFhubvJhCKE.

Frere-Jones, Sasha. 2008. "Living Pains: Mary J. Blige's Chronic Brilliance." *New Yorker*. February 3. https://www.newyorker.com/magazine/2008/02/11/living-pains.

Fuhr, Michael. 2016. *Globalization and Popular Music in South Korea: Sounding Out K-pop*. New York: Routledge.

Gabler, Neal. 1989. *An Empire of Their Own: How the Jews Invented Hollywood*. New York: Anchor Books.

Gainer, Nichelle. 2014. *Vintage Black Glamour*. London: Rockett 88.

Galloway, A. Scott. 2017. "The Isley Brothers—Go for Your Guns." *Radio Facts*. October 26. https://radiofacts.com/that-time-when-the-isley-brothers-created-their-second-perfect-album-and/.

Gammage, Marquita Marie. 2015. *Representations of Black Women in the Media: The Damnation of Black Womanhood*. New York: Routledge.

Garofalo, Reebee. 1993. "Black Popular Music: Crossing Over or Going Under?" In *Rock and Popular Music: Politics, Policies, Institutions*, edited by Tony Bennett et al., 229–45. London: Routledge.

Gates Jr., Henry Louis. 1998. *The Signifying Monkey: A Theory of African-American Literary Criticism*. Oxford: Oxford University Press.

Generasia. n.d. "Welcome to *generasia*." Accessed September 19, 2019. http://www.generasia.com/wiki/.

George, Nelson. 1999. *Hip-Hop America*. New York: Penguin.
George, Nelson. 1988. *The Death of Rhythm and Blues*. New York: Penguin Books.
GhostWriter. 2016. "Hyun Jin Young, The Very First SM Artist." *Allkpop*. May 11. https://www
 .allkpop.com/article/2016/05/way-back-wednesday-hyun-jin-young-the-very-first-sm-artist.
Glasby, Taylor. 2018. "Meet Jay Park, The Korean Hip Hop Polymath with America in His
 Sights." *Dazed*. February 15. http://www.dazeddigital.com/music/article/39032/1/jay-park
 -korea-hip-hop-r-b-interview.
Glasby, Taylor. 2017. "Meet Dean, the Rising Star Bringing Korean R&B to the World." *Hero
 Magazine*. March 6. http://hero-magazine.com/article/90012/meet-dean-the-multi-skilled
 -star-bringing-korean-rb-to-the-world/.
"G.O.D—Observation MV HD (지오디 - 관찰 뮤직비디오 HD)." 2012. YouTube. Posted by
 GrooveOverDoseTV, June 15. https://www.youtube.com/watch?v=wifIwg-XpLU.
Goldblatt, David. 2013. "Nonsense in Public Places: Songs of Black Vocal Rhythm and Blues
 or Doo-Wop." *Journal of Aesthetics and Art Criticism* 71 (1): 101–10. doi: 10.1111/j.1540-6245
 .2012.01546.x.
Goodall, Nataki. 1994. "Depend on Myself: T.L.C. and the Evolution of Black Female Rap."
 Journal of Negro History 79 (1): 85–93. doi: 10.2307/2717669.
Goodwin, Andrew. 1992. *Dancing in the Distraction Factory: Music Television and Popular
 Culture*. Minneapolis: University of Minnesota Press.
Gordon, Larry. 2015. "Korean-Language Classes Are Growing in Popularity at U.S. Colleges."
 Los Angeles Times. April 1. http://www.latimes.com/local/education/la-me-korean-language
 -20150401-story.html.
Gracyk, Theodore. 2007. *Listening to Popular Music, or How I Learned to Stop Worrying and
 Love Led Zeppelin*. Ann Arbor: University of Michigan Press.
Green, Michael Cullen. 2010. *Black Yanks in the Pacific: Race in the Making of American Military
 Empire after World War II*. Ithaca, NY: Cornell University Press.
Greenblatt, Stephen. 2010. "Cultural Mobility: An Introduction." In *Cultural Mobility: A Manifesto*, edited by Stephen Greenblatt, Ines G. Zupanov, Reinhard Meyer-Kalkus, Heike Paul,
 Pal Nyiri, and Friederike Pannewick, 1–23. Cambridge: Cambridge University Press.
Greenwald, Jeff. 2002. "Hip-Hop Drumming: The Rhyme May Define, but the Groove Makes
 You Move." *Black Music Research Journal* 22 (2): 259–71. doi: 10.2307/1519959.
Greig, Charlotte. 1989. *Will You Still Love Me Tomorrow?: Girl Groups from the 1950s On*.
 London: Virago Press.
Grossberg, Lawrence. 1992. "Is There a Fan in the House?: The Affective Sensibility of Fandom." In *The Adoring Audience: Fan Culture and Popular Media*, edited by Lisa A. Lewis,
 50–65. London and New York: Taylor and Francis.
Grossberg, Lawrence, Cary Nelson, and Paula Treichler. 1992. "Cultural Studies: An Introduction." In *Cultural Studies*, edited by Lawrence Grossberg, Cary Nelson, and Paula Treichler,
 1–16. New York: Routledge.
Ha, Jarryn. 2015. "Uncles' Generation: Adult Male Fans and Alternative Masculinities in South
 Korean Popular Music." *Journal of Fandom Studies* 3 (1) (March): 43–58. https://doi.org
 /10.1386/jfs.3.1.43_1.
Hamera, Judith. 2012. "The Labors of Michael Jackson: Virtuosity, Deindustrialization, and
 Dancing Work." *PMLA* 127 (4): 751–65. doi: 10.1632/pmla.2012.127.4.751.
Hamilton, Jack. 2016. "How Rock and Roll Became White." *Slate*. October 16. http://www.slate
 .com/articles/arts/music_box/2016/10/race_rock_and_the_rolling_stones_how_the_rock
 _and_roll_became_white.html.

Han, Geon-soo. 2003. "African Migrant Workers' Views of Korean People and Culture." *Korea Journal* 43 (1): 154–73.

Harper, Phillip Brian. 1989. "Synesthesia, 'Crossover,' and Blacks in Popular Music." *Social Text* 23: 102–21. doi: 10.2307/466423.

Harris, Keith. 1999. "'Untitled': D'Angelo and the Visualization of the Black Male." *Wide Angle* 21 (4): 62–83. doi:10.1353/wan.2004.0003.

Harvie, Charles, and Hyun-hoon Lee. 2003. "Export-Led Industrialization and Growth: Korea's Economic Miracle, 1962–1989." *Australian Economic History Review* 43 (3): 256–86. doi: https://doi.org/10.1046/j.1467-8446.2003.00054.x.

Hazzon, Dave. "Korea's Black Racism Epidemic." *Groove Korea*. February 11. http://groove-korea.com/article/koreas-black-racism-epidemic-0/.

"[HD] G.O.D—Dear Mother/to My Mother MV ENG SUB/ROM (지오디 - 어머님께 뮤직비디오 HD)." 2013. YouTube. Posted by GrooveOverSubs, July 1. https://www.youtube.com/watch?v=6vPzSt8muF4.

Henderson, Alex. 2003. "K-Ci & Jo-Jo." In *All Music Guide to Soul*, edited by Vladimir Bogdanov, John Bush, Chris Woodstra, and Stephen Thomas Erlewine, 382. San Francisco: Backbeat Books.

Hennion, Antoine. 1989. "An Intermediary between Production and Consumption: The Producer of Popular Music." *Science, Technology, and Human Values* 14 (4): 400–424. https://www.jstor.org/stable/689684.

Herman, Tamar. 2018. "SHINee Looks Back on Debut Song 'Replay' Ten Years Later." *Billboard*. June 21. https://www.billboard.com/articles/columns/k-town/8462058/shinee-replay-interview-ten-years-later.

Herman, Tamar. 2017a. "Every Wonder Girls Single Ranked from Worst to Best: Critic's Take." *Billboard*. February 9. https://www.billboard.com/articles/columns/k-town/7685988/every-wonder-girls-single-ranked.

Herman, Tamar. 2017b. "BTS and Steve Aoki Drop 'Mic Drop' Remix Feat. Desiigner: Watch." *Billboard*. November 24. https://www.billboard.com/articles/columns/k-town/8046914/bts-steve-aoki-k-pop-drop-mic-drop-remix-desiigner-edm.

Herman, Tamar. 2015. "Meet Hyukoh, the Indie Rock Band Topping the Korean Charts in a World of K-Pop." *Noisey*. August 13. https://noisey.vice.com/en_us/article/rpy3zk/hyukoh-22-comes-and-goes-south-korea-indie-rock-interview.

Herman, Tamar, Jeff Benjamin, and Caitlin Kelley. 2017. "The Best K-pop Songs of 2017." *Billboard*. December 14. https://www.billboard.com/articles/events/year-in-music-2017/8070355/best-k-pop-songs-of-2017-top-20.

Hills, Matt. 2002. *Fan Cultures*. Abingdon: Routledge.

Hip-Hop Evolution. 2016. "The Foundation." Episode 1. Season 1. Directed by Darby Wheeler. Netflix.

Hip-Hop Evolution. 2016. "The Birth of Gangsta Rap." Episode 3. Season 1. Directed by Darby Wheeler. Netflix.

Hirshey, Gerri. 1984. *Nowhere to Run: The Story of Soul Music*. Boston: Da Capo Press.

Hoffman, Heiko. 2005. "From the Autobahn to I-94." *Pitchfork*. November 28. http://pitchfork.com/features/articles/6204-from-the-autobahn-to-i-94/.

Hogarth, Hyun-key Kim. 2013. "The Korean Wave: An Asian Reaction to Western-Dominated Globalization." *Perspectives on Global Development and Technology* 12 (1–2): 135–51. doi: 10.1163/15691497-12341247.

Holcombe, Charles. 2011. *A History of East Asia: From the Origins of Civilization to the Twenty-First Century*. Cambridge: Cambridge University Press.
"How Epik Is Epik High's Comeback?" 2012. *seoulbeats*. October 29. http://seoulbeats.com/2012/10/how-epic-is-epik-highs-comeback/.
Howard, Keith. 2006. *Korean Pop Music: Riding the Wave*. Dorset, UK: Global Oriental.
"[Interview] Record Producer Yoo Young-Jin—Part 1." 2010a. *10asia*. June 11. http://www.asiae.co.kr/news/view.htm?idxno=2010061109310268065.
"[Interview] Record Producer Yoo Young-Jin—Part 2." 2010b. *10asia*. June 11. http://www.asiae.co.kr/news/view.htm?idxno=2010061113544954123.
"[Interview] Shinhwa Members Say 'Shinhwa' Is Their Life-Long Career." 2015. *Korea.net*. March 3. http://www.korea.net/NewsFocus/Daily-News/view?articleId=1101&flag=2&lgroupId=A120200.
"Interview with Korea's g.o.d." 2001. *CNN.com*. http://edition.cnn.com/2001/WORLD/asiapcf/east/06/27/korea.god/.
Iwabuchi, Koichi. 2010. "Undoing Inter-national Fandom in the Age of Brand Nationalism." *Mechademia* 5: 87–96. https://www.jstor.org/stable/41510958.
Jackson, John L. 2005. *Real Black: Adventures in Racial Sincerity*. Chicago: University of Chicago Press.
Jackson, Kennell. 2005. "Introduction: Traveling While Black." In *Black Cultural Traffic: Crossroads in Global Performance and Popular Culture*, edited by Harry Justin Elam Jr. and Kennell Jackson, 1–42. Ann Arbor: University of Michigan Press.
"The Jackson 5 Dancing Machine Live at Soul Train." 2014. YouTube. Posted by Marley Jackson, August 2. https://www.youtube.com/watch?v=CuyOGuXiGAk.
Jara. 2015a. "'No. 5' Album Review." *FunCurve*. October 28. http://www.funcurve.com/music/2pm-no-5-album-review/.
Jara. 2015b. "SHINee—'Odd' Album Review." *FunCurve*. October 19. http://www.funcurve.com/music/shinee-odd-album-review/.
Jenkins, Henry. 2013. *Textual Poachers: Television Fans and Participatory Culture*. 2nd ed. New York: Routledge.
Johnson, Jennie Alice. 2003. "Exploring Korea's Pop Culture: An Interview with the Reigning Korean Hip-Hop Group, Jinusean." *Harvard Asia Pacific Review* 7 (1): 83–87.
Joora. 2014. "8 Artists with That 'Unique Voice.'" *allkpop*. April 19. https://www.allkpop.com/article/2014/04/8-artists-with-that-unique-voice.
Journal of Popular Music Studies. n.d. "About." Accessed August 27, 2019. https://jpms.ucpress.edu/content/about.
Jung, Eun-young. 2011. "The Place of Sentimental Song in Contemporary Korean Musical Life." *Korean Studies* 35: 71–92. https://www.jstor.org/stable/23719454.
Jung, Eun-young. 2010. "Playing the Race and Sexuality Cards in the Transnational Pop Game: Korean Music Videos for the US Market." *Journal of Popular Music Studies* 22 (2): 219–36. doi: 10.1111/j.1533-1598.2010.01237.x.
Jung Bae. 2012. "Album Review: Shinhwa—The Return." *hellokpop*. April 15. http://www.hellokpop.com/review/album-review-shinhwa-the-return/.
Jung, Sun, and Hirata Yukie. 2012. "Conflicting Desires: K-pop Idol Girl Group Flows in Japan in the Era of Web 2.0." *ejcjs* 12 (2).
Jung, Sung. 2011. *Korean Masculinities and Transcultural Consumption: Yonsama, Rain, Oldboy, K-pop Idols*. Hong Kong: Hong Kong University Press.

Katz, Mark. 2014. "What Does It Mean to Study Popular Music?: A Musicologist's Perspective." *Journal of Popular Music Studies* 26 (1): 22–27. https://doi.org/10.1111/jpms.12057.

Kawaiineyo. 2008. "DBSK ["O"Jung.Ban.Hap] (Third Korean Album)." *Memories of Love*. September 18. https://memoriesoflove.wordpress.com/2008/09/18/dbsk-o-jungbanhub-third-korean-album/.

KCCA. n.d. "Introduction." http://eng.kocca.kr/en/contents.do?menuNo=201433.

Kelley, Robin D. G. 1997. *Yo' Mama's Disfunktional: Fighting the Cultural Wars in Urban America*. Boston: Beacon Press.

Kim, Chang-nam. 2012. *K-pop: Roots and Blossoming of Korean Popular Music*. Seoul: Hollym.

Kim, Do Kyun, and Min-Sun Kim. 2011. *Hallyu: Influence of Korean Popular Culture in Asia and Beyond*. Seoul: Seoul National University Press.

Kim, Monica. 2017. "How Hyuk Oh, the Korean Indie Rock Star, Is Changing the Sound and Style of Seoul." *Vogue*. October 16. https://www.vogue.com/article/hyukoh-korean-music-artist-anti-kpop-fashion-style.

Kim, Nadia Y. 2006. "'Seoul-America' on America's 'Soul': South Koreans and Korean Immigrants Navigate Global White Racial Ideology." *Critical Sociology* 32 (2–3): 381–402. doi: 10.1163/156916306777835231.

Kim, Rebecca. 2015. *The Spirit Moves West: Korean Missionaries in America*. Oxford: Oxford University Press.

Kim, Su-yeon. 2011. "Tablo Uncut: An Interview with Epik High's Charismatic Leader: Part IV." *MTVIggy*. November 3. http://www.mtviggy.com/interviews/tablo-uncut-an-interview-with-epik-high's-charismatic-leader/4/.

Kinnon, Joy Bennett. 1998. "K-Ci & JoJo: Music's Hottest Duo." *Ebony* 53 (12): 80, 82, 178.

KisforKARENX3. 2011. "SNSD to Greet Fans at Soshified Fanmeet at SM Town NYC." *soompi*. October 21. http://www.soompi.com/2011/10/21/snsd-to-greet-fans-at-soshified-fanmeet-at-sm-town-nyc/.

Konser, Relawan. 2014. "[Special] Interview with Urban Zakapa." *Relawan Konser*. October 24. https://relawankonser.com/2014/10/24/interview-urban-zakapa-october-2014/.

"Korean Entertainment Agency Takes Its Acts Globally." 2011. YouTube. Posted by Stanford Graduate School of Business, May 12. http://youtu.be/bGP5mNh9z08.

"Korean Hip-Hop: K-Hop Goes Global." 2012. *Newsweek*. January 23. http://www.thedailybeast.com/newsweek/2012/01/22/korean-hip-hop-k-hop-goes-global.html.

"K-pop Indie Gem: Urban Zakapa." 2011. *seoulbeats*. September 23. http://seoulbeats.com/2011/09/k-indie-gem-urban-zakapa/.

Kpop Vocalists' Vocal Analyses. n.d. "F.A.Q." Accessed August 29, 2019. https://kpopvocalanalysis.net/faq/.

Kwon, Seung-Ho, and Joseph Kim. 2014. "The Culture Industry Policies of the Korean Government and the Korean Wave." *International Journal of Cultural Policy* 20 (4): 422–39. doi: 10.1080/10286632.2013.829052.

Lee, Jamie Shinhee. 2004. "Linguistic Hybridization in K-Pop: Discourse of Self-Assertion and Resistance." *World Englishes* 23 (3): 429–50. doi: 10.1111/j.0883-2919.2004.00367.x.

Lee, Mary. 2008. "Mixed Race Peoples in the Korean National Imaginary and Family." *Korean Studies* 32: 56–85. doi: 10.1353/ks.0.0010.

Lee, Sangjoon. 2015. "Introduction: A Decade of Hallyu Scholarship: Toward a New Direction in Hallyu 2.0." In *Hallyu 2.0: The Korean Wave in the Age of Social Media*, edited by Sangjoon Lee and Abé Mark Nornes, 1–28. Ann Arbor: University of Michigan Press.

Lee, Sangjoon, and Abé Mark Nornes. 2015. *Hallyu 2.0: The Korean Wave in the Age of Social Media*. Ann Arbor: University of Michigan Press.

Legg, Andrew. 2010. "A Taxonomy of Musical Gesture in African American Gospel Music." *Popular Music* 29 (1): 103–29. doi: 10.1017/S0261143009990407.

Leight, Elias. 2018. "How American R&B Songwriters Found a New Home in K-pop." *Rolling Stone*. May 2. https://www.rollingstone.com/music/music-news/how-american-rb-songwriters-found-a-new-home-in-k-pop-627643/.

Lena. 2010. "Interview with Drunken Tiger." *KoME U.S.A.* March 3. http://www.kome-world.com/us/articles-9463-interview-with-drunken-tiger.html.

Lendrum, Alexander. 2017. "HIGHGRND: The Underground K-Pop Sub-Label That's Redefining the Genre." *Unrated*. January 4. http://unrtd.co/highgrnd-the-underground-k-pop-sub-label-thats-redefining-the-genre/.

Lennon. 2013. "[Interview] Yang Hyun-suk, CEO of YG Entertainment—Part 2." *Kstar10*. January 17. http://kstar10.tenasia.co.kr/?construct=K_newContent&fz=news&newCode=ARTS&gisaNo=27909.

Leonard, Marion, and Robert Strachan. 2003. "Dance." In *Bloomsbury Encyclopedia of Popular Music of the World: Volume II: Performance and Production*, edited by John Shepard, David Horn, Dave Laing, Paul Oliver, and Peter Wicke, 651–60. Continuum.

Lewis, Nate. 2018. "Michael McDonald Speaks from the Soul." *Blues and Soul Magazine*. July 24. http://www.bluesandsoul.com/feature/262/michael_mcdonald_speaks_from_the_soul/.

Lie, John. 2014. *K-pop: Popular Music, Cultural Amnesia, and Economic Innovation in South Korea*. Oakland: University of California Press.

Lie, John. 2012. "What is the K in K-pop?: South Korean Popular Music, the Culture Industry, and National Identity." *Korea Observer* 43 (3): 339–63.

Light, Alan. 2008. "The Kalimba Story." Liner notes for Earth, Wind and Fire box set *The Eternal Dance*. New York: Columbia Records.

Lim, Hyun-chin, and Joon Han. 2003. "The Social and Political Impact of Economic Crisis in South Korea: A Comparative Note." *Asian Journal* 31 (2): 198–200. http://www.jstor.org/stable/23654666.

Lindsay. 2012. "K-pop Sub-genres: Get Retro with New Jack Swing." *seoulbeats*. October. http://seoulbeats.com/2012/10/k-pop-sub-genres-get-retro-with-new-jack-swing/.

Lindvall, Helienne. 2011. "Behind the Music: What Is K-Pop and Why Are the Swedish Getting Involved?" *Guardian*. April 20. http://www.guardian.co.uk/music/musicblog/2011/apr/20/k-pop-sweden-pelle-lidell.

Locke, Kaito. 2017. "[Album Review] Zion.T—OO." *United Kpop*. March 7. http://ukp.link/YAVAV.

Luo, Benny. 2017. "Meet the Most Famous Black Man in Korea." *Nextshark*. May 30. https://nextshark.com/sam-okyere-most-famous-black-man-korea/.

"Lyn Preaches Love in 'I Like This Song' and We Love It." 2013. *seoulbeats*. September 1. http://seoulbeats.com/2013/09/lyn-preaches-love-in-i-like-this-song-and-we-love-it/.

Lyon, Chris. 2015. "DEAN | HIPHOPKR Exclusive Interview." *Hip Hop Korea*. December 12. https://hiphopkr.com/interviews/d%ce%be%ce%b4n-hiphopkr-exclusive-interview-2/.

Madrid-Morales, Dani, and Bruno Lovric. 2015. "'Transatlantic Connection': K-pop and K-drama Fandom in Spain and Latin America." *Journal of Fandom Studies* 3 (1): 23–41. doi: https://doi.org/10.1386/jfs.3.1.23_1.

Maliangkay, Roald. 2015. "Uniformity and Nonconformity: The Packaging of Korean Girl Groups." In *Hallyu 2.0: The Korean Wave in the Age of Social Media*, edited by Sangjoon Lee and Abé Mark Nornes, 90–107. Ann Arbor: University of Michigan Press.

Malone, Jacqui. 1988. "'Let the Punishment Fit the Crime': The Vocal Choreography of Cholly Atkins." *Dance Research Journal* 20 (1): 11–18. doi: 10.2307/1478812.

Mark. 2013. "Aegyo Hip Hop: Cultural Appropriation at Its Messiest." *seoulbeats*. January 5. http://seoulbeats.com/2013/01/aegyo-hip-hop-cultural-appropriation-at-its-messiest/.

Marsh, David. 1992. "Gotta Find Me an Angel." Liner notes for *Aretha Franklin Queen of Soul: The Atlantic Recordings*, 25–30. New York: Atlantic Records.

Marshall, Wayne. 2006. "Giving Up Hip-Hop's Firstborn: A Quest for the Real after the Death of Sampling." *Callaloo* 29 (3): 868–92. doi: https://www.jstor.org/stable/4488375.

Matsumoto, Jon. 2012. "The K-pop Explosion." *Grammy.com*. May 3. http://www.grammy.com/news/the-k-pop-explosion.

Maultsby, Portia K. 2006. "Funk." In *African American Music: An Introduction*, edited by Mellonee V. Burnim and Portia K. Maultsby, 293–314. New York: Routledge.

McClure, Steve. 2001. "Japan Hits the Road." *Billboard* 113 (8): APQ1, APQ4.

McLeod, Kembrew. 1999. "Authenticity within Hip-Hop and Other Cultures Threatened with Assimilation." *Journal of Communication* 49 (4): 134–50. doi: 10.1111/j.1460-2466.1999.tb02821.x.0.

MCST: Ministry of Culture, Sports and Tourism. n.d. "Vision." http://www.mcst.go.kr/english/ministry/vision/vision.jsp.

Melendez, Monique. 2016. "Crush Talks Erasing Musical Boundaries at KCON New York 2016: Exclusive." *Billboard*. June 27. https://www.billboard.com/articles/columns/k-town/7416610/crush-interview-kcon-new-york-2016.

Meyer, Leonard. 1956. *Emotion and Meaning in Music*. Chicago: University of Chicago Press.

Miller, Monica. 2009. *Slaves to Fashion: Black Dandyism and the Styling of Black Diasporic Identity*. Durham: Duke University Press.

Ming, Cheang. 2017. "How K-Pop Made a Breakthrough in the US in 2017." CNBC. December 29. https://www.cnbc.com/2017/12/29/bts-and-big-hit-entertainment-how-k-pop-broke-through-in-the-us.html.

Mitchell, Gail. 2000. "Reinventing the Real: R&B Gets Its Groove Back." *Billboard*, June 3: 41, 47, 52.

Mitchell, Tony. 2001. "Introduction: Another Root—Hip-Hop Outside the USA." In *Global Noise: Rap and Hip-Hop Outside the USA*, edited by Tony Mitchell, 1–38. Middletown, CT: Wesleyan University Press.

Miyakawa, Felicia M. 2007. "Turntablature: Notation, Legitimization, and the Art of the Hip-Hop DJ." *American Music* 25 (1): 81–105. doi: 10.2307/40071644.

"ML | Adventures with YG Entertainment." 2011. YouTube. Posted by MovementLifestyle, February 7. http://youtu.be/iOCpvvNuOaY.

Mobius, J. Mark. (1966). "The Japan-Korea Normalization Process and Korean Anti-Americanism." *Asian Survey* 6 (4): 241–48. doi: 10.2307/2642122.

Mody, Seema. 2017. "China Lashes Out as South Korea Puts an American Anti-Missile System in Place." CNBC. April 29. http://www.cnbc.com/2017/03/17/thaad-anti-missile-system-makes-china-lash-out-at-south-korea.html.

Mokoena, Tshepo. 2017. "Why Is Black Music Still Rarely Classified as Mainstream Pop?" *Noisey*. March 21. https://noisey.vice.com/en_us/article/z4k8aj/why-is-black-music-still-rarely-classified-as-mainstream-pop.

MoonSoshi9. 2012. "Writers Review February 2012: 'The Boys' and 'MR. TAXI' Repackages." *Soshified*. March 1. https://www.soshified.com/2012/03/writers-review-february-2012-the-boys-and-mr-taxi-repackages.

Moore, Allan F. 2012. *Song Means: Analysing and Interpreting Recorded Popular Song*. Farnham, UK, and Burlington, VT: Ashgate.

Moore, Allan F. 2002. "Authenticity as Authentication." *Popular Music* 21 (2): 209–23. doi:10.1017/S0261143002002131.

"[MV] Fin.K.L (핑클) _ Blue Rain." 2019. YouTube. Posted by 1theK (원더케이), May 23. https://youtu.be/PZ-rMQtWoTc.

"[MV] god_Saturday Night." 2018. YouTube. Posted by 1theK (원더케이), August 21. https://www.youtube.com/watch?v=srdN65FoZSQ.

"[MV] Yoonmirae (윤미래) _ Black Happiness (검은 행복)." 2015. YouTube. Posted by 1thK, December 24. https://youtu.be/1DK-MPh7vKk.

"[MV] Yoonmirae (윤미래) _ KawiBawiBo (가위바위보)." 2018. YouTube. Posted by 1theK, April 20. https://youtu.be/gAzdJCPdkJ4.

Moorefield, Virgil. 2005. *The Producer as Composer: Shaping the Sounds of Popular Music*. Cambridge, MA: MIT Press.

Morelli, Sarah. 2001. "'Who Is a Dancing Hero?': Rap, Hip-Hop, and Dance in Korean Popular Culture." In *Global Noise: Rap and Hip-Hop Outside the USA*, edited by Tony Mitchell, 248–58. Middletown, CT: Wesleyan University Press.

Morgan, Marcyliena, and Dionne Bennett. 2011. "Hip-Hop and the Global Imprint of a Black Cultural Form." *Daedalus: Journal of the American Academy of Arts & Sciences* 140 (2): 176–96. doi: 10.1162/DAED_a_00086.

Motoway065. 2008. "Album Review—Wonder Girls—Nobody: The Wonder Years Trilogy." *soompi*. December 1. https://www.soompi.com/2008/12/01/album-review-wonder-girls-nobody-the-wonder-years-trilogy/.

Mukherjee, Roopali. 2006. "The Ghetto Fabulous Aesthetic in Contemporary Black Culture: Class and Consumption in the *Barbershop* Films." *Cultural Studies* 20 (6): 599–629. doi: 10.1080/09502380600973978.

Murphy, John P. 1990. "Jazz Improvisation: The Joy of Influence." *Black Perspective in Music* 18 (1–2): 7–19. https://www.jstor.org/stable/1214855.

"MUSIC VIDEO: Wheesung—Incurable Disease." 2007. YouTube. Posted by linhieee, August 20. https://youtu.be/ptKqKYz9U_k.

Nakassis, Constantine V. 2013. "Citation and Citationality." *Signs and Society* 1 (1): 51–77. doi: 10.1086/670165.

Neal, Mark Anthony. 2005. "White Chocolate Soul: Teena Marie and Lewis Taylor." *Popular Music* 24 (1): 369–80. https://www.jstor.org/stable/3877524.

Neal, Mark Anthony. 1999. *What the Music Said: Black Popular Music and Black Public Culture*. Routledge: New York.

"New Edition—Cool It Now (Official Video)." 2009. YouTube. Posted by NewEditionVEVO, October 7. https://youtu.be/RZUq6N7Gx1c.

Nick. 2017. "Song Review: Zion.T—The Song." *Bias List*. February 1. https://thebiaslist.com/2017/02/01/song-review-zion-t-the-song/.

Nini. 2015. "[Inside the Music] VIBE and 4MEN Talk about 'K-Soul' and US Tour." *hellokpop*. February 1. http://www.hellokpop.com/news/exclusive/inside-the-music-vibe-and-4men-talks-about-k-soul-and-us-tour/.

Noh, Dong-eun. 2003. "Singing Culture of Koreans: A Multifaceted Soundtrack of Life." *Koreana: A Quarterly on Korean Art and Culture* 17 (3): 72–77.

Norfleet, Dawn M. 2006. "Hip-Hop and Rap." In *African American Music: An Introduction*, edited by Mellonee V. Burnim and Portia K. Maultsby, 353–89. New York: Routledge.

Nye, Joseph, and Youna Kim. 2013. "Soft Power and the Korean Wave." In *The Korean Wave: Korean Media Go Global*, edited by Youna Kim, 31–42. New York: Routledge.

Oak, Jessica. 2014. "EXO Keeps Their Astounding Momentum Going with 'Overdose.'" *Billboard*. May 7. https://www.billboard.com/articles/columns/k-town/6077666/exo-keeps-their-astounding-momentum-going-with-overdose.

Oak, Jessica. 2013. "Dynamic Duo Reflect on 14 Years in K-pop: Exclusive Q&A." *Billboard Korea*. September 6. http://www.billboard.com/articles/columns/k-town/5687190/dynamic-duo-reflect-on-14-years-in-k-pop-exclusive-qa.

Ock, Hyu-ju. 2017. "[Newsmaker] Why Koreans Want to Leave 'Hell Joseon.'" *Korea Herald*. December 10. http://www.koreaherald.com/view.php?ud=20171210000292.

Oh, Chang-hun, and Celeste Arrington. 2007. "Democratization and Changing Anti-American Sentiments in South Korea." *Asian Survey* 47 (2) (March/April): 327–50. doi: 10.1525/as.2007.47.2.327.

Oh, David. "Black K-pop Fan Videos and Polyculturalism." *Popular Communication* 15 (4): 269–82. doi: 10.1080/15405702.2017.1371309.

Oh, Ingyu. 2013. "The Globalization of K-pop: Korea's Place in the Global Music Industry." *Korea Observer* 44 (3): 389–409.

Oh, Ingyu, and Hyo-Jung Lee. 2013. "K-pop in Korea: How the Pop Music Industry Is Changing a Post-Developmental Society," *Cross-Currents: East Asian History and Culture Review* (9): 105–24. https://cross-currents.berkeley.edu/e-journal/issue-9/oh-and-lee.

Oh, Ingyu, and Gil-Sung Park. 2012. "From B2C to B2B: Selling Korean Pop Music in the Age of New Social Media." *Korea Observer* 43 (3): 365–97.

Ollison, Rashod. 2015. "Before Adele and Sam Smith: The British Pop-Soul Invasion of the '80s." *Virginian-Pilot*. October 29. https://pilotonline.com/entertainment/music/behind-the-groove/article_ceb5ac7b-672a-53db-a0e0-fc4a1e0aabdf.html.

Palmer, Joe. 2015. "SM Entertainment: The 'Brand.'" *KultScene*. April 20. http://kultscene.com/sm-entertainment-the-brand/.

Pan, Deanna. 2012. "Is 'Gangnam Style' a Hit Because of Our Asian Stereotypes?" *Mother Jones*. September 24. http://www.motherjones.com/mixed-media/2012/09/gangnam-style-asian-masculinity%20.

Pareles, Jon. 1992. "Review/Pop; A Girl Group for a Changing World." *New York Times*. September 17. https://www.nytimes.com/1992/09/17/arts/review-pop-a-girl-group-for-a-changing-world.html.

Park, Gil-sung. 2013. "Manufacturing Creativity: Production, Performance and Dissemination of K-pop." *Korea Journal* 53 (1): 14–33.

"Park Hyo Shin's Interview @ Dong-A Ilbo." 2007. *Reika no Rakuen*. February 1. https://reikanorakuen.wordpress.com/2007/02/01/park-hyo-shins-interview-dong-a-ilbo/.

Park, Si-soo. 2014. "Anti-Hallyu Voices Growing in Japan." *Korea Times*. February 21. http://www.koreatimes.co.kr/www/news/nation/2016/09/386_152045.html.

Park Sun-young. n.d. "Shinsedae: Conservative Attitudes of a 'New Generation' in South Korea and the Impact on the Korean Presidential Election," *East-West Center*. http://www.eastwestcenter.org/news-center/east-west-wire/shinsedae-conservative-attitudes-of-a-new-generation-in-south-korea-and-the-impact-on-the-korean-pres.

Pennycook, Alastair. 2007. "Language, Localization, and the Real: Hip-Hop and the Global Spread of Authenticity." *Journal of Language, Identity, and Education* 6 (2): 101–15. doi: 10.1080/15348450701341246.

Perkins, William Eric. 1996. "The Rap Attack: An Introduction." In *Droppin' Science: Critical Essays on Rap Music and Hip Hop Culture*, edited by William Eric Perkins, 1–45. Philadelphia: Temple University Press.

Perry, Imani. 2004. *Prophets of the Hood: Politics and Poetics in Hip Hop*. Durham, NC: Duke University Press.
Petchauer, Emery. 2009. "Framing and Reviewing Hip-Hop Educational Research." *Review of Educational Research* 79 (2): 946–78. doi: 10.3102/0034654308330967.
Peterson, Richard, and Andy Bennett. 2004. "Introducing Music Scenes." In *Music Scenes: Local, Translocal and Virtual*, edited by Andy Bennett and Richard Peterson, 1–15. Nashville, TN: Vanderbilt University Press.
"Queen Latifah—Just Another Day." 2010. YouTube. Posted by UPROXX Video, December 15. https://youtu.be/YkGY5EzA-h4.
Railton, Diane, and Paul Watson. 2011. *Music Video and the Politics of Representation*. Edinburgh: Edinburgh University Press.
"[RAIN/비] 2nd—How to Avoid the Sun [태양을 피하는 방법] [Official MV- 2003.10.16]." 2012. YouTube. Posted by RAIN's Official Channel, July 15. https://www.youtube.com/watch?v=VGa2_bAHeQ8.
"RAIN 3rd—Its raining M/V Full v. (2004.10.08)." 2012. YouTube. Posted by RAIN's Official Channel, July 9. https://www.youtube.com/watch?v=9VqpPtb7RJg.
Raine0211. 2016. "The 14 Most Unique Voices in K-pop." *soompi*. June 25. https://www.soompi.com/2016/06/25/14-unique-voices-k-pop/.
Ramsey, Guthrie P. 2004. *Race Music: Black Cultures from Bebop to Hip-Hop*. Berkeley: University of California Press.
Randall, Annie J. 2008. *Dusty! Queen of the Postmods*. Oxford: Oxford University Press.
Random J. 2010. "Album Review: 2PM—1:59PM." *Random JPop*. January 4. http://randomjpop.blogspot.com/2010/01/album-review-2pm-159pm.html.
Rashid, Sam. 2012. "Everything You Need to Know about Psy, the Man behind Gangnam Style." *National Post*. October 2. https://nationalpost.com/entertainment/everything-you-need-to-know-about-psy-the-man-behind-gangnam-style.
Raymer, Miles. 2014. "Yes, Indie R&B Actually Exists." *Fortune*. June 6. http://fortune.com/2014/06/06/indie-r-b/.
"[Review] 'I Am the Best.'" 2011. *allkpop*. https://www.allkpop.com/article/2011/06/review-i-am-the-best-by-2ne1.
Rhythm.Connection. 2013. "Bringing the Beat: Five Influential Producers in Korean Hip-Hop." *Korea-Canada Blog*. June 17. https://korcan50years.com/2013/06/17/bringing-the-beat-five-influential-producers-in-korean-hip-hop/.
"R.I.P Epik High 2003–2012 [RANT]." 2012. *MyOppaIsBetterThanYours*. October 20. https://myoppaisbetterthanyours.wordpress.com/2012/10/20/r-i-p-epik-high-2003-2012-rant/.
Ripani, Richard J. 2006. *The New Blue Music: Changes in Rhythm and Blues, 1950–1999*. Jackson: University Press of Mississippi.
Rischar, Richard. 2004. "A Vision of Love: An Etiquette of Vocal Ornamentation in African American Popular Ballads of the Early 1990s." *American Music* 22 (3): 407–43. doi: 10.2307/3592985.
Ritz, David. 1970. "Happy Song: Soul Music in the Ghetto." *Salmagundi* 12: 43–53. https://www.jstor.org/stable/40546579.
Rivera, Nicole. 2012. "Big Bang—'Alive.'" *Pop Reviews Now*. February 29. http://popreviewsnow.blogspot.com/2012/02/big-bang-alive.html.
Rose, Tricia. 1994. *Black Noise: Rap Music and Black Culture in Contemporary America*. Middletown, CT: Wesleyan University Press.

Rosenstone, Robert. 1980. "Learning from Those 'Imitative' Japanese: Another Side of the American Experience in the Mikado's Empire." *American Historical Review* 85 (3): 572–95. doi: 10.1086/ahr/85.3.572.

"Roundtable: Thoughts and Experiences of Black K-pop Fans." 2015. *seoulbeats*. March 12. http://seoulbeats.com/2015/03/roundtable-thoughts-experiences-black-K-pop-fans/.

Rudinow, Paul. 1994. "Race, Ethnicity, Expressive Authenticity: Can White People Sing the Blues?" *Journal of Aesthetics and Art Criticism* 52 (1): 127–37. doi: 10.2307/431591.

Russell, Mark James. 2008. *Pop Goes Korea: Behind the Revolution in Movies, Music, and Internet Culture*. Berkeley, CA: Stone Bridge Press.

"S.E.S—Im Your Girl MV [HD Enhanced]." 2010. YouTube. Posted by bbvoxlover, May 9. https://youtu.be/WpmTLDtr4qY.

Saivickna. 2015. "Primary—2.0—Album Review." *Soju Wave*. September 15. http://sojuwave.com/2015/09/17/primary-2-album-review/.

Salaam, Mtume ya. 1995. "The Aesthetics of Rap." *African American Review* 29 (2): 303–15. doi: 10.2307/3042309.

Sanjek, David. 1997. "One Size Does Not Fit All: The Precarious Position of the African American Entrepreneur in Post–World War II American Popular Music." *American Music* 15 (4): 535–62. http://www.jstor.org/stable/3052385.

Schloss, Joseph G. 2004. *Making Beats: The Art of Sample-Based Hip-Hop*. Middletown, CT: Wesleyan University Press.

Schumaker, Thomas G. 2004. "'This is Sampling Sport': Digital Sampling, Rap Music, and the Law in Cultural Production." In *That's the Joint!: The Hip-Hop Studies Reader*, edited by Murray Foreman and Mark Anthony Neal, 443–58. New York: Routledge.

Schwartz, Terri. 2012. "Psy and MC Hammer: The Story behind the Epic American Music Awards Mash-up." *Zap2it*. November 19. http://blog.zap2it.com/pop2it/2012/11/psy-and-mc-hammer-the-story-behind-the-epic-american-music-awards-mash-up.html.

Seabrook, John. 2012. "Factory Girls: Cultural Technology and the Making of K-pop." *New Yorker*. October 8. http://www.newyorker.com/reporting/2012/10/08/121008fa_fact_seabrook?currentPage=all.

Shapiro, Peter. 2005. *Turn the Beat Around: The Secret History of Disco*. New York: Faber and Faber.

Sharon. 2016. "Crush Reveals American and Korean Artists Who Inspired Him." *seoulbeats*. August 6. http://www.hellokpop.com/news/crush-reveals-american-korean-artists/.

Shephard, Julienne Escobedo. 2017. "Legendary New Jack Swing Producer Teddy Riley on His Legacy, Making Sexy Music for Women and K-pop." May 25. *Jezebel*. https://themuse.jezebel.com/legendary-new-jack-swing-producer-teddy-riley-on-his-le-1795546414.

Sherlock, Steve. 2014. *The Performativity of Value: On the Citability of Cultural Commodities*. Lanham, MD: Lexington Books.

Sherman, Maria. 2015. "Epik High Discuss 'Sad Fun' Hip Hop & K-pop at SXSW 2015." *fuse*. March 26. www.fuse.tv/2015/03/epik-high-interview-sxsw.

Shim, Doobo. 2006. "Hybridity and the Rise of Korean Popular Culture in Asia." *Media, Culture and Society* 28 (1): 25–44. doi: 10.1177/0163443706059278.

Shin, Hyun-joon. 2009. "Have You Ever Seen the *Rain*? And Who'll Stop the *Rain*?: The Globalizing Project of Korean Pop (K-pop)." *Inter-Asia Cultural Studies* 10 (4): 507–23. doi: 10.1080/14649370903166150.

Shin, Hyun-joon, Mori Yoshitaka, and Ho Tung-hung. 2013. "Introduction: Special Issue—East Asian Popular Music and Its (Dis)contents." *Popular Music* 32 (1): 1–5. doi: https://doi.org/10.1017/S0261143012000505.

Shin, Solee I., and Lanu Kim. 2013. "Organizing K-pop: Emergence and Market Making of Large Korean Entertainment Houses, 1980–2010." *East Asia* 10 (4): 255–72. doi: 10.1007/s12140-013-9200-0.

"SHINHWA (신화)—All Your Dreams." 2013. YouTube. Posted by SHINHWASubs&Cuts, November 30. https://www.youtube.com/watch?v=DKp-SEKAizI.

"Shinhwa—Hae Gyul Sah (Solver)[HQ]." 2010. YouTube. Posted by usakoMV, April 14. https://www.youtube.com/watch?v=8U_dozTbUjI.

Sisario, Ben. 2010. "Teena Marie, an R&B Hitmaker, Is Dead at 54." *New York Times*. December 28. https://www.nytimes.com/2010/12/28/arts/music/28marie.html.

Shuker, Roy. 2017. *Popular Music: The Key Concepts*. New York: Routledge.

Shuker, Roy. 2001. *Understanding Popular Music*. London and New York: Routledge.

Sinker, Mark. 1992. "Black Science Fiction." *The Wire*. 96. https://www.thewire.co.uk/issues/96.

SJP. 2015. "Primary, OhHyuk (오혁): Lucky You!" *Korean Indie*. April 7. https://www.koreanindie.com/2015/04/07/primary-ohhyuk-lucky-you/.

"SM Entertainment Is Branching Out in 2016 with New Culture Technology." 2016. *Officially KMusic*. February 5, http://officiallykmusic.com/sm-entertainment-branching-2016-new-culture-technology/.

Son, Min-jun. 2006. "Regulating and Negotiating in T'ŭrot'ŭ, a Korean Popular Song Style." *Asian Music* 37 (1): 51–74. https://www.jstor.org/stable/4098488.

Song, Myoung-Sun. 2014. "The S(e)oul of Hip-Hop: Locating Space and Identity in Korean Rap." In *The Korean Wave: Korean Popular Culture in Global Context*, edited by Yasue Kuwahara, 133–48. New York: Palgrave Macmillan.

Sontag, Deborah. 2006. "A Strong Forecast for Korean Pop's Rain." *New York Times*. January 26. https://www.nytimes.com/2006/01/27/arts/a-strong-forecast-for-korean-pops-rain.html.

"[SS Interview] Zion.T 'Photosynthesizing from the Sun Named YANG HYUN SUK . . . Really Respect TEDDY.'" 2017. *YG-Life*. February 2. http://www.yg-life.com/archives/85732?lang=en.

Stachniak, Zander. 2015. "With 'Exodus,' EXO Prove They're Here to Stay: A Review." *Critical Kpop*. April 1. http://www.criticalkpop.com/2015/04/with-exodus-exo-prove-theyre-here-to-stay.html#sthash.OzW3bYkD.Ql5uznrY.dpbs.

Stephens, Robert W. 1984. "Soul: A Historical Reconstruction of Continuity and Change in Black Popular Music." *Black Perspective in Music* 12 (1): 21–43. http://www.jstor.org/stable/1214967.

Stephens, Vincent. 2001. "The Day (Music Release)." *Popular Music and Society* 25 (3–4): 132–34. doi: 10.1080/03007760108591804.

Sterling, Marvin D. 2010. *Babylon East: Performing Dancehall, Roots Reggae, and Rastafari in Japan*. Durham, NC: Duke University Press.

"Stop Calling EDM EDM!" 2015. *Magnetic Magazine*. October 7. http://www.magneticmag.com/2015/10/stop-calling-edm-edm-here-is-a-proper-definition/.

Stroupe, Craig. n.d. "Cultural Work." *Craig Stroupe*. https://www.d.umn.edu/~cstroupe/ideas/cultural_work.html. Accessed September 5, 2019.

Sullivan, Caroline. 2004. "CD: John Legend, Get Lifted." *Guardian*. December 9. https://www.theguardian.com/music/2004/dec/10/popandrock.shopping2.

Sung, Sang-yeon. 2010. "Constructing a New Image. Hallyu in Taiwan." *European Journal of East Asian Studies* 9 (1): 25–45. doi: 10.1163/156805810X517652.

"SUPER JUNIOR 슈퍼주니어 'A-CHA' MV." 2011. YouTube. Posted by SMTOWN, September 26. https://youtu.be/GvTaLTTanJc.

Sykes, Charles. 2006. "Motown." In *African American Music: An Introduction*, edited by Mellonee V. Burnim and Portia K. Maultsby, 431–52. New York: Routledge.

Taylor, Paul C. 1997. "Funky White Boys and Honorary Soul Sisters." *Michigan Quarterly Review* 36 (2): 320–36.

Taylor, Shawn. 2007. *A Tribe Called Quest's People's Instinctive Travels and the Paths of Rhythm*. New York: Continuum.

"The Temptations—My Girl." 2016. YouTube. Posted by Island Music, January 13. https://www.youtube.com/watch?v=C_CSjcm-z1w.

"The Temptations – The Way You Do the Things You Do (1965). 2012. YouTube. 3:09. Posted by Abdul Jalil, May 20, https://www.youtube.com/watch?v=gjzBbYr4Eik.

"They Will Even Hear Sound of Our Breath." 2007. *Dong-A Ilbo*. August 29. http://english.donga.com/srv/service.php3?biid=2007082953018.

"TLC—What About Your Friends (Album Version)." n.d. YouTube. Posted by TLC. https://youtu.be/92gHq1s6G-c.

Toop, David. 2004. "Uptown Throwdown." In *That's the Joint!: The Hip-Hop Studies Reader*, edited by Murray Forman and Mark Anthony Neal, 233–45. New York: Routledge.

Toussaint, Eric. 2006. "South Korea: The Miracle Unmasked." *Economic and Political Weekly* 41 (39): 4211–19. https://www.jstor.org/stable/4418764.

Um, Hae-kyung. 2013. "The Poetics of Resistance and the Politics of Crossing Borders: Korean Hip-Hop and 'Cultural Reterritorialisation.'" *Popular Music* 32 (1): 51–64. doi: 10.1017/S0261143012000542.

"Usher—Yeah! Ft. Lil Jon, Ludacris." 2015. YouTube. Posted by Usher, April 17. https://www.youtube.com/watch?v=GxBSyx85Kp8.

"Usher—You Make Me Wanna . . . (Official Video Version)." 2009. YouTube. Posted by Usher, October 25. https://www.youtube.com/watch?v=bQRzrnH6_HY.

Vecchiola, C. 2011. "Submerge in Detroit: Techno's Creative Response in Urban Crisis." *Journal of American Studies* 45 (1): 95–111. doi: 10.1017/S0021875810001167.

Vincent, Ricky. 2000. "Hip-Hop and Black Noise: Raising Hell." In *That's the Joint!: The Hip-Hop Studies Reader*, edited by Murray Foreman and Mark Anthony Neal, 481–92. New York: Routledge.

Vincent, Ricky. 1996. *Funk: The Music, the People, and the Rhythm of the One*. New York: St. Martin's Griffin.

Wall, Tim. 2003. *Studying Popular Music Culture*. London: Hodder & Stoughton Educational.

Walters, Barry. 2012. "Frank Ocean, Miguel, and Holy Other Usher in PBR&B 2.0." *SPIN*. August 22. https://www.spin.com/2012/08/frank-ocean-miguel-and-holy-other-usher-in-pbrb-2o/.

Ward, Brian. 1998. *Just My Soul Responding: Rhythm and Blues, Black Consciousness, and Race Relations*. Berkeley: University of California Press.

Warwick, Jacqueline. 2007. *Girl Groups, Girl Culture: Popular Music and Identity in the 1960s*. New York: Routledge.

Weber, Lindsey. 2018. "No. 9: 'Palette,' IU: A Declaration of Womanhood, K-pop Style." *New York Times Magazine*. March 8. https://www.nytimes.com/interactive/2018/03/08/magazine/25-songs-future-of-music.html#/intro.

Werner, Craig. 1999. *A Change Is Gonna Come: Music, Race, and the Soul of America*. New York: Plume.

Werner, Craig. 1994. *Playing the Changes: From Afro-Modernism to the Jazz Impulse*. Urbana: University of Illinois Press.

Wexler, Jerry, and David Ritz. 1992. "Listen at Her . . . Listen at Her!" Liner notes to *Aretha Franklin Queen of Soul: The Atlantic Recordings*, 7–17. New York: Atlantic Records.
"What Is Pop Music?" n.d. *English Club*. https://www.englishclub.com/vocabulary/music-pop.htm. Accessed September 5, 2019.
Wheeler, Elizabeth. 1991. "'Most of My Heroes Don't Appear on No Stamps': The Dialogics of Rap Music." *Black Music Research Journal* 11 (2): 193–216. doi: 10.2307/779266.
White, Shane, and Graham White. 1998. *Stylin': African American Expressive Culture from Its Beginnings to the Zoot Suit*. Ithaca, NY: Cornell University Press.
Wicke, Peter, David Liang, and David Horn. 2003. *Bloomsbury Encyclopedia of Popular Music of the World: Volume II: Performance and Production*, edited by John Shepard, David Horn, Dave Laing, Paul Oliver, and Peter Wicke, 181–206. London: Continuum.
Wilson, Rob. 1991. "Theory's Imaginary Other: American Encounters with South Korea and Japan." *boundary 2* 18 (3): 220–41. doi: 10.2307/303210.
"Wonder Girls 'NOBODY (Kor. Ver)" M/V." 2008. YouTube. Posted by wondergirls, December 14. https://youtu.be/QZBn1e9pr2Q.
Yeeun. 2008. "[Review] Epik High—Pieces, Part 1 (5th Album)." *yeeun2grace*. April 20. https://yeeun2grace.wordpress.com/2008/04/20/epik-high-5th-pieces-part-1/.
Yoo, Reera. 2015. "Kim Tae-woo Back on Center Stage." *KoreAm*. January 9. http://kore.am/kim-tae-woo-back-on-center-stage/.
Yoon, Sunny. 2009. "The Neoliberal World Order and Patriarchal Power: A Discursive Study of Korean Cinema and International Co-Production." *Visual Anthropology* 22 (2–3): 200–210.

INDEX

1TYM, 54–55, 122, 141
2AM, 50
2NE1, 56, 67, 72, 90, 122, 141
2PM, xxi, 49–53, 58, 78, 119, 154
4MEN, xxi, 89–90, 94–95

African American cultural production, x, xvii, 144
African American popular music, ix–xiv, xvii, xix–xx, 3–41, 45–46, 54–55, 65–67, 69, 95, 114, 128, 139, 148–49, 151–54, 156, 158; aesthetics, x, xiii, xxii, 24–26, 40, 54–55, 65, 72, 96, 114, 122, 125, 127, 145, 154, 157–58; choreography, xviii, xxi, 32–33, 43–44, 46, 50, 54, 60, 65–75, 86, 109, 112–13, 120; instrumentation, x–xi, xx–xxi, 25, 28–30, 46, 47, 65, 89, 114, 117, 134, 145, 148, 151–52, 155; performance, x, xviii, xxi, 22, 24–25, 32–33, 38, 43–44, 46, 65–74, 79, 89, 109–15, 117, 136, 138–39, 155; vocals, x–xi, xx–xxii, 25–30, 46, 54–64, 89, 96, 103, 114, 117, 127, 134, 149, 151–52, 154–55, 157–58
African Americans, xiii, xix–xxi, 18–24, 33, 45–46, 65–66, 80, 82–83, 85–86, 90, 114–15, 144
African American Vernacular English (AAVE), 124
Akdong Musician, 7
American Music Awards, ix, 3, 13, 16, 149
American studies, xvii–xviii, xx
Amoeba Culture, 107–8, 127–28, 133–34. *See also* Dynamic Duo

Aoki, Steve, ix
AOMG, 7, 119
Arashi, 76
Asiansoul, The, 4, 78. *See also* Park Jin-young
Atkins, Cholly, 32, 67

b-boys, 66, 121
Baby Vox, 51
Badu, Erykah, 107, 150
Baker, Anita, 63, 100
Bambaataa, Afrika, 132, 135, 145
BEAST, 52, 105. *See also* Jang Hyun-seung
Beenzino, 124, 153
Beyoncé, 83
Bi. *See* Rain
BigBang, 56, 90, 122
BigHit Entertainment, 26
Big Mama, xxi, 7, 90, 95, 99–102, 109–11, 117, 157–58
Billboard, ix, 7, 21, 34, 46, 57, 63, 84, 86, 145, 157
Bizzy, 8, 121
black American popular music. *See* African American popular music
Black Eyed Peas, 3
blackface, 20
black K-pop fans, 39
Blackstreet, 51, 58
Blige, Mary J., 105, 138
blues, xi, xii–xx, 23–24, 27–30, 39–40, 58, 55, 80, 82, 85–86, 90, 99, 101, 103, 115–16, 145, 155, 157
BoA, 57

Index

British soul, 117, 157
Brown, Bobby, 57, 66
Brown Eyed Soul, xxi, 7, 95–100, 117, 129, 152
Bruno Mars, 10, 26
BTS, ix, xxii, 2, 7, 26, 61, 87; *BTS American Hustle Life*, ix

Carey, Mariah, 100, 105
CBMASS, 105, 127, 130
Chanyeol, 34. *See also* EXO
Charles, Ray, 22, 49, 99, 101
Choiza, 127, 129. *See also* Dynamic Duo
Chong, Jae, 90, 128. *See also* Solid
choreography, x, xx, 3, 6–7, 47–48, 50, 58, 61, 63, 66–75, 77, 79, 91, 112–14, 120, 152; complementary, 67; complex, x, 6, 29, 33, 58, 68; moonwalk, 68, 72; synchronized, 32, 47, 66
Chun Doo-hwan, 18
Ciara, 46
Clon, 120–21
colonialism, xvii, 87, 156
Combs, Sean, 33–34, 60
Coolio, ix
Crush, 106–7, 109
cultural appropriation, xi, 23, 26, 40–41, 114–15
cultural production, xi, xvi, 83; African American, x, xvii, 39, 115, 144, 159; fan, xxi; Korean, xix, 13, 37, 83, 88; K-pop as, xviii
cultural studies, xi
Cypress Hill, 30, 55

D'Angelo, 107–8, 112–13, 150
Dean, 34, 106–7, 164–65, 169
Desiigner, ix
Deux, 120–21
digital music, 81, 84, 150, 152
disco, xi, xv, 4, 19, 21, 23–25, 29–30, 37, 39–40, 48–49, 52, 55–56, 59, 62, 70, 74, 82, 86, 94, 98, 101, 108, 123, 128, 145, 149, 153, 156
DJs, 16, 121, 128, 143–44
Dok2, 108, 122, 134
Dominic, Simon. *See* Simon D
doo-wop, 25, 27, 32, 73, 93, 100
Dr. Dre, 30, 134
Drunken Tiger, 121, 141. *See also* Tiger JK
dubstep, 6, 31

Dumbfoundead, 34, 125
Dynamic Duo, xxii, 7, 96, 105, 107, 122–23, 125–30, 134–35, 148

Earth, Wind & Fire, 65, 95, 97–99
East Asia, xi–xvi, xix, 4, 14, 22, 81, 116
Edmonds, Kenneth "Babyface," 57, 103–4
electronic dance music (EDM), 24, 31, 51, 53–57, 61–62, 103–4, 107, 133
Elliott, Missy, 60
"Elvis Effect," 39
enka, 44
Epik High, xxii, 7, 105, 122–27, 130–36, 141, 144, 148
Eurodisco, 30
Euro-pop, 6, 31
EXO, 7, 34, 57, 89, 150–51

fandom: fan reviewers, x–xi, xiv–xvi, xxi, 4–5, 34, 36–40, 51, 56–57, 59, 64, 73, 91, 133, 135, 141, 153–55, 158; female, 35, 70, 92; global, x–xii, xiv–xvi, xviii, xx–xxi, 5, 8, 10, 14–17, 34–38, 41, 70, 81, 89, 91, 119, 122–23, 149, 152–54, 158; knowledge, xiv, xvi, 36–39, 41, 81, 153–55; stereotypes, 35, 153; transcultural, xv–xvi, 34–35, 153; transnational, 35, 56
fan studies, xiv, xvi, xx
Fin.K.L, 51, 73, 79
Fly to the Sky, xxi, 89–95, 109, 119
Franklin, Aretha, 40, 99–102, 111, 157
funk, xxi, 23–25, 28–30, 44, 46, 48–51, 55–56, 63, 65, 70, 82–83, 91–92, 96–97, 108–9, 115, 128, 131, 135–36, 138, 150–52

Gaeko, 123, 127, 129. *See also* Dynamic Duo
Gap Band, 48
Gaye, Marvin, 107
genre, xi, xiii, xv–xvii, xx–xxii, 5–10, 23–31, 33, 37–38, 41, 43–46, 55–56, 58–63, 65, 67, 83–84, 89–91, 96, 102–3, 105–8, 114–15, 119, 123–24, 127–28, 130–34, 138, 142–43, 147–50, 152–55, 158
Girls' Generation, 16–17, 31, 36, 46, 57–58, 65, 79, 150–51; *Soshified*, 17, 36
Gladys Knight and the Pips, 32
globalization, xvii–xviii, xx, xxii, 148, 156, 158–59

g.o.d, xxi, 43, 46–50, 52–53, 60–61, 78, 152
Gordy, Berry, xxi, 75–77, 80–85, 87
gospel, xxi, 23, 25–27, 29–30, 47, 49, 83, 85, 89, 91, 94–104, 117, 129–30, 151–53, 157–58
GOT7, 50, 78
Graham, Larry, 29, 98–99
Groove Overdose. *See* g.o.d

Hallyu. *See* Korean wave
Happyface Entertainment, 94
Heize, 151
HIGHGRND, 131, 149
hip-hop: African American, 65, 120, 124–27, 136, 138, 145; American, ix, 7, 34, 65, 120–21, 124–27, 131, 136, 138, 145; authenticity, ix, 40, 116, 120, 124–27, 132, 134, 140–42; innovation, 30, 127, 133, 136, 139, 143–45; intertextuality, xx, xxii, 119, 127–28, 144, 148–49, 158; Korean, x, xxii, 7–8, 54, 96, 107, 119–45, 148, 150, 158; political and social commentary, 40, 120–21, 124, 126–27, 139–42; styles, xxii
Holland-Dozier-Holland, 27, 86
H.O.T., 14, 33, 46–47, 79. *See also* Yoo Young-jin
House Rulez, 7
Houston, Whitney, 57, 91, 100
Hwanhee, 91–93, 109
Hyukoh, 135, 147, 149, 158
Hyuna, 52, 123

"idol" system, xxi, 6, 46, 66, 75, 79, 81, 87, 91; training, xxi, 6, 46, 49, 75–77, 79, 81, 84, 86–87, 91
imperialism, 116, 156
indie: groups, 7, 131, 135, 147–50; music, 107, 149–50, 158
INFINITE, 67, 79
Ingram, James, 49, 104
Insooni, 20
IU, 7

Jackson 5, 68
Jackson, Janet, 29, 58, 60
Jackson, Michael, 4, 33, 47, 57, 67–69, 79, 82–83
Jang Hyuk, 47
Jang Hyun-seung, 52

Japanese K-pop market, 14, 39, 50, 59, 63, 65, 77, 122
Japanese popular music industry, 81
Jaurim, 7
Jay-Z, 7, 106, 119
jazz, xiv, xix, 23, 31–32, 38, 49, 56, 59, 83, 97–99, 102–4, 106–7, 109, 115–16, 131, 133–35, 145, 149, 155, 158
Jellyfish Entertainment, 90
Jimmy Jam, 29
Jinusean, 55, 121–22, 141
Jisun, 132–33
Johnny's Entertainment, 50, 75–76
Jones, Quincy, 49, 57, 134
Jonghyun, 57–59. *See also* SHINee
Jung Ji-hoon. *See* Rain
Jun.K, 50
JYJ, 63, 96
JYP Entertainment, 4, 7, 47, 49–50, 52, 69–70, 74–75, 78

K-Ci & JoJo, 51, 93–94
KCON, 8, 123
Kim Hyun-joong, 7
Kim Tae-woo, 47, 49–50. *See also* g.o.d
Kim Young-Sam, 18
King, Rodney, 20
kkonminam, 85
Korea-China relations, 15
Korea Creative Content Agency, 13–14
Korea-Japan relations, 14–15, 18
Korea-US relations, 11, 15, 17–19, 116
Korean Kittens, 22
Korean R&B, x, xxi–xxii, 7, 22, 34, 89–117, 119, 127, 129, 145, 150–52, 154, 157
Korean studies, xvii–xix
Korean television, xvii–xix, 6, 8, 12, 20, 37, 43, 47, 52, 61, 66, 75, 92, 122–23, 128, 158
Korean War, 11, 17–19, 116
Korean wave, xv–xvi, xviii, xix, 13, 36–37, 66, 87, 122, 156
K-pop: authenticity, ix, xiv, xxii, 38–41, 114–15, 124–27, 140–41, 148, 152, 155, 158; citational practices in, x–xii, xiv–xv, xx–xxii, 5, 16–17, 21, 24–28, 30–34, 36, 38–41, 43–46, 48–50, 52, 56, 58, 60, 62, 65–72, 89, 95, 100, 106–7, 109–13, 117,

119–20, 127–30, 136, 138–39, 150, 152, 157; concerts, 4, 8, 14, 17, 36, 43, 47, 59, 65, 79, 81, 89, 95, 154; English in, xii, xiv–xv, 15, 31, 37, 51, 55, 63, 72, 121, 124–25; hybridity in, x, xvi, xx, 5, 10, 15, 17, 21–22, 24, 31, 41, 148, 156; industry, xix, 11–14, 39, 53–54, 77, 79, 81, 110, 123–24, 147; musical emulation in, x, xii, xx–xxii, 5, 24–25, 30, 41, 46, 53, 56, 58, 60–62, 64–65, 73, 75, 81, 86, 88–91, 95, 97–99, 113–14, 117, 119, 127, 148, 152, 156–57; musical enhancement in, x, xi, xx–xxii, 5, 25, 30–31, 41, 58, 62, 65, 88, 96, 103, 106, 114, 117, 119, 127, 131, 145, 148, 158; promotion of, xi, xxi, 3, 6, 8, 12–14, 16, 44, 59, 61, 63, 75–77, 80, 91–92, 109, 117, 120, 122, 149; teenage fans of, 4–5, 8, 35, 94; transnational impulse of, 56; umbrella, x–xi, xxi–xxii, 5, 7, 10, 65, 75, 89, 119, 123, 139, 148–49, 152–53

K-pop websites: *allkpop*, 37, 57, 120; *generasia*, 7; *hellokpop*, 37; *jpopasia*, 7; *seoulbeats*, 37, 39, 40, 141, 147–48; *soompi*, 37, 73

Kraftwerk, 56, 135, 145

K. Will, 8, 123

Lady Gaga, 72
Lee Moon-sae, 108–9
Lee Soo-man, 26, 46, 76, 87. *See also* SM Entertainment
Legend, John, 151
Lewis, Terry, 29
Lidel, Pelle, 16
Loco, 7
Lyn, xxi, 7–8, 103–6, 117, 123

masculinity, xvi, 50, 65, 72, 112, 114
Mase, 4
Mason, Harvey, Jr., 53, 56–57
Masta Wu, 113, 122, 141
McDonald, Michael, 26, 103–4
MC Hammer, 3–4
McKnight, Brian, 49, 91
MC Mong, 7
MC the Max, 8, 123
MCs, 28, 30, 105, 107, 128, 143
melisma, 27, 52, 92–93, 100, 102, 112, 129
Melvin and the Blue Notes, 29–30

MFBTY, 8, 121, 123. *See also* Bizzy; Tiger JK
MFSB, 29
military service, 43, 61, 127, 131
Ministry of Culture, Sports and Tourism, 13
Mithra Jin, 130, 133
Motown, 4, 22, 27–28, 45, 52, 67, 73–78, 80–82, 85–86, 88, 101–2, 109, 115
MTV, 33, 66–69
musical emulation. *See* K-pop
musical enhancement. *See* K-pop
musical intertextuality, 65, 136
musicology, xi–xiii, 26
music producers, ix, xxi–xxii, 16, 33, 53–54, 134
music videos, x, xviii, xxi–xxii, 6, 12, 32–34, 43, 50, 52, 63, 66–73, 81, 89, 92, 109, 111–13, 117, 119, 122, 134, 136–39, 154; African American fashion style in, xi, 33–34, 45, 65–66, 72–74, 102, 111, 113–14, 122, 136, 158; sex, 72, 112, 136–38; women in, xxi–xxii, 50, 52, 71–73, 109, 111–12, 136–39

Nakasone, Rino, 58
Na-ul, 7, 95–96, 129. *See also* Brown Eyed Soul
Nell, 7
N.W.A, 140

Ohio Players, 48, 65
O'Jays, 30
Okyere, Sam, 20
Omarion, 4, 70
One Direction, 8

pal-ship-pal-man-won-sae-dae, 13
pansori, 112
Park, Jay, xxii, 7, 50, 106, 119, 136–37
Park, Teddy, 54–55
Park Hyo-shin, xxi, 90, 103
Park Jin-young, 4, 47, 70, 74, 78. *See also* JYP Entertainment; Asiansoul, The
Parliament, 29, 65
Pendergrass, Teddy, 29
popular music studies, xi, xx
ppong, 6, 31, 44–45
ppongjjak, 44–45
Primary, xxii, 123, 127, 130, 134–36, 149, 158
Prince, 56, 82–83, 109

promotion, xi, xxi, 3, 6, 8, 12–14, 16, 44, 59, 61, 63, 75–77, 80, 91–92, 109, 112, 120, 122, 149
Psy, xviii, 3–4, 15–16, 41, 43, 124
Public Enemy, 140

Queen Latifah, 139

racial binary, x, xxii, 89, 114, 116
racism, 16, 19, 67, 82, 116, 142
Rain, xvi, xxi, 4, 52, 65, 69–72, 78, 109, 112–13, 152
R&B: African American, 57, 91, 103; American, xii, 4, 56–57, 91, 93, 112–13, 151; authenticity, x, xiv, xx, xxi–xxii, 5, 32, 34, 38, 40–41, 96, 111, 114–17, 127, 134, 140, 142, 148, 152, 154–55, 157–58; genres, x, xii, xvii, xx–xxi, 4–5, 28, 30–31, 44, 46, 49, 55, 58, 89, 93, 106, 128, 130, 134, 152, 154–55; global, x, xiv, xvii, xx, xxii, 44, 83, 89, 114, 117, 119, 139–40, 145, 148, 152, 154–56, 158; intertextuality, x, xii, xiv, xx–xxii, 5, 24–25, 30, 41, 43, 58, 65, 89, 95, 114, 117, 119, 127–28, 136, 148, 152, 154–56, 158; Korean, x, xxi–xxii, 7, 22, 34, 89–117, 119, 129, 145, 150–52, 154, 157
rap, 9, 23, 29, 31, 45, 48, 51, 61–62, 83, 92, 105, 120–22, 127–34, 137–38, 140, 142–45; artists, ix, xi, xxii, 3–4, 6–7, 20, 30, 34, 44–45, 50, 52–58, 60–62, 71, 91–92, 105, 108–9, 113, 119–21, 124–26, 136–39, 151, 153, 155; East Coast, 30, 134, 140; gangster, 126, 134; West Coast, 20, 134, 140, 145
Red Velvet, 7, 151
representation, 84, 142; African American, x, xviii; Asian, 65, 87; women, xxi, 109–12
Rhythm and Blues. *See* R&B
Rihanna, 46
Riley, Teddy, 51, 53, 57
Roc Nation, 7, 119. *See also* Jay-Z
Roh Tae-woo, 18
Roots, The, 131, 134, 150

sampling, xxii, 29–30, 44, 119, 127–28, 130–35, 142
Se7en, 4
Seo Taiji, 44–45, 90. *See also* Seo Taiji and Boys
Seo Taiji and Boys, 31, 44–45, 65–66, 78, 90, 121, 126

S.E.S, 43, 51, 73
SHINee, xxi, 33, 57–61, 65, 89, 150, 152
Shinhwa, xxi, 8, 43, 58, 60–63, 89, 152
Simmons, Kimora Lee, 33
Simon D, 7, 108, 126
sinsaedae, 12–13
Sly and the Family Stone, 29, 48, 95, 98–99. *See also* Graham, Larry
SM Entertainment, 16–17, 26, 31, 33, 46, 51, 54, 57–58, 60–61, 63; SMAP, 76
Snoop Dogg, 30
SNSD. *See* Girl's Generation
social media, ix, 14, 16–17, 35, 81, 119, 122, 124; Daum, 124; Facebook, 17, 37, 124; Instagram, 17, 81; Naver, 14, 124; Reddit, 8, 153; Twitter, 16–17, 58, 81, 122, 124; Vryl, 14; YouTube, 3, 8, 10, 14, 35, 37, 81, 91, 119, 124, 152–54
Solid, 22, 90
soul, xiii, xix, xxi, 9, 22–25, 29–31, 40–41, 45, 51, 60, 70, 73, 80, 82–83, 92–117, 128–29, 131, 136, 145, 149–52, 155, 157–58
Sound of Philadelphia, The, 29–30, 56, 145
South Korea: economy, 11; financial crisis, xix, 11–13; government, xix, 11–14, 86, 116; "Hell Joseon," 13; politics, xvii–xviii, xix, 11–12, 15, 18, 126; soft power, xix, 87
SPIN, 9, 34
Spinners, 30
SS501, 7
Standing Egg, 7
stereotypes: African American, 19, 75, 85, 109; Asian, 44; Asian men, 16; Asian women, 75, 109, 138; fans, 153; negative, 19, 75
streaming websites: Crunchyroll, 36; Viki, 37
Super Junior-M, 14
Supremes, 32, 74, 102

Tablo, 7, 122–23, 125–27, 130–31, 133
Taemin, 33, 57–59. *See also* SHINee
Taeyeon, 151. *See also* Girls' Generation
Tasha. *See* Yoon Mi-rae
techno, 4, 45, 55–56, 132
Teddy. *See* Park, Teddy
Temptations, 68
Tiger JK, 8, 121, 123, 141
Timberlake, Justin, 4, 123

TLC, 51–52, 73
Tohoshinki. *See* TVXQ
trance, 31
Tribe Called Quest, A, 131, 145
trot, 31, 45
Trouble Maker, 52. *See also* Hyuna; Jang Hyun-seung
TVXQ, xxi, 14, 16, 33, 36, 58, 63–65, 89, 96, 150
Tyrese, 4, 70

Underdogs, 57, 106
urban contemporary, 25, 44, 52–53, 67, 92, 94, 100, 105
Urban Zakapa, 7, 147–49, 153
Usher, 4, 70–72, 112–13

Variety, 85
Vibe (group), 151
Vibe (magazine), 34

Ward, Hines, 20
Warren G., ix
Wheesung, xxi, 109, 112–14, 117, 152
White, Barry, 30
will.i.am, 3
Wonder, Stevie, 49, 90, 150
Wonder Girls, xxi, 4, 7, 49–50, 52–53, 73–75, 152. *See also* Hyuna; Yubin
Woollim Entertainment, 130
Wooyoung, 50

Yang Hyun-suk, 44, 78. *See also* Seo Taiji and Boys; YG Entertainment
YG Entertainment, 7, 44, 54–55, 67, 75, 78, 90, 100, 108, 112–13, 122, 131, 141, 149
Yoon Mi-rae, xxii, 8, 20, 121, 123, 136, 138–39
Yoo Young-jin, 16, 33, 54, 60, 67, 78–79. *See also* SM Entertainment
Younha, 96, 133
Yubin, 52–53
Yunho, 33, 63. *See also* TVXQ

Zion.T, xxi, 103, 106–9, 117, 134, 152

ABOUT THE AUTHOR

Crystal S. Anderson is affiliate faculty in Korean Studies, Department of Modern and Classical Languages at George Mason University, where she studies transnational American Studies and Global Asias. She is author of *Beyond "The Chinese Connection": Contemporary Afro-Asian Cultural Production*. Her work has appeared in *African American Review*, *MELUS*, *Ethnic Studies Review*, and *Extrapolation*.

www.ingramcontent.com/pod-product-compliance
Lightning Source LLC
Chambersburg PA
CBHW030623230426
43661CB00053B/2123